™

San Diego

The Best Sights
and How To Photograph Them

San Diego

The Best Sights and How To Photograph Them

Andrew Hudson

Contributors:

Bob Krist . . . . .Foreword
   Photography columnist, National Geographic Traveler
Richard Amero . . . . .Balboa Park
   Historian
Bob Couey . . . . .SeaWorld
   Photo Services Manager, SeaWorld San Diego
Ron Garrison . . . . .San Diego Zoo
   Photo Services Manager, Zoological Society of San Diego
Jerry Schad . . . . .Mountains and Deserts
   Author of 'Afoot & Afield in San Diego County'
James Blank . . . . .Skylines
   Postcard photographer
Dianne Brinson . . . . .Photography Law
   Attorney

San Diego

Andrew Hudson

A compendium of the most visually
distinctive places in San Diego
County that you can easily and
dependably photograph.

Map

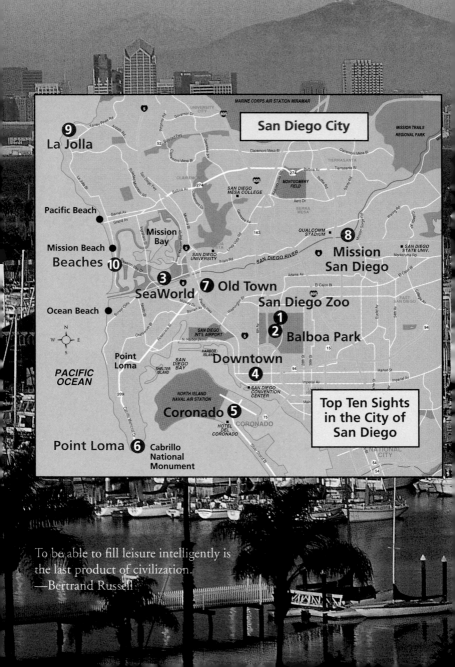

San Diego City

MARINE CORPS AIR STATION MIRAMAR

MISSION TRAILS
REGIONAL PARK

9 La Jolla

Pacific Beach

**Mission
Bay**

8 Mission
San Diego

Mission Beach

Beaches **10**

3 **SeaWorld**

7 Old Town

Ocean Beach

San Diego Zoo

1

2 Balboa Park

**PACIFIC
OCEAN**

Point
Loma

Downtown

4

Coronado **5**

**Top Ten Sights
in the City of
San Diego**

Point Loma **6** Cabrillo
National
Monument

To be able to fill leisure intelligently is
the last product of civilization.
—Bertrand Russell

Orange County
Riverside County
Camp Pendleton
Pala
Palomar Observatory
Mission San Luis de Rey
Oceanside
San Diego Wild Animal Park
Anza-Borrego Desert State Park
Carlsbad
Vista
Julian
Escondido
Encinitas
Del Mar
Cuyamaca Rancho State Park
Detail left
Laguna Mountain Recreation Area
San Diego
N W E S
Imperial Beach
San Diego County
Tijuana
M e x i c o

To take photographs is to hold one's breath when all faculties converge in the face of fleeting reality. It is at that moment that mastering an Image becomes a great physical and intellectual joy.
—Henri Cartier-Bresson

8

Contents

Resources

County

Other

Top Ten

Top Ten Sights of
San Diego

San Diego Zoo

Known for its pandas and koalas, the city's most famous attraction makes for a great day out and terrific photos.

San Diego Zoo

Balboa Park

With more museums, architecture, flora and fauna than any other city park in the world, Balboa Park is the gem of San Diego.

Balboa Park

SeaWorld

Join Shamu and friends for a whale of a good time at this entertaining adventure park.

SeaWorld

Downtown

Renovated and revitalized, down-town combines the Victorian-style Gaslamp Quarter and modern buildings with ships, marinas and imaginative malls.

Coronado

The magnificent Hotel del Corona-do, a lavish Victorian dream made entirely of wood, anchors this ele-gant Navy town. Don't miss the great views of San Diego's skyline from the Ferry Landing.

Point Loma

On the tip of Point Loma is Cabrillo National Monument, honoring the 'discoverer' of America's West Coast. There are great views of the Bay as well as two lighthouses, a whale-watching station and several tide pools.

Old Town

The first permanent civilian settle-ment in California, Old Town is now a feast of restaurants and museums. Nearby, in Presidio Park, are the remains of the original Spanish fortress and mission.

Mission San Diego

Known as "the mother of the mis-sions," this is the first and oldest of California's chain of 21 romantic Spanish missions.

La Jolla

One of California's most scenic and exclusive communities, La Jolla has a beautiful shoreline, rugged cliffs, galleries and restaurants. Don't miss the Birch Aquarium at Scripps and Torrey Pines State Reserve.

Beaches

Reeling in the Southern California scene, the districts of Pacific Beach, Mission Beach and Mission Bay are popular for sunbathing, rollerblad-ing, surfing, sailing and people-watching.

Publisher's Cataloging in Publication Data:
Hudson, Andrew, 1963-

PhotoSecrets San Diego: the best sights and
how to photograph them / Andrew Hudson;
contributors Bob Krist, Jerry Schad... [et al]
1st ed.   p, cm. – (PhotoSecrets guidebooks)
Includes index. Preassigned LCCN: 98-65786
ISBN 0-9653-87-3-1   Ingram 893457
1. San Diego County (Calif.)–Guidebooks. 2.
Outdoor photography–California–San Diego
County. 3. Travel photography–California–San
Diego County. I. Title. II. Title: San Diego III.
Series: PhotoSecrets (Series)
F868.S15H84 1998   917.94'9804'53

First edition © 1998–2003, PhotoTour
Books, Inc. First published in 1998, reprinted
with updates in 2000 and 2003.

Printed in Korea. Distributed to the trade by
National Book Network ☎ 800-462-6420.

The information in this guide is intended to
be accurate however the author and publisher
accept no responsibility for any loss, injury,
inconvenience or other unfortunate consequences arising from the use of this book.

Conceived, photographed, written, designed,
published and marketed by Andrew Hudson.
PHOTOSECRETS is a registered trademark of
Photo Tour Books, Inc.

Photo Tour Books, Inc.
9582 Vista Tercera
San Diego CA 92129

Visit the web site:
photosecrets.com

Left: Discovering San Diego. On the road at
the Cabrillo National Monument.

Foreword

By Bob Krist

Bob Krist writes the 'Photography' column for *National Geographic Traveler*. His photographs regularly appear in *National Geographic, National Geographic Traveler, Travel/Holiday* and *Islands*.

A great travel photograph, like a great news photograph, requires you to be in the right place at the right time to capture that special moment on film. Professional photographers have a short-hand phrase for that uncanny ability to be in just the right spot when it counts, "F8 and be there."

There are countless books that can help you with photographic technique, the "F8" portion of that equation. But until now, there's been no help available for the other, more critical portion of that equation, the "be there" part. To find the right spot, you had to expend lots of time and shoe leather to essentially reinvent the wheel.

In my career as a professional travel photographer, well over half my time on location is spent seeking out the good angles. It's time consuming, dull, and very frustrating.

Andrew Hudson's PhotoSecrets does all that legwork for you, so you can spend your time photographing instead of wandering about. It's like having a professional location scout in your camera bag. Hudson has thoroughly scoured the city like only a resident can and will tell you where and when to go to get the best pictures of San Diego and the environs. I wish I had one of these books for every city I photograph on assignment.

San Diego is one of the most beautiful cities in North America and PhotoSecrets can help you capture that beauty on film with a minimum of hassle and a maximum of enjoyment.

The Story Of This Book

I first fell in love with San Diego when I moved here in October 1990. I'd driven cross-country from Philadelphia to set up a West Coast sales office for a videoconferencing firm. I met my partner, Jennie, the following February and we settled into Pacific Beach followed by La Jolla.

On July 25, 1994, while on a round-the-world trip, I was sitting in the Indian embassy in Singapore poring over my guidebooks to plan a trip to Thailand. I wanted to visit the beach used in the 1974 James Bond film *The Man with the Golden Gun,* where a limestone tower rises out of the sea. I'd seen the beach pictured in magazines but none of the guidebooks I had showed where it was. Surely I wasn't the only person who enjoyed using a camera to explore? I thought there ought to be a guidebook cataloging the classic views of an area and giving photography information. The idea for PhotoSecrets was born.

In April 1996, wanting to create something, I left the safety of a full-time job and dove into a world I knew nothing about—publishing. A year later, in June 1997, my first book appeared on bookshelves—*PhotoSecrets San Francisco and Northern California.*

Since I was busy trying to sell and publicize my first book, I thought I'd find an "easy" subject for my second project. What could be simpler than San Diego? How wrong I was! Upon inspection, San Diego turned out to be vastly more diverse and visual than I'd thought, with at least as much to photograph as the "great" cities of the world.

It's taken twelve solid months to put this book together—I hope you enjoy it! *PhotoSecrets San Diego* should help you maximize your time and learn more about America's Finest City. From a fellow fan of travel and photography, have fun!

Andrew Hudson.

Author's Welcome

By Andrew Hudson

Photo by Jennie Van Meter

Andrew Hudson is the publisher of PhotoSecrets books. His first book, *PhotoSecrets San Francisco and Northern California*, won the Benjamin Franklin Award for Best First Book. He lives in La Jolla, San Diego.

Thank you for picking up this copy of PhotoSecrets. As a fellow fan of travel and photography, I know this book will help you find the most visually stunning places and come home with equally stunning photographs.

I first came to San Diego in 1990 and, like many other new residents, I soon fell in love with its climate, people and pleasures. No where else can you combine such perfect weather with such a variety of photogenic sights, outdoor activities and distinctive neighborhoods. While researching this book, I've had great fun exploring San Diego, and I know you will too.

PhotoSecrets is designed to quickly show you all the best sights. As you travel, this book will give you tips for the best places to stand, ideas for composition and lighting, and historical background for each sight. It'll be like travelling with a location scout and a pro-photographer in your pocket. Now, pack some extra film and start exploring!

Andrew Hudson

Acknowledgements

Credits

Author, photographer, designer and publisher:
.... Andrew Hudson

Contributors:
Foreword ...... Bob Krist
Balboa Park History......
.... Richard Amero
Skylines ..... James Blank
Backcountry .. Jerry Schad
SeaWorld ..... Bob Couey
Zoo . Ron Gordon Garrison
Law ...... Dianne Brinson

Consultants:
General . Jennie Van Meter
Design ..... Rob Mikuteit
Mac... Andy Cunningham
Editing...... Andy Harris,
Cy Hudson, Steve Roy,
Dave and Liane Ousley
Accounting . .Barry J. Kohn
Legal ..... Peter H. Karlen

Suppliers:
Film............ Nelson's
Developing ...... Chrome
PhotoCD....... Dale Labs
Printing.. Doosan Dong-A,
South Korea

"A good traveler has no well-defined plan and is not intent on arriving."
—Lao Tzu (570–490 BC), Chinese philosopher

"I am but a small child wandering upon the vast shores of knowledge, every now and then finding a small bright pebble to content myself with."
—Plato

This is my second book project and again it wouldn't have been more than a daydream without the encouragement of my love, Jennie Van Meter. In the early days and the late nights, it was only Jennie's belief in this book that kept me working on it. Thanks Coco—one day I'll be able to hire you!

Thanks to my Mumb and Dad for their loving support and interest. My Mumb carries my Yosemite book in her handbag and proudly shows it to everyone she meets, and Dad's editing was perceptive and useful. Hello to my brother Patrick who is winding his way through South America at the moment, and to Jennie's parents and sisters.

Three people in particular generously spent a lot of unpaid time and effort helping me, and this book is richer for their contributions (although they aren't!). Richard Amero exhaustively researched the architecture of Balboa Park and for many months answered my endless and often witless questions. James Blank offered unlimited enthusiasm, experiences and photos and I look forward to working with him on future books. Bob Couey at SeaWorld was an ardent campaigner and provided a wealth of photo tips.

Other people who went above-and-beyond the call of duty include: Jerry Schad for his poetic article; Debbie Stetz, Park Ranger and Historian at Cabrillo National Monument; and Janet Bartel, Historian for Mission San Diego.

I'd also like to thank the following for their invaluable contributions: Laurie Krusinski, Ron Gordon Garrison, Ken Kelley and Georgeanne Irvine at the Zoological Society of San Diego; Mardi Snow, Sue Fouquette and Paul Sirois at Balboa Park; Shelley Stefonyszyn, Rick Crawford and Sally West at the San Diego Historical Society; Therese Muranaka at the Serra Museum; Dr. Clare Crane of SDSU and James Horne for the Villa Montezuma; Corrine Brindley, Kina Skudi, Ken Bohn and Mike Aguilera at Sea-

"Though we travel the world over to find the beautiful, we must carry it with us or we find it not."
—Ralph Waldo Emerson

"I would say to any artist: 'don't be repressed in your work, dare to experiment, consider any urge, if in a new direction all the better.'"
—Edward Weston to Ansel Adams.

"The real voyage of discovery consists not in seeking new landscapes but in having new eyes."
—Marcel Proust (1871–1922), French writer

"The writer does the most who gives his reader the most knowledge and takes from him the least time." *—Sydney Smith*

"Every good and excellent thing in the world stands moment by moment on the razor edge of danger and must be fought for."
—Thornton Wilder

World; Lisa Yamaguchi Pak and Cherilyn Megill at Horton Plaza; Kelly Conte and Kathi Thompson at Seaport Village; Cynthia Hansen at the Gaslamp Quarter Historical Foundation; Lauren Ash Donoho at the Hotel del Coronado; Jill Votaw, U.S. Navy Public Affairs; Ron Quinn, ex-Historian for Old Town State Historic Park; Elder Grant Furse at the Mormon Battalion Visitors Center; Cindy Clark at the Stephen Birch Aquarium; Bob Wohl at Torrey Pines State Reserve; Jim Bremner at DesertUSA.com; Brian Cahill at Anza-Borrego Desert State Park.

The elegant design template is thanks to Rob Mikuteit at Mikuteit Design.

Thanks to everyone who took the time to review, promote and/or sell PhotoSecrets books. Thanks also to Vickie Visa and Marcie Mastercard for financing this extravagant venture.

Thanks to everyone at NBN (National Book Network) for being such a wonderful distributor. Miriam Bass and Jed Lyons saw the potential of this concept in 1996 based on just a few sheets of paper and boldly signed a publisher who had, at the time, no books. Thanks to James Penfield, Spencer Gale, Ray Wittrup, Rich Freese, Michael Sullivan, Jock Hayward, Tracy Bauer, Tressa Keith and others for their important contributions.

Hello to our many San Diego friends including A1 (Andy Cunningham); A2 (Andy Harris); Steve Roy and Kelli Burn-Lucht; Dave and Liane Ousley; Mary, Chuck, Ben and Katie Allen; Jane Trenaman; Martin and Laura Carrington; everyone at the Old Rohr Sailing Club.

Hello also to my family (Patrick; Mumb and Dad; Gracie; Nan; Yve, John, Richie, Jenny; Fi, Dan, Cameron and Emily; Sue, John, Sarah and Alex; Liz, Malcolm, Rachel and James; Ive and Bill; Ken and Wendy; Rich and Sylvia; Olive and Kim) and all my friends from Redditch, Coventry, Manchester, New York, Philadephia and elsewhere.

About This Book

"Whether it's a major travel assignment or a family vacation, the more specifics you know about the location, the better your pictures will be."
—Bob Krist, National Geographic Traveler

1 Plan

Decide which sites to visit by reviewing the pictures. Use the 'When' information to plan your day around the best light.

2 Visit

For each sight, the text describes what it is and why it's interesting. 'Where' tells you how to get there and 'When' gives you the best time of the day for photography.

3 Shoot

Start by taking the photographs in the book. The maps and tips tells you how. Then branch off with your own interpretations. Try different angles, work the subject. Use the accompanying pictures for ideas.

What this book is

A compendium of the most visually distinctive places in and around San Diego that you can easily and dependably photograph. All photos were taken with standard 35mm equipment (nothing expensive) from easily accessible places (no helicopters or special entry required) and don't depend on a particular date or season. You *can* take every shot in this book.

Why you need this book

To identify the major sights; to find the classic views; to see what's been done before; to use as a spring-board to your unique interpretations.

What's not in this book

Places to stay; places to eat; museums—unless there's something worth photographing; pictures of festivals and events—see the list at the back; great shots which are mainly of people or the weather; places that you need to hike a long way to find; nature or wildlife photography—this is just travel.

Got any tips?

PhotoSecrets is intended to be a 'community of interest' reference book. If you find errors or omissions, sights not mentioned, better angles or have any tips, please let us know. That way the second edition will be even better!

Updates

For a current list of updates, visit our web site at:
http://www.photosecrets.com

Layout

The title pages for each subject have a standard format so that you flick through the book and find the sights you're most interested in.

Find the spot

Dot: *Where to stand*

Arrow: *Best direction to face*

Title Listed in the contents and index

Slide Identifies the Top Ten sights

Scene Shows what the area is like

Quote For atmosphere and historical reference

What What the sight is and why it's interesting

Where Getting there

When Best time of day for lighting

Best Time

🕐 *Morning*

🕐 *Anytime*

🕐 *Afternoon*

Cost Entrance prices are given as adult/child. Discounts may apply. Prices may change.

Tab Helps you navigate sections of the book

San Diego Zoo

Est. 1921

36

The "World-Famous" San Diego Zoo® is the city's best-known attraction and one of the largest and most famous zoos in the world. San Diego's ideal climate allows the animals to be displayed outdoors all year round. Instead of barred cages, many animals are displayed in open, moated enclosures, similar to their natural environment.

Over 4,000 animals of 800 species are exhibited, including the only pair of pandas in the U.S., the largest koala colony outside of Australia, and Galapagos tortoises. Other highlights include two of the world's largest walk-through aviaries, Polar Bear Plunge, Hippo Beach, Gorilla Tropics, Tiger River, Pygmy Chimps at Bonobo Road and Sun Bear Forest.

The Zoo is set in 100 subtropical acres, beautifully landscaped with more than 6,500 varieties of plants including towering eucalyptus, graceful palms, bird-of-paradise and hibiscus. The plants create the natural environments for many animals and, for some, provide the leaves and fruit of their native habitats.

The Zoo has a "second campus," the 2,200-acre *San Diego Wild Animal Park*, 30 miles north.

Above and right: Female Bai Yun is the more playful and attractive of the Zoo's two pandas.

"A zoo is just about the most fascinating place in the world."
—Dr. Harry M. Wegforth, founder of the San Diego Zoo.

Where In Balboa Park, north of downtown. Access via Park Boulevard or Pershing Drive.

When Opens at 9am (may be 7:30pm in summer); closing times vary between 4pm (winter) and 5pm (summer).

Cost $16/$7. Deluxe package with bus tour, aerial tram and children's zoo: $19/$11. Subject to change. Call 619-234-3153 for current information.

Giant Pandas

San Diego Zoo is home to the only giant panda pair in the U.S. Bai Yun (female) and Shi Shi (male) are on a 12-year loan from China and are treated as VIPs (Very Important Pandas). There are less than 1,000 pandas in the world and only 16 outside China.

Tip Find a handrail for support. For sharp images you need to keep your camera steady. Since the animals are often moving, a tripod is generally more trouble than it's worth. Instead use a wall or handrail.

Tip Be patient. The pandas are shy and operate on their own schedule. Exhibit times are posted at the zoo's entrance. The pandas are most active in the morning, particularly at feeding time. The best shots capture a glint of light in the panda's dark eyes.

Most pictures are in the 2:3 aspect ratio of 35mm film. Full-page pictures are in the 10" x 8" size of a standard enlargement.

Tip On-the-spot tips and ideas

Nearby Places to go afterwards

Map Shows the best camera locations. Maps are always to scale and always point vertically north. They are for illustration—you will need a good road atlas.

Tips and Tricks

Above: **Find a foreground with an interesting shape.**
Below: **Clouds obscure the sun and create rays.**

Right: **Wait until the sun is almost touching the horizon, so that it's brightness matches that of the sky. Frame just the sky and water for maximum effect.** *Below:* **30 minutes later the high clouds pop up with color.**

Look away from the sun for more-even lighting.

Travel **photographers** are like magicians—they have a bag of tricks and choose the right ones for the occasion. Here are some tricks for you to practice.

Sunsets

The biggest problem with sunsets is the sun. It's just too bright. Unlike human eyes, camera film cannot handle high contrasts so including the sun in a photograph will usually give you a picture of a big white splodge. Your picture will be overexposed with little color or detail. There's no easy way around this, so the trick is to either wait until the sun is on the horizon (when it's dimmer), or photograph the sunset without the sun. Look for clouds to obscure the sun or photograph a part of the sky away from the sun.

The sky often has the most color after the sun has set—the afterglow. Pick a day when there's a sprinkling of very high, whispy clouds as they'll turn a bright golden color about 15-30 minutes after sunset.

Pictures of just the sky can be boring so find a simple foreground to add depth and interest. Your foreground will be silhouetted, so find a subject that has an interesting outline. I like piers and palm trees. To photograph people, use a flash to add light on their faces.

Position the horizon low in your frame so that you mostly capture the colorful sky and any reflecting water.

Water makes a good fore-ground —you get double the effect. An FL-D filter gives a purple tint.

Find a subject that has a lot of lights. This is easier in the holiday season. Choose a view with an even coverage of light.

Dusk

Many of my favorite photographs are taken at dusk. This is a magic moment when camera film can produce images even better than the human eye can see in real life. The delicate mix of natural and artificial light creates romantic, colorful and fascinating scenes.

Timing

The key element of dusk photography is timing. You want the brightness of the sky to equal the brightness of the artificial lights. During dusk, the sky's light level is descending rapidly and you only have a window of a few minutes to capture the perfect mix. This occurs about 10-30 minutes after sunset. Any later and the sky loses color and will appear black, which is a waste.

You could use a light meter to continually measure the light level but I find it easier just to shoot a whole roll of film over the 20-30 minute range and pick out the best shot.

Equipment

This is low-light photography so a good tripod is a must. Automatic exposure works fine, but take additional shots with +1/2 and +1 stops of exposure just in case. Filters aren't necessary but you can get a nice purple effect (top) with an FL-D filter. This counteracts the green color of tungsten lighting. A 'saturated' slide film like Fuji Velvia captures the richest colors. You can lend a cool blue cast to the scene by using tungsten-balanced film.

Subject

Find a subject that is evenly lit and decorated with artificial light. Set up early, around sunset, and wait patiently for the perfect light.

Animals

Now you can't come to San Diego and not photograph some animals! Like people, animals are best photographed by cropping tightly into the face. To do this, you'll need a long lens, preferably reaching to 200 or 300mm. To avoid blurred images, always get a good support. Lean on a barrier or against a wall, or even on a friend's shoulder—that's what friends are for. Don't lean your lens against glass as you'll scratch the surface.

Use a long lens to concentrate on the face.

Overflow the frame with the animal's face to produce impact. Focus on the eyes as they're the key feature. As with people, try to photograph animals from eye level for an intimate feel.

Include a person for scale and emotion.

Use a long lens to contract distances.

Water

The main trick for fountains and waterfalls is to use a shutter speed of 1/8s. This blurs moving water to create a soft, romantic look. Crop out the edge of the water so it appears that you're in the water.

Distant Objects

A long lens reduces the apparent distant between objects. You can use this to combine subjects in a way the eye doesn't see them. For example, the plane to the left appears closer to the buildings than it really is.

A long lens "flattens" an image.

Buildings

Pictures of buildings can appear flat and lifeless, so find a strong foreground to add depth and warmth. Plants and water are good as they offer color and natural textures to contrast the building's hard surfaces.

Use a wide-angle lens to emphasize the foreground and exaggerate depth. I like a 28mm lens, but many professionals prefer a 20mm. Set the lens to f16 or f22 to provide a wide depth-of-field and keep both the foreground and background in focus. This will reduce the shutter speed so a tripod may be useful. Simplify the border of your frame to emphasize the subject.

Overflow the bottom of the frame with flowers or water and use a wide-angle lens to draw the eye into the shot.

Shooting an hour or two before sunset produces golden colors to add warmth and long shadows to show texture.

Getting Great Colors

Get that deep, warm 'National Geographic' look by concentrating on color. Here's how:

• Use 'saturated' film. Lower-speed film (ISO 100) holds deeper colors than faster film (ISO 200); and slide film holds deeper colors than print film. I love Fujichrome Velvia, an ISO 50 slide film.

• Use a polarizer. This is a low-cost filter that produces deep blue skies. I use it on almost every daytime shot.

• Shoot in the 'magic hours'—the first and last few hours of the day. Plan your photography for when the sun is low in the sky and the sunlight appears warm and golden.

Warnings

For a brief discussion of some of the legal issues that affect photographers and photographs, see page 308.

Taking photographs can be illegal and/or dangerous and result in liability. You are responsible for your safety, actions and judgment. The publishers, authors and distributors of this book accept no responsibility or liability for:

• Your conduct;

• Any actions stated, inferred, or contemplated by this book, including, without limitation, the taking of photographs, and;

• The accuracy of information, including prices and entrance fees, contained in, or inferred by, this book.

Commercial photographers in particular should be aware of copyright, trademark, defamation, and other laws and of the legal consequences and ramifications of taking photographs of various subject matter and selling and licensing their photographs.

DO NOT:

• Stop a vehicle on, or at, a freeway, on/off ramp, bridge, a no-parking area, or other dangerous or illegal places to take a photograph;

• Trespass on private property, ignore 'no entry' or 'do not enter' signs, disturb the privacy of individuals or organizations, or photograph private homes;

• Take a photograph while driving a vehicle;

• Take a photograph when warned not to;

• Take a photograph from, or ask your subject(s) to pose near dangerous places such as, but not limited to, a road, cliff edge, river, slippery rocks, narrow hiking trail, beyond guard rails, an open window, railway tracks, storm drain, around uncaged wild animals, or by climbing a building, tree, lamppost, sculpture or other structure not intended for that purpose.

Things Change
The only constant is change. Prices and fees may be higher than quoted, and opening times, views, and facts may have changed since publication.

Statues and Murals
Reproducing images of artwork, such as statues and murals, even when temporary or in public view, may require the permission of the copyright owner.

Commercial Photographers

If you are photographing or using a location for commercial purposes (advertising, TV, film, etc. or anything involving models, props or product) you will probably need permission from the property owners and local authorities. Although some information is provided, these requirements are beyond the scope of this book.

The permission process can take days or weeks so contact the appropriate people ahead of time. They are usually very willing to assist you and have forms for the purpose. Fees and insurance may be required.

For more information, contact the San Diego Film Commission at 1010 Second Avenue, Suite 1600, San Diego, CA 92101. Tel: 619-234-3456.

State Parks

All commercial photographers in state parks must be permitted through the California Film Commission. Contact Pamela Lockhart on 800-858-4749. Upon arrival at a state park, commercial photographers must announce themselves and their intentions prior to any commercial photography session.

DO NOT:

• Reproduce or sell photographs of or including: paintings, sculpture, statues, murals, illustrations, posters, photographs (including postcards) or any other work of art without first obtaining the permission of the copyright owner(s)—usually the artist(s) and/or property owner(s);

• Reproduce or photograph trademarks without obtaining the permission of the trademark owner(s);

• Photograph or distribute photographs of famous people without their consent;

• Photograph or distribute photographs of private individuals in embarrassing, private, obscene, scandalous, libelous, unlawful or defamatory situations;

• Photograph or distribute photographs of people or property where the image may be used for commercial purposes, such as product packaging, endorsement, promotion or advertisements, without the permission of the individual(s) and/or organization(s) concerned;

To 'distribute' includes to display on an Internet website, to attach to an e-mail message, or to store or transmit by any other electronic means.

Always consult a qualified attorney before you distribute copies of any photographs you take, particularly when you are publicly distributing such photographs for commercial purposes.

The above warnings do not list each and every possible area of illegality, danger, or liability but are intended to illustrate some of the areas of risk in taking and distributing photographs. If you have any questions regarding the taking or distributing of any photographs, consult your attorney and your insurance advisor.

Introduction

Background to San Diego

"**A**merica's Finest City" is the slogan for San Diego and it certainly rings true. Blessed with an almost perfect climate, California's most attractive beaches, and one of the world's great natural harbors, San Diego is a year-round resort. Even in February, as half the country lumbers under snow, you'll find San Diegans sunbathing on the beaches, rollerblading on the boardwalks, surfing the coastlines, sailing the bays, and hiking the deserts. Throughout the year's seasons, San Diegans exude the casual and energetic lifestyle that is Southern California.

With a population of 1.2 million people, San Diego is the nation's seventh-largest city (ranking behind New York, Los Angeles, Chicago, Houston, Philadelphia and Phoenix) and the second-largest city on the West Coast. San Diego County contains 70 miles of coastline, 30 beaches, and 4,205 square miles of land, over half of which is publicly-owned. The county rises from sea level in the west to 6,533 feet at Hot Springs Mountain in the northeast.

To the east are high mountains which give way to California's largest state park—the Anza-Borrego Desert. In the north is Camp Pendleton Marine Corps Base—the largest amphibious training base in the United States—separating San Diego from the metropolitan areas of Orange, Riverside and Los Angeles Counties. South of San Diego is the Mexican border and the long peninsula of Baja California. Tijuana, Mexico's fourth-largest city, is a mere 30 minutes drive from downtown San Diego. With a population of 1.3 million people, Tijuana is comparable in size to its American neighbor, San Diego.

Based on San Diego County's rich history, geographical variations, cultural influences, and a thriving tourist industry, the area offers a multitude of fun things to see, do, and photograph. San Diego is a cultural city, fostering one of the most active theater scenes in the country and more than 90 museums. Not-to-be-missed attractions include the world-famous San Diego Zoo, displaying more than 900 species of animals; Balboa Park (which encompasses the Zoo), offering more museums, theaters, and varieties of plant life than any other park in America; and the original SeaWorld San Diego, a 150-acre marine theme park.

In sharp contrast to the vast, sprawling metropolis of Los Angeles, its neighbor to the north, San Diego County features small, pocket communities, easily connected by an effective city freeway system. Within the metro area lies the affluent culture of La Jolla and its Mediterranean architecture; the college-crowd surf towns of Pacific Beach and Mission Beach; the elegant residences of Point Loma and Coronado; the Arts-and-Crafts architecture of Kensington and North Park; the bohemian Hillcrest; the nightlife and shopping districts in downtown; the biotech and communication industries of Torrey Pines and Sorrento Valley; military bases around San Diego Bay and at Miramar and Camp Pendleton; and the Mexican heritage of Old Town. It's this accessible variety that is the joy and essence of San Diego.

Balboa Park.

History

Zooming In On San Diego's Past

"On this day, Thursday Sept 28 1542, we discovered a port, closed and very good, which we named San Miguel." — Juan Rodríguez Cabrillo in his log. San Miguel was later renamed San Diego.

"Thanks be to God, I have arrived at this Port of San Diego. It is beautiful to behold and does not belie its reputation." — Father Serra, 1769.

San Diego is the oldest city and one of the most historic places in California. Much of this history beckons your camera.

10,000 years ago, prehistoric tribes roamed today's San Diego County. You can still see their pictographs in Anza-Borrego Desert State Park. The earliest-known tribe was the San Dieguitos, and the last native people are the Cahuilla and Kumeyaay Native Americans, now resident on several reservations.

In 1542, 78 years before the Pilgrims landed at Plymouth Rock, San Diego became the first place on America's West Coast to be discovered by Europeans. Juan Rodríguez Cabrillo, exploring on behalf of Spain, sailed into the bay and named it 'San Miguel.' Today you can visit **Cabrillo National Monument** on Point Loma which overlooks the explorer's landing spot and has stunning views of the city.

In 1602, Sebastián Vizcaíno mapped the bay and renamed it after a fifteenth-century Franciscan, Saint Didacus, known to the Spanish as *San Diego de Alcalá*.

In 1769, San Diego became the first permanent European settlement in the western U.S. Worried about the encroachment of British and Russian fur trappers in the north, Spain expanded out of today's Mexico and its Baja (lower) California peninsular to colonize Alta (upper) California. Father Junípero Serra established a mission (a church to convert the native population) and a *presidio* (fort). You can visit the excavated ruins on **Presidio Hill**, the "Plymouth Rock of the West." The adjacent Junípero Serra Museum makes a great photograph.

California's most historic and unifying landmarks are the 21 Spanish missions, each a day's walk apart, linking San Diego to Sonoma. **Mission San Diego de Alcalá** was the first in the chain and you can visit this still-active church in Mission Valley. Three other missions grace San Diego County, near Oceanside, Pala and Julian.

Following Mexico's independence from Spain in

1821, California's role changed from colonization to commerce. From 1825–32, San Diego was the capital of Mexico's Baja and Alta California. The original town center of that period, and the early American period (1846–72), is preserved in **Old Town State Historic Park**. The mission system was disbanded around 1833 and the lands and cattle divided up to create large, wealthy ranches (*ranchos*). One of the best examples of a Spanish-Mexican ranch house is **Rancho Guajome Adobe** (1853) in Vista.

Mexico opened up the ports to foreign ships, and cattle hides were traded for exotic goods from the American Colonies, England and South America. The **Maritime Museum of San Diego** displays the 1863 English square-rigged trade ship *Star of India*.

Skirmishes from the Mexican-American War of 1846–48 are remembered at **Fort Stockton Memorial** in Presidio Park and **San Pasqual Battlefield State Historic Park** near the **San Diego Wild Animal Park**. In 1850, San Diego became the first county of California and, two years later, California joined the Union to become the 31st state.

"I thought San Diego must be a Heaven on Earth... It seemed to me the best spot for building a city I ever saw."
— *Alonzo Horton, 1867.*

In 1867, a merchant from San Francisco, Alonzo Horton, laid the foundation for today's modern city. He bought 960 acres of a previous development by William Heath Davis, subdivided it in a grid, and promoted South San Diego—New Town. The following year, Horton and Ephraim Morse set aside 1,400 acres as a city park, today's **Balboa Park**.

In 1885 the transcontinental railroad —a spur south from Los Angeles—reached San Diego and sparked a real-estate boom. Magnificent stores and houses were built along Fifth Avenue and Broadway. They are preserved today as the **Gaslamp Quarter**, a 16-block area in downtown of restored buildings dating from 1850 to the 1920s. Other Victorians are displayed at **Heritage Park** (1886–89) by Old Town, **Villa Montezuma** (1887) east of downtown, and **Heritage Walk** in Escondido. The coastal cities of La Jolla, Carlsbad and

Timeline

Coronado were developed, and eucalyptus trees—now a dominant feature of San Diego—were imported from Australia and grown for railroad ties. There are railroad museums in Balboa Park, Escondido and Campo.

In 1888, on San Diego's neighboring island of Coronado, the largest seaside hotel in the country was opened—the **Hotel del Coronado**. Today the hotel, with its distinctive red conical towers, is the only remaining example of California's opulent Victorian beach resorts. You can visit Coronado via the gracefully curving **San Diego-Coronado Bay Bridge** (1969) and get terrific skyline views from the **Ferry Landing**.

Boom was followed by bust, allowing another San Franciscan—sugar magnate heir John D. Spreckels—to buy the Del and most of Coronado in 1889. Spreckels financed the "impossible railroad," the *San Diego and Arizona* (1906–1919) which traveled east over the Anza-Borrego Desert, as well as **Spreckels Organ** (1915) in Balboa Park and the **Giant Dipper** (1925) rollercoaster in Belmont Park.

In 1897, English newspaper heiress Ellen Browning Scripps moved to **La Jolla**. She bought much of the land around La Jolla's coast and donated it to the community. Thanks to Ms. Scripps, today residents and visitors alike enjoy Children's Pool, **La Jolla Cove**, **Torrey Pines State Reserve**, and much of San Diego Zoo.

In 1914 the Panama Canal was opened, shortening the sea route between America's coasts. Seizing the opportunity to launch San Diego—the "First Port of Call"—as a major city, a world's fair was created. City Park was renamed **Balboa Park** and developed into a showplace. Architect Bertram Goodhue created a fantasy city of Spanish-Colonial style buildings. Horticulturists Kate Sessions and John Morley turned the barren Balboa Park into a land of sub-tropical trees and exotic flowers.

Although the "official" fair was held in San Francisco, San Diego's smaller 1915–16 Panama-California International Exposition had a more lasting effect. The

San Diego has a significant aeronautical history. John J. Montgomery made the first controlled-wing, heavier-than-air flight in 1883—20 years before the Wrights; Glenn Curtiss made the first seaplane flight in 1911; and in 1927, Claude Ryan built the first aircraft to fly across the Atlantic, Charles Lindbergh's *Spirit of St. Louis*. A replica can be seen at the San Diego Aerospace Museum.

San Diego is also a significant center of marine research. The renowned Scripps Institution of Oceanography was founded in 1903 and you can visit their Stephen Birch Aquarium in La Jolla. One of the city's most popular attractions is SeaWorld San Diego (1964)—the first Sea-World marine park.

buildings now house some of the park's thirteen museums, the largest collection in the country outside of Washington, D.C. The animals of the Exposition were acquired by Dr. Harry Wegeforth in 1916 to form the basis of the world-famous **San Diego Zoo** and the **San Diego Wild Animal Park**.

In 1941, after the bombing of Pearl Harbor, the U.S. Navy moved its Pacific naval headquarters to San Diego. The bay is now one of the largest and busiest U.S. Navy ports in the world. The bay was dredged to accommodate aircraft carriers and the material was used to join North Island to Coronado (1940), and to create Coronado's Ocean Beach (1945), Shelter Island (1950) and Harbor Island (1969). In the 1950s, the City dredged a large swamp at the mouth of the San Diego River to create **Mission Bay Park**, a 4,600-acre watersports playground. On the edge of Mission Bay is now one of San Diego's premier attractions— SeaWorld.

In 1974, plans were laid for the revitalization of **downtown** San Diego. New additions include **Seaport Village** (1980), **Horton Plaza** (1985), and many defining office buildings and hotels.

Today, the largest industries are manufacturing ($18B), military ($9B) and tourism ($4B). There are over 14 million overnight visitors to San Diego and the city's most popular attractions are the San Diego Zoo, Balboa Park, and SeaWorld.

PhotoSecrets   San Diego

Top Ten Sights

San Diego Zoo®

Above and right: Female Bai Yun is the more playful and attractive of the Zoo's two adult pandas.

"A zoo is just about the most fascinating place in the world."
—Dr. Harry M. Wegeforth, founder of the San Diego Zoo.

Where
In Balboa Park, north of downtown. Access via Park Boulevard or Pershing Drive.

When ⏱
Open 365 days a year. Hours: 9 a.m. to 4 p.m. Summer (Jul–Aug) hours: 9 a.m. to 9 p.m.

Cost
$19.50/$11.75. Deluxe package with bus tour and aerial tram: $32/$19.75. Subject to change. Info: 619-234-3153.

CONTENTS:

Zoo

The 'World-Famous' San Diego Zoo® is the city's best-known attraction and one of the largest and most famous zoos in the world. San Diego's ideal climate allows the animals to be displayed outdoors all year round. Instead of barred cages, many animals are displayed in open, moated enclosures, similar to their natural environment.

Over 4,000 animals of 800 species are exhibited, including the only family of pandas in the U.S., the largest koala colony outside of Australia, and Galapagos tortoises. Other highlights include two of the world's largest walk-through aviaries, Polar Bear Plunge, Hippo Beach, Gorilla Tropics, Tiger River, Pygmy Chimps at Bonobo Road and Sun Bear Forest.

The Zoo is set in 100 subtropical acres, beautifully landscaped with more than 6,500 varieties of plants including towering eucalyptus, graceful palms, bird-of-paradise and hibiscus. The plants create the natural environments for many animals and, for some, provide the leaves and fruit of their native habitats.

The Zoo has a "second campus," the 2,200-acre *San Diego Wild Animal Park*, 30 miles north.

Giant Pandas ⏱

The Zoo's most famous residents. Female Bai Yun gave birth to a girl, Hua Mei, on 8/21/99 and a boy (not named at press time) on 8/19/03. Along with male Gao Gao, the pandas are on loan from China. For exhibit times call 888-MY-PANDA.

Tip
Find a handrail for support. For sharp images you need to keep your camera steady. Since the animals are often moving, a tripod is generally more trouble than it's worth. Instead use a wall or handrail.

Tip

Be patient. The pandas are shy and operate on their own schedule. Exhibit times are posted at the zoo's entrance. The pandas are most active in the morning, particularly at feeding time. The best shots capture a glint of light in the panda's dark eyes.

Faces of the San Diego Zoo

This page: Indo Chinese tiger. Opposite from top left: pygmy chimpanzee baby; Sumatran orangutan; male lowland gorilla; Alaskan brown bear cub. All photos by Ron Garrison.

Map of the Zoo

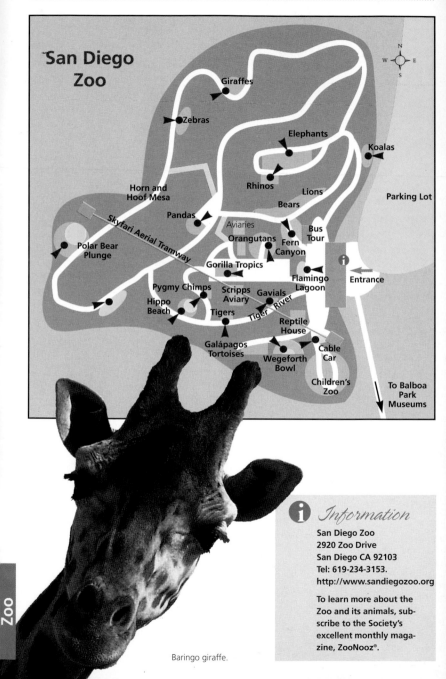

San Diego Zoo

Giraffes

Zebras

Elephants

Koalas

Horn and Hoof Mesa

Rhinos

Lions

Bears

Parking Lot

Pandas

Skyfari Aerial Tramway

Aviaries

Bus Tour

Orangutans

Fern Canyon

Polar Bear Plunge

Gorilla Tropics

Flamingo Lagoon

Entrance

Pygmy Chimps

Scripps Aviary

Gavials

Hippo Beach

Tigers

Tiger River

Reptile House

Galápagos Tortoises

Wegeforth Bowl

Cable Car

Children's Zoo

To Balboa Park Museums

Baringo giraffe.

ℹ️ *Information*

San Diego Zoo
2920 Zoo Drive
San Diego CA 92103
Tel: 619-234-3153.
http://www.sandiegozoo.org

To learn more about the Zoo and its animals, subscribe to the Society's excellent monthly magazine, ZooNooz®.

Zoo

The Skyfari Aerial Tramway 🕐 is best photographed as it rises over the duck pond, near the Children's Zoo.

Where

In Balboa Park, just north of the main buildings. Free parking off Park Blvd. From I-5, take the Pershing Drive exit north to Florida Drive and Zoo Place.

When 🕐

Morning is best as the animals are most active at this time. On hot summer afternoons, the animals may retreat to the shade and doze. Cooler weather and seasons (winter) are best. When it's raining the animals may seek shelter out of view.

You can easily spend an entire day here, if not more. To avoid the crowds, come early on weekdays. The pandas are very popular but not always on display—their exhibit times are posted at the entrance and there's a hotline at 1-888-MY PANDA.

Pets are not permitted. Prices, exhibits and times subject to change.

Getting Around:

The best approach is to spend all day walking along the five miles of pathways. Make sure you bring comfortable walking shoes. There are exhibits and refreshments all over, so just aim for your favorite animals.

A good introduction is the 40-minute guided bus tour which departs from the Flamingo Lagoon area by the main entry plaza. The open-sided double-decker buses leave every few minutes on a three-mile round trip, and the commentary is fun and informative. There are good views of many animals, although you can't see

the pandas, pygmy chimpanzees, gorillas or sun bears.

Alternatively the Kangaroo Bus, which is also guided, follows the same route but allows you to ride all day and hop on and off at nine different stops.

The Skyfari® Aerial Tramway (extra charge) is a third-of-a mile trip to the far end of the Zoo. Starting from the main entrance, open-air gondolas whisk you over the treetops, 180 feet above the ground, to the Horn and Hoof Mesa. The ride is relaxing but doesn't give you close-up views of the animals.

Tip

Zoom in to the face. As with people, the most powerful shots of animals are usually just of the face. Use a 200mm or 300mm lens to zoom in.

Sumatran orangutan.

History of the Zoo

Derived from "It Began with a Roar!" by Dr. Harry M. Wegeforth and Neil Morgan.

"The account of the Zoo's founding is one of the most impressive stories of disinterested public service that San Diego or any other city may boast."
—San Diego Sun

"No one person gave so much of personal energy, interest, devotion and very life to the development of a public project as Doctor Harry gave to the creation of the Zoo."
—Tom Faulconer, Zoo Director.

"Practically alone, [Wegeforth] raised all the private funds with which the magnificent Zoo was built. He visualized and planned all of its unique features. He traveled at his own expense all over the world."
—From an early guidebook.

Zoo

San Diego Zoo was founded by Dr. Harry M. Wegeforth (1882–1942), a local doctor who became a keen photographer.

The son of a German oil refiner, Wegeforth was born in Baltimore, MD. From an early age he became enthralled with animals, possibly from a visit to the Barnum and Bailey circus. In 1908, in search of a place to open a new medical practice, the newly-qualified doctor found his way to the warm climate of San Diego. He opened an office in downtown San Diego at Fifth and Broadway, and was later joined by his brother, Paul, in 1915.

In the book *It Began with a Roar!,* Wegeforth tells the story of the founding of the Zoo:

"On September 16, 1916, as I was returning to my office after performing an operation, I drove down Sixth Avenue and heard the roar of the lions in the cages at the Exposition then being held in Balboa Park. I turned to my brother, Paul, who was riding with me, and half jokingly, half wishfully, said, 'Wouldn't it be splendid if San Diego had a zoo! You know … I think I'll start one.'

"I had long nurtured the thought of a San Diego Zoo and now—suddenly—I decided to try to establish one. Dropping my brother at our office, I went down to the *San Diego Union* where I talked long and earnestly with Mr. Clarence McGrew, the city editor. Next morning, [an article proposing a zoo] appeared in the *Union*, prominently featured."

Three men offered support and October 2 the Zoological Society of San Diego (the "Society") was formed. Granted supervision of the Exposition animals, and given other animals by enthusiastic residents, the Society soon had a minor collection. The crew of a

Founder Dr. Harry Wegeforth riding one of the Zoo's first elephants in 1923.

The White Elephants

Wegeforth found it easier to pay for animals if he bought them on credit and then displayed them. In a famous incident, investor John D. Spreckels declined to pay for the Zoo's first elephants by joking that he only funded "white elephants." So Wegeforth had the beasts covered entirely in white powder. When Spreckels saw them, he laughed and promptly paid for the elephants and their compound.

"Watch out for this Wegeforth. If you're a patient, you get your tonsils or your appendix cut out. But if you're working on the Zoo, you get cut off at the pockets."
—*John D. Spreckels.*

Navy ship even donated its pet bear—Caesar—which "grew like a weed" and wrecked several cages. With a donation from Ellen Browning Scripps, a new type of restraint was built for Caesar—the Zoo's first open-moated enclosure.

More animals were acquired from the municipal Zoo and a traveling circus. To transport them, Wegeforth drove with a bear in his car and rode elephants through the streets of San Diego.

In a battle to become automonous from the Park Commission, the Society gave its animals to the City in 1921 in exchange for permanent use of the present 126-acre location. The Zoo is thus owned by the people of San Diego and administered by the Zoological Society of San Diego.

Belle Benchley, who came to the San Diego Zoo in 1925 as a substitute bookkeeper, was promoted by Wegeforth to become the world's first woman zoo director. She wrote two bestsellers which promoted the Zoo and she campaigned persistently to make San Diego Zoo the first zoo outside of Australia to display koalas.

To counter the rise of animal dealers, Wegeforth established the Association of Zoological Parks and Aquariums to exchange animals and information.

Wegeforth traveled to every continent in search of animals and plants to build his zoo. He died in 1942, from pneumonia and malaria contracted while on an animal-buying expedition through India.

In 1972, the Society opened a second location near Escondido—the *San Diego Wild Animal Park*—where many of the larger animals could roam free.

Today the Society also maintains the Center for Reproduction of Endangered Species (CRES) which applies modern medical and scientific methods to save exotic animal species from extinction.

Tip
The **flamingos** ⏱ are the first animals you'll see. Their bright plumage makes for colorful photos. Concentrate on their most distinctive features—the long neck and slender legs.

Camera Den

Situated next to the clock tower at the main entrance, the Camera Den offers Kodak® film, batteries, single-use cameras, postcards, souvenirs and guidebooks.

Members of the Zoological Society of San Diego receive free admission for one year to the San Diego Zoo and San Diego Wild Animal Park. On Founder's Day (the first Monday in October—named in honor of founder Dr. Harry Wegeforth) the Zoo is free. The entire month of October is free for children age 11 and under.

Tip
Focus on the eyes. The most important part of any face is usually the eyes, so try to keep the eyes in focus. The mouth is the next-most important feature, and is easier to focus on with a manual focus camera.

No this isn't "Jurassic Park," it's an alligator. He's got his eye on you—don't stroke his teeth!

Caribbean Flamingo ⏱

Greeting you at the entrance plaza is a display of flamingos. The Caribbean is the largest and most brightly hued of the six species of flamingo. The pink plumage is a result of the pigments present in their crustacean diet.

Tiger River ⏱

To the left of the flamingos is a small path into Tiger River. Recreating an Asian rainforest, this area was the Zoo's first bio-climactic exhibit. Bamboo and other plants are watered by mist-simulating monsoon rainfall. The winding path takes you past gharials, pythons, fishing cats and Malayan tapirs before reaching the eye-catching tigers.

Three windows allow you different views of Indo Chinese tigers. There are fewer than 2,000 Indo-Chinese tigers in the world.

Queensland Koala ⏰

Koalas are the unofficial symbol of San Diego. The Australian authorities were hesitant to allow the fragile marsupials outside of their native habitat. After much discussion, the San Diego Zoo was the first zoo outside of Australia to display koalas. Over 80 koalas have been born at the Zoo, making its collection of koalas the largest outside Australia.

Koalas are one of the most narrowly specialized mammals on Earth, eating only the leaves and young shoots of eucalyptus trees, and only those from 25 varieties of the more than 600 varieties native to Australia.

Nearby are Parma wallabies and Goodfellow's tree kangaroos.

Tip

Photograph the koalas first. Their exhibit has several purpose-built 'trees' for them to pose in, and a wooden deck for you to photograph from. The exhibit faces east so the best light is in the early morning. Use a 200mm lens to zoom in tight. A flash will help to light the koala's eyes and fur.

More koalas can be seen through viewing windows. Look out for Onya-Birri, a rare albino (white) koala.

Queensland koala.

Fern Canyon ⏰ is a verdant retreat. The best view is from the lower bridge looking up the canyon.

Left: North Chinese leopard. *Above:* Galápagos tortoise.

Galápagos Tortoise 🕐

These were Dr. Wegeforth's favorite animal. Nearby are American alligators and a komodo dragon.

Children's Zoo

The Zoo is dedicated to children and in this mini-zoo the conservationists of tomorrow can meet spider monkeys, tree kangaroos and naked mole-rats. There's a petting paddock and an area to watch chicks hatch.

Don't miss the nursery, used for hand-raising animals that have been injured or rejected by their mothers. If there are animals present, you can photograph the babies through glass windows.

Aviaries 🕐

There are three walk-through aviaries, which allow you to watch and photograph exotic birds. The multi-level Scripps Aviary is the oldest and largest. Carefully placed feeders allow some very close-up viewing.

Pygmy Chimps at Bonobo Road ⊕

This is the first exhibition in the U.S. of these endangered pygmy chimps. In their native Republic of Congo they are called 'bonobos.' Bonobos live in female-dominated groups. There are fewer than 100 in captivity.

Gorilla Tropics® ⊕

The recently remodeled Gorilla Tropics (above) displays magnificent lowland gorillas at a simulated African rainforest.

Shows

Live animal shows are presented at the Wegeforth Bowl and the Hunte Amphitheater.

Tip
Use a neutral background. Try to photograph the animals with a simple, mid-toned background. With giraffes, use the mid-toned tree leaves rather than sky as a background. A bright sky may confuse your light meter and make the shot underexposed. A complicated background will distract from your subject.

Horn and Hoof Mesa "

On the flat plains of the west side roam several hoofed species from Africa such as zebras and giraffes.

Borneo orangutan

Tip
Capture expression. To add life and interest to your photographs, wait for the animals to interact with each other and express character and emotion.

Hippo Beach^{SM}   1995

With a 105-foot-long observation window, this exhibit allows you to photograph two hippos, Funani and Jabba, underwater. The two-ton creatures seem awkward on land but are graceful and lithe when swimming in their 150,000 gallon pool. Now you can appreciate why Walt Disney cast hippos as ballerinas!

Nearby are three more hippos, this time made of sand and glue. Lifeguard Mitch, Kahuna Kevin and Surfer Sally are sand sculptures by Gerry Kirk, 1996.

Polar Bear Plunge^{SM}   1996

Come face-to-face with earth's largest carnivore! Designed as a 2.2-acre summer tundra habitat, this is one of the largest polar bear exhibits in the world. A two-level underwater viewing area allows you to watch the playful bears swimming and jumping in their 12-foot-deep, 130,000-gallon pool of chilled water. You can photograph the animals through the 'bear-proof' acrylic window.

Also displayed in the complex are Siberian reindeer, arctic foxes and a variety of arctic birds.

Tip
Include people for scale and
reaction. Stand a few feet
back from the glass to
include some people in the
shot. Try to capture that eye-
to-eye contact between the
hippo or polar bear and a
person. Children usually
make the best subjects.
A fill-flash will illuminate the
otherwise darkened people.
Shoot at an angle to the
glass to reduce reflection
from the flash.

Photographing the Zoo

By Ron Gordon Garrison

Ron Gordon Garrison is the Photo Services Manager for the Zoological Society of San Diego. He has been photographing the animals of San Diego Zoo and San Diego Wild Animal Park since 1965 and supplies most of the images for the Society's magazine, ZooNooz®.

If you wish to sell or commercially reproduce images you have taken of the Zoo animals, you need permission first. Send a written request to:

The Zoological Society
  of San Diego
Public Relations Department
P.O. Box 551
San Diego CA 92112-0551
Tel: 619-685-3291
Fax: 619-557-3970

You are free to use a tripod and flash in the zoo, unless advised otherwise. Some animals, particularly gorillas, are sensitive to flash so there may be 'no flash' signs. As always, be careful with a tripod as people may trip over the legs.

Zoo

I've been photographing the zoo now for over 30 years, and still I love every minute. There's always something new to capture—a new animal or attraction —and the scenery is fabulous. I've traveled to many countries in Africa and Asia to photograph for the Society, but I've never found a better place to photograph so much wildlife than right here in San Diego.

I recommend using an SLR camera with a variety of lenses, depending upon the view. Simplifying the view is very important. The most powerful images are made when you crop tightly into the face of one animal. For this I use a 135–300mm lens, set at the widest aperture, and sometimes with a 2x convertor. With a long lens, a tripod is necessary to get sharp images. Autofocus is very useful as the animals move quite a lot.

Using a flash can highlight the face and add a twinkle to the eyes. However, if you have a built-in flash, it's usually better to switch it off as it creates glare on glass and doesn't work on subjects farther than about ten feet away from you.

Light meters are 'fooled' by very bright or very dark subjects. When photographing a white polar bear on a white background, automatic exposure will make the image turn out gray. To retain the white, overexpose by a stop (+1 exposure compensation). Similarly, if you're photographing the face of a black gorilla, underexpose by a stop (-1).

How to shoot through glass or wire

Several of our animals are exhibited behind glass, which can produce glare. To avoid this, shoot at an angle to the glass. Alternatively, shoot straight on and get very close to the surface. Don't touch the glass as you can can scratch it, instead use your hands or a rubber lens hood as a buffer. If you're using a flash, use a PC cord and hold it off to one side of the camera.

To shoot through wire, get close to the wire and use your widest aperture.

Right: Scarlet macaw.

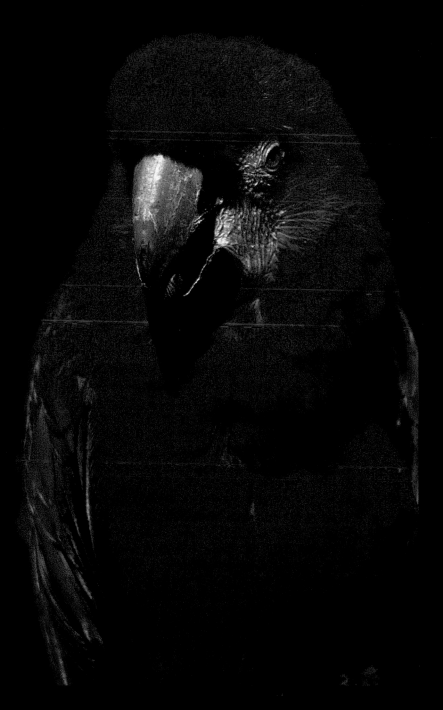

Balboa Park

"Balboa Park is one of the largest, most unusual and strikingly beautiful parks in the world."
—John Nolen,
City Planner, 1926.

The 1994 Weisman Travel Report rated Balboa Park as the number one city park in the United States. The Report was issued by an agency that rates city parks in the United States based on the number of cultural facilities they contain.

CONTENTS:

Home to the world-famous San Diego Zoo, and the site of two international expositions, Balboa Park contains more museums, theaters, animals, architecture, flora, sports facilities, and things to photograph, than any other city park in the world.

Established in 1868 in an era of civic pride and daring beginnings, Balboa Park is a contemporary of New York's Central Park (1857) and San Francisco's Golden Gate Park (1870). Now encompassing about 1,200 acres, Balboa Park is comparable in size to its counterparts (at 843 and 1,107 acres respectively) but contains a greater number of attractions.

The park was little used until the 1915 Panama-California Exposition, which was held on a mesa (flat tableland) in the central portion of the park. Buildings were constructed along a promenade, 'El Prado,' and central plaza, 'Plaza de Panama,' and their fantasy Spanish Colonial architecture has since inspired much of Southern California's Spanish look.

In 1935, a second exposition added more buildings just south of El Prado around a second plaza, 'Pan-American Plaza.' The buildings of both expositions now house thirteen museums, the largest complex west of the Mississippi and second in number only to Washington's Smithsonian Institution.

The animals of the 1915 Exposition became the nucleus of the San Diego Zoo, today the city's most famous attraction. Since 1921, the Zoo has been located on several mesas and canyons just north of El Prado and now occupies about 10% of the park. Although operated by the non-profit Zoological Society of San Diego, the Zoo is owned by the City of San Diego and is part of Balboa Park.

Today, Balboa Park is the city's biggest attraction, drawing many visitors and residents alike. There's a wide variety of activities and enough photographic opportunities to keep a photographer busy for a week.

Right: The Museum of Man (California Tower) from Alcazar Garden.

Balboa Park

Map of Balboa Park

Where

Balboa Park is northeast of downtown San Diego, about two miles from the Convention Center. The best approach to the museums is from the west on Laurel Street. You'll cross Cabrillo Bridge and enter through the impressive West Gate.

From I-5 north: Take the airport exit and turn east on Laurel St.
From I-5 south: Take the Bering Road exit and follow Pershing Drive onto Zoo Place.
From Hwy 163 north: Follow the signs to Park Boulevard.
From downtown: Take Sixth Avenue north and turn right on El Prado (Laurel Street).

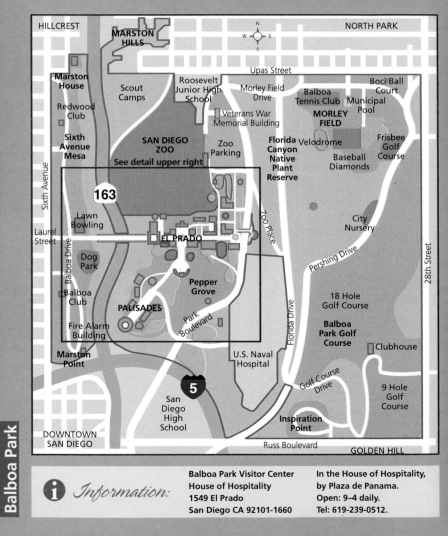

Information: Balboa Park Visitor Center
House of Hospitality
1549 El Prado
San Diego CA 92101-1660

In the House of Hospitality, by Plaza de Panama.
Open: 9–4 daily.
Tel: 619-239-0512.

Balboa Park

Main Buildings/Museums

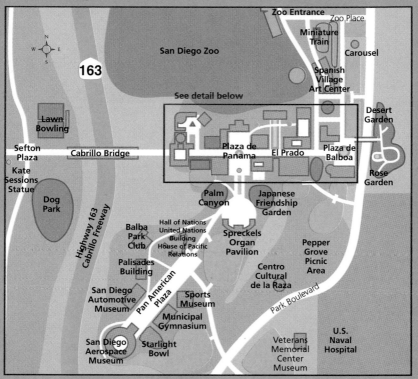

El Prado Buildings/Museums

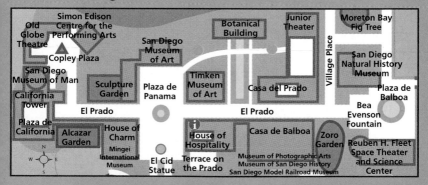

Maps © PhotoSecrets Publishing.

History of Balboa Park

By Richard Amero

Historian Richard W. Amero kindly supplied most of the information in this book about the architecture and history of Balboa Park. Visit his website at:
http://members.home.net/ramero/amero.htm

"These lands are to be held in trust forever ... for the purposes of a free and public park and for no other or different purpose."
—*City decree, 1871.*

"The setting of the park between a vast mountain system on the one hand and the broad ocean on the other is unique. Harbor, bay, islands, sea, promontories, mountains, and miles of open country—each with its own unusual and distinct characteristics, are all incorporated in the park scheme; they form an inseparable and a vital part of it; hundreds of square miles of land and sea are thereby added to the territory of the park."
—*Samuel Parsons, Jr., landscape architect, 1902.*

Balboa Park

In 1867, businessman Alonzo Horton arrived from San Francisco with a grand vision for San Diego. The great cities of the day were forming city parks—New York in 1857 and San Francisco in 1870—so Horton and merchant Ephraim W. Morse persuaded the Board of Trustees of the Town of San Diego to do the same.

In 1868, an almost perfect rectangle of 1,400 acres was set aside "for a park"—a bold move for a town of only 2,300 people. Kate Sessions started planting in the park in 1892 and encouraged George Marston to hire a renowned landscape architect, Samuel Parsons, Jr., in 1903. Trained in the "picturesque" English romantic style, Parsons developed City Park, as it was then called, with winding pathways and grand vistas.

Developing the Park

In 1909, G. Aubrey Davidson proposed a World Exposition in City Park. In six years time the Panama Canal would open, reducing the sea route to California from the East Coast by 8,000 miles. San Diego would be the first port of call and this was cause for celebration. San Diego's leaders, inspired by the real-estate boom of London's Regents Park and the success of Chicago's 1893 World Colombian Exposition, felt that developing City Park into an area of beauty would bring admiration, commerce and residents—and increase property values and city revenues.

A few months later however, San Francisco proposed a similar exposition. In a highly political battle, San Francisco was chosen as the 'official' fair. Undeterred, San Diego resolved to proceed.

Colonel D. C. "Charlie" Collier was elected Director-General of the exposition. He traveled the world, on his own money, for research and promotion. Collier chose human progress as the theme and 400-acres of on the west side of the park as the site.

Kate Sessions— The Mother of Balboa Park

In 1884, Katherine Olivia Sessions (1857–1940) arrived in San Diego from San Francisco to become a school teacher. She taught at the Russ School, a squatter on City Park land.

When her salary was reduced a year later, Sessions became a horticulturist in Coronado. She designed beautiful gardens for the city's rich and for the Hotel del Coronado, and opened a shop at Fifth and C streets in downtown San Diego.

By 1892, when the land of her Coronado nursery became too valuable, she proposed a deal with the City. Sessions was loaned 36 acres in the NW corner of City Park in which she put a 10-acre nursery. As rent, each year she was to plant 100 trees within the park and to donate another 300 trees and plants to the City for parks and streets.

From 1892 to 1903, when her nursery moved to Mission Hills, Sessions planted about 10,000 trees and shrubs in Balboa Park. Most were grown from seeds which she imported from all over the world— Australia, Asia, South America, Spain, Baja California and New England.

Sessions was the first woman to receive the International Meyer Medal in genetics. She remained a promoter of Balboa Park as, first and foremost, a horticultural park.

Kate Sessions in a 1998 statue by Ruth Hayward, near Sefton Plaza.

Why 'Balboa' Park?

The first problem was the name. In 1910, the San Diego Park Commission renamed the park after the 'discoverer' of the Pacific Ocean, Vasco Nunez de Balboa. Balboa was a Spanish conquistador who crossed the Atlantic Ocean to Panama, climbed the mountains and, on September 25, 1513, became the first European to see a new ocean. He called it *Mar del Sur*, the South Sea, later renamed the Peaceful Sea, the Pacific Ocean.

Architect Bertram Goodhue

To design the fairgrounds, the town's leaders hired landscaper John Charles Olmsted. Based in Brookline, Mass., Olmsted had designed park systems for Boston, Seattle, and Portland, Oregon. Architects Bertram Grosvenor Goodhue from New York and Irving Gill from San Diego were hired to design simple, Mission-style buildings for Olmsted's 'natural' plan.

However, Goodhue encouraged the Exposition management to favor architecture over nature. Within a few months, Olmsted and Gill resigned due to creative differences and Goodhue took charge. He changed the focus to a Spanish-Colonial architectural complex with Persian Islamic fixtures, claiming that this style recalled the Spanish-Mexican beginnings of San Diego.

Goodhue worked from his New York office, visiting San Diego occasionally. His on-site representative, Carleton M. Winslow, helped design most of the buildings while Frank P. Allen, Jr., the Director-of-Works, designed other structures and supervised construction.

Goodhue, Winslow and Allen incorporated details from buildings in Italy, Spain and Mexico in buildings they created in Balboa Park. Believing that Exposition

Spanish Colonial

Spanish Colonial architecture is derived from that of the Moors (Muslims who occupied Spain for 300 years), Italians and Central Americans. It combines rococo and baroque flourishes from the Renaissance with the vivid decoration of Indian craftsmen in New Spain.

The Balboa Park buildings contain elements of missions and churches in Southern California and Mexico, and of palaces and homes in Mexico, Spain and Italy.

Muslim details such as minaret-like towers, reflecting pools, colored tile inlays, and human-size urns highlight the buildings. There are arcades, arches, bells, colonnades, domes, fountains, views through gates of shaded patios, and vistas of broad panoramas provided variety. A low-lying cornice line helps preserve a sense of continuity.

"Among the ten greatest examples of architecture in the United States." — *John Nolen.*

"It is so beautiful that I wish to make a plea: that you keep these buildings here permanently." —*Former President Theodore Roosevelt, 1915.*

architecture should provide "illusion rather than reality," Goodhue conjured up an idealized 17th century Spanish-Colonial city on a broad mesa overlooking San Diego's downtown and harbor. The cloud-capped towers, gorgeous palaces, and inviting gardens sparkled in the sunlight and, at night, evoked an atmosphere of mystery and romance.

Goodhue hoped the style—eclectic Spanish-Revival style buildings and arcades, vines climbing their walls, and gardens of sub-tropical plants—would supply a festive alternative to the formalized and monumental Neo-Classical style buildings then in vogue for hotels, banks and civic centers in the United States.

The popularity of the buildings in Balboa Park heralded the craze for Spanish architecture and street names that characterizes Southern California today. Hearst Castle in San Simeon, and even an entire city— Santa Barbara, took on the look of Spain. Although Mexican critics called the architecture "Hollywood Spanish," Mexican architects used the same ideas in homes for rich clients and hotels for tourists.

1915–16 Panama-California International Exposition

On New Year's Day, 1915, a fireworks display in Balboa Park concluded with a flaming sign, "The Land Divided—The World United—San Diego the First Port of Call." There were exhibits from various industries, most California counties, seven states and a few foreign countries. The park was a fantasy world that dazzled and entertained, offering a style of magnificence that San Diego could become worthy of.

1935–36 California-Pacific International Exposition

The 1935–36 California-Pacific International Exposition, inspired by Chicago's 1933–34 Century of Progress Exposition, was intended to pull the city out of its Great Depression doldrums. As an added attraction, young women promoted healthful and natural

Balboa Park

From 1911-35, Englishman John Morley was responsible for the planting of the park, carefully selecting plants that could adapt to the dry climate.

Today there are 15,000 trees of over 350 different species, the majority of which are not native to San Diego. Native trees include sycamores, sumacs, Torrey pines, and coastal live oaks. Non-native but notable trees include the coast redwood, fan palms, elm, pepper trees, and the predominant eucalyptus trees.

"Botanically speaking, I would call Miss Sessions a perennial, evergreen and ever-blooming."
—*George Marston, 1935.*

The tableau and cartouche on the east side of Casa del Prado, facing Balbo Plaza.

living at the popular Zoro Gardens nudist colony.

This time, San Diego architect Richard Requa was in charge. He preserved the 1915 structures and added additional buildings south of El Prado around Pan American Plaza. Continuing the 'New Spain' theme, he borrowed decorative ideas from Mayan temples in Yucatan and Pueblo Indian buildings in New Mexico. Nonetheless, Requa's buildings are plain and sterile compared to Goodhue's opulent and fanciful creations.

Preservation

Most of the 1915 buildings were of temporary wood and plaster construction. After modernistic replacements were proposed, shocked citizens formed the Balboa Park Protective Association to prevent demolition of the original buildings. The Association gave way in 1967 to the Committee of 100. Led by Bea Evenson and architectural consultant Sam Hamill, the Committee rebuilt Casa del Prado in 1971 and Casa de Balboa in 1982. The 1915 Exposition buildings along El Prado and the 1935 buildings around Pan American Plaza were listed as a National Historic Landmark in 1978.

Cabrillo Bridge

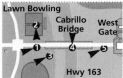

Lawn Bowling

Cabrillo Bridge

West Gate

Hwy 163

On November 4, 1915, stunt pilot Joe Boquel entertained the crowds in his plane. He tried to do a "corkscrew" by Cabrillo Bridge. He crashed and died, five minutes before he was to have been awarded an Exposition gold medal.

Originally there was a reflecting pool beneath the bridge but it dried up and was replaced by Highway 163.

Lawn Bowling ⊕

Clad in white from head to toe, members of the San Diego Lawn Bowling Club engage in their gentle sport. The object is to roll the weighted black balls near the white "jack" ball. There are two regulation 120x120-foot bowling greens, built in 1932.

Where

By the NW corner of Cabrillo Bridge. Games are usually played each afternoon from 1 to 3:30pm, except on Mondays. The lawns support up to sixteen simultaneous games.

Tip

Get low, towards the height of the ball, to get a dynamic perspective.

Sir Francis Drake was the most famous lawn bowler. Upon learning that the Spanish Armada was approaching England, he chose to finish his game of bowls before heading to battle.

Cabrillo Bridge ⊕   1914 Frank P. Allen, Jr.

The grand entrance to Balboa Park is across the elegant Cabrillo Bridge. Designed by Frank P. Allen, Jr., the bridge is 450 ft. long, 40 ft. wide and 120 ft. high.

Balboa Park

The plain, cantilever-style, seven-arched design is similar to the Roman-style aqueduct in Queretaro, Mexico. The cantilever principle was new at the time, but the arched design dates back to Roman viaducts.

Tip
Use leading lines. I love this shot as the gently curving streaks of car lights sweep your eye into the distant skyline.
This is an easy shot to take. Around sunset, stand on Cabrillo Bridge, overlooking Highway 163. Use a 50mm lens and shoot through the guard fence. Take several shots, 10-20 minutes after sunset. Using a medium aperture (f5.6) and a long exposure such as a few second will turn the carlights into long streaks.

"The most beautiful highway I've ever seen."
—John F. Kennedy, 1963, about Hwy 163 around Cabrillo Bridge.

West Gate ⏱   1915   Carleton M. Winslow

The West Gate was the main entrance to the 1915 Panama-Pacific Exposition and above the archway are symbolic sculptures. The male "Mar Atlanticum" and female "Mar Pacificum" pour water from their vases to represent the Panama Canal joining the world's two great oceans.

Above the figures is the crest of the City of San Diego and between them is the date of the exposition—1915. The West Gate was designed by Carleton M. Winslow in a neo-Classical style with sculpture by the Piccirilli Brothers of New York City.

Museum of Man

Also known as the California Building

1915 California Building; 1916 San Diego Museum; 1935 Palace of Science; 1942 San Diego Museum of Man. 1915 by Bertram Goodhue.

"The California Building is second in beauty only to the State Capitol in Sacramento."
—San Diego Union reporter, 1913.

"Behold the spreading dome, catching the light of the rising and setting sun. Look upward to the glorious tower rising so serenely in the sky; observe with quiet thoughtfulness the figures of saints and heroes which adorn the southern front."
—George W. Marston, dedication ceremony, 1915.

On August 14, 1916, Billy Webber, "the human fly," climbed the tower in 90 minutes. This is not recommended.

Balboa Park

The San Diego Museum of Man (also known by its original name, the California Building) is the most architecturally significant structure in San Diego. With it, architect Bertram Goodhue, assisted by Carleton S. Winslow, introduced a romantic new style to the U.S. that has come to dominate much of Southern California—Spanish Colonial-Revival.

Although Spanish in derivation, the building has an unusual Byzantine-inspired, Greek-cross plan derived from Madonna de San Biagio in Montepulciano, Italy. It is decorated with Mexican motifs such as the blue and yellow ceramic tiles on the tower and dome. Everything was constructed locally—the tiles made in National City and the ornaments in Chula Vista.

The building has three main points of interest: the tower, the dome, and the façade.

California Tower ⊕

This 200-foot high bell tower is an architectural landmark of San Diego. The tower, decorated with ceramic tiles and glass beads, is gracefully divided into three stages similar to the three stages of the tower of the Cathedral of Morelia, Mexico. The stages change from quadrangle to octagon to circle as they rise. The tower is capped by a weather vane shaped like a Spanish galleon.

Inside is the 100-bell Ona May Carillon that plays Westminster chimes every 15 minutes, and a five minute chime at noon. Installed in 1967 by Dr. Frank Lowe, in memory of his mother, the bells are controlled from two keyboards on the third floor. It takes a skilled carilloneur to play the keyboard, although it's usually played automatically by plastic rolls (like a player-piano).

Tip
Left: It's difficult to photograph the entire California Building ⊕ as there are obstructions all around. Copley Plaza, by the Old Globe Theatre, is best, but watch out for the large eucalyptus tree.

Dome ⊕

The glorious central dome is colorfully adorned with blue, yellow and white inlaid ceramic tiles. The starburst design is patterned after that of the great dome of the Church of Santa Prisca and San Sebastián at Taxco, Mexico. The dome itself is reminiscent of the magnificent Byzantium Haga Sophia of Istanbul. Several smaller domes flow towards the back of the building but they are hidden by an annex of the Old Globe Theater.

A Latin inscription at the base of the dome is a tribute to the fertility of California, reading, in translation: "A land of wheat and barley, and vines and fig trees, and pomegranates; a land of olive oil and honey." Also look out for California's state motto: "Eureka."

Tip
From Copley Plaza, zoom into the California Dome ⊕ to capture its distinctive starburst tile pattern. You can see the same style repeated downtown, at the Santa Fe railroad station and the Balboa Theater in Horton Plaza.

Façade ⊕

Facing the Plaza de California, the south façade is the main entrance to the Museum of Man.

South Façade

San Diego's Spanish-Colonial Founders

1. Father Luis Jayme;
2. George Vancouver;
3. Sebastián Vizcaíno;
4. King Philip III of Spain;
5. Father Junípero Serra;
6. King Charles I of Spain;
7. Juan Rodríguez Cabrillo;
8. Gaspar de Portolá;
9. Father Antonio de la Ascención.

Also featured are the coats of arms of (a) Spain; (b) Mexico; (c) San Diego.

Museum of Man

The Museum of Man exhibits the anthropology and archaeology of early cultures, particularly the Native Indians of the American Southwest. It has survived petitions to change its name to the 'Museum of Men and Women' and the 'Museum of Humanity.'

During W.W.II, the Navy occupied this building. They removed several monolithic statues by sawing them into door--sized pieces.

The museum contains one of the county's finest anthropological collections, emphasizing American Indian cultures. Open 10–4:30, $6/3, 619-239-2001. Free on the third Tuesday of the month.

The south façade of the Museum of Man has plain walls punctuated by a richly ornate frontispiece in the Churrigueresque style. The design was inspired by the former Jesuit Church of San Francisco Javier in Tepotzlan, Mexico, and other churches and palaces.

The doors are made of Philippine mahogany. Surrounding them are statues and busts of people from the Spanish heritage of San Diego.

1542: Juan Rodríguez Cabrillo (7) was the first European to 'discover' San Diego bay. He named the bay San Miguel Harbor. Cabrillo was exploring the coast of Alta California and was sponsored by Charles I of Spain (Emperor Charles V of the Holy Roman Empire) (6).

1602: Don Sebastián Vizcaíno (3) led the second party of European sailors to the region. Entering shortly before the feast day of San Diego de Alcalá, he renamed the bay 'San Diego.' Father Antonio de la Ascención (9), a Carmelite priest, was Vizcaíno's cartographer. King Philip III of Spain (4) was Vizcaíno's patron.

1769: Leading an overland military and religious colonization party, Gaspar de Portolá (8) arrived in San Diego along with Father Junípero Serra (5). Serra founded the Roman Catholic Mission of San Diego, and thereby the town of San Diego, on July 16, 1769, starting a chain of 21 missions through California. Portolá became the first Spanish governor of California.

1775: Father Luis Jayme (1), who had accompanied Serra to San Diego, became the first Christian martyr in California. He lost his life protecting the San Diego mission from an Indian uprising.

1783: George Vancouver (2) was the first English navigator to visit San Diego.

The Old Globe Theater and Copley Plaza.

Tip

Look for details. This small fountain ⏱ is on the east side of the Museum of Man. 'Small' shots like this add variety to your collection of photos.

Simon Edison Centre for the Performing Arts ⏱ 1982

Combines the Old Globe Theater, the Cassius Carter Stage and the outdoor Lowell Davies Festival Theater.

The Tony-winning Old Globe Theater is named, and was originally modeled, after Shakespeare's 16th-century Globe Theater in London, England. During the 1935–36 exposition, the theater had an open-air, in-the-round Elizabethan stage where 40-minute versions of "the bard's" greatest hits were performed.

In 1978 the complex was destroyed by arson and the 1982 replacement is a traditional indoor stage.

The adjacent Lowell Davies Festival Theater is outdoor and in-the-round.

Tours are given of the backstage scene shops and costume rooms (some weekends, 11am, $3, 619-231-1941). Plays: 619-239-2255; ticket information: 619-234-5623. Same-day bargain tickets are available at Times ArtsTix (tel: 619-238-3810) by Horton Plaza.

El Prado

The main east-west thoroughfare is named after the "Paseo del Prado" city walk in Madrid, Spain.

Alcazar Garden ⏱

1935 by Richard Requa.

Right: The classic view of California Tower is from the formal Spanish-style Alcazar Garden. Over 7,000 annuals have been planted for year-round color. Square flower beds with trimmed hedges surround colorful tiled fountains.

Originally called the Montezuma Garden in the 1915 exposition, the name and design were changed for the 1935 exposition to honor the gardens of Alcazar Castle in Seville, Spain.

Balboa Park

Plaza de Panama

Plaza de Panama

1915 by Goodhue and Stein.
This plaza, now home to a fountain and a statue of El Cid, was the hub of the 1915–16 Panama-California Exposition.

El Cid

In the 11th century, Rodrigo Diaz de Bivar, a Christian knight under King Sancho, helped force the Muslim Moors out of Spain. He was called "The Valiant Military Leader"—El Cid Campeador—and immortalized in an epic poem.

Fountain 🕐

In the center of Plaza de Panama is a fountain which makes a good foreground to the California Tower. Designed by Laird Plumleigh in 1995, the fountain was donated by Elizabeth North in memory of her parents.

El Cid Statue 🕐

1927 by Anna Hyatt Huntington.

On the south side of Plaza de Panama is a statue of El Cid, the legendary Spanish medieval hero.

The bronze sculpture was cast in 1927 by Anna Hyatt Huntington. Her husband, Archer Milton Huntington, had inherited vast wealth from coal mining and shipbuilding. The Huntingtons loved Spain and gave this statue and other gifts to support Spanish culture. They gave other statues from the original mold to the cities of Seville, San Francisco, New York, and Buenos Aires.

The statue is best photographed in the morning when El Cid faces the rising sun.

Balboa Park

Decorative Styles

Plateresque

The façade of the Museum of Art is in the *plateresque* style. Developed in 16th century Spain, during the Early Renaissance, the style consisted of low-relief ornamentation applied to the surface of buildings. It resembled the fine bossing on plates by silversmiths (*platero* in Spanish).

Baroque

The Casa del Prado is in the Spanish *Baroque* style. Notice the twisted candy-cane columns on the twin pavilions facing El Prado. Baroque became popular all over Europe in the 17th century, particularly in Roman Catholic countries.

Churrigueresque

The façade of the Museum of Man is in the *Churrigueresque* style, the most flamboyant form of Spanish Baroque. A mass of exuberant and frenetic stucco in deep relief, often contrasted by stark walls, is intended to overwhelm. It is derided as being "decorative toothpaste."

The style was initiated in Spain in the late 17th- and early 18th-century by José Benito Churriguera and his family.

One of the few genuinely historic examples in the U.S. is the 1776–97 Mission San Xavier del Bac in Tucson, Arizona—a favorite photographic subject of Ansel Adams.

San Diego Museum of Art ⏱

1926 by William Templeton Johnson 1935 Palace of Fine Arts.
Replaced the 1915 Sacramento Valley Building demolished in 1923.

Echoing the University of Salamanca (1529) in Spain, the ornate façade is in the Plateresque style. It contains sculptures and busts of five 17th century Spanish Baroque painters—Ribera, Velasquez, Murillo, Zurbaran and El Greco—whose work is displayed in the museum. The museum also displays works by Dali, Matisse, O'Keefe and Toulouse-Lautrec.

The interior has an attractive rotunda with a staircase and carved wood roof.

Tue–Thurs, 10–4:30. $8/$6/$3. 619-232-7931. Closed Monday. Free on the third Tuesday of month.

House of Charm

House of Hospitality

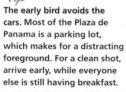

Tip

The early bird avoids the cars. Most of the Plaza de Panama is a parking lot, which makes for a distracting foreground. For a clean shot, arrive early, while everyone else is still having breakfast.

"Woman of Tehuantepec" by Donal Hord. Inside the House of Hospitality is this statue of an Aztec woman pouring water.

House of Charm ⏱

1915 by Carlton Winslow. 1915 Indian Arts Building; 1916 Russia & Brazil Building; 1935 House of Charm. Rebuilt in 1996.

The Mission style east façade, facing the Plaza de Panama, was modeled after the Sanctuary of Guadalupe in Guadalajara, Mexico.

Inside is the Mingei International Museum of Folk Art. During the 1935 exposition, the building housed cosmetics, hence the name "House of Charm."

Tues–Sat 10–4. $5/2. 619-239-0003.

House of Hospitality

1915 by Goodhue and Winslow.1915 Foreign Arts Building; 1935 House of Hospitality. Rebuilt in 1997.

The west façade (above) resembles the Hospital of Santa Cruz in Toledo, Spain. It is the only façade in the Park that faces west and radiates a sandy-gold at sunset.

Inside is a courtyard designed after the State Museum in Guadalajara, Mexico. It is is surrounded by columns and arcades in a Tuscanstyle.

Timken Museum of Art

1965 by Frank L. Hope. Replaced the 1915 Home Economy Building.

The Timken houses the privately-owned Putnam collection of 14th–19th century European Old Masters. There are works by Rembrandt, Rubens, El Greco, Cezanne and Pisarro, and 18th–19th century American painters such as John Copley and Eastman Johnson.

The shoebox internationalstyle building is conspicuous for being one of two buildings facing the Plaza de Panama that are not in a Spanish style.

Casa de Balboa

1915 by Frank P. Allen, Jr. 1915 Commerce & Industries Building; 1916 Canadian Building; 1935 Palace of Better Housing; 1936 Electric Building. Burned down in 1978 and rebuilt in 1981 as the Casa de Balboa.

The two north pavilions echo the Palace of the Count of Ecala in Queretaro, Mexico. The Casa de Balboa houses three museums:

The Museum of San Diego History

This museum of San Diego's American history (1848 onwards) contains one of the country's largest archives of historic photographs. The museum also displays maps, household goods and furniture. There is a store and a 100-seat audio/visual theater. Tue–Sun 10–4:30. $5/$4/$2. 619-232-6203. Free on the second Tuesday of the month.

MoPA
—The Museum of Photographic Arts

Opened in 1983, MoPA is one of the first and finest museums in the U.S. dedicated to photographic art. The museum displays about six shows per year covering the entire history of the medium. Shows have included historic, daguerreotype, fine art, contemporary, documentary, photojournalistic and holographic photography. There's also a great book store. A 250-seat theater iwas added in March 1999.

Open daily 10–5. $6/$4/free. Guided tours available Sundays at 2 p.m. Free on the second Tuesday of the month. 619-238-7559.

The San Diego Model Railroad Museum

The largest operating model railroad museum in North America. The museum showcases four working scale models of actual railroads in Southern California. Don't miss the model of the San Diego and Arizona Railway over Carrizo Gorge, or the Southern Pacific and Santa Fe track over Tehachapi Pass. There's also a hands-on model railroad for children to operate.

Tue–Fri. 11–4; Sat and Sun. 11–5. $4/free. Free on the first Tuesday of the month. 619-696-0199.

The exotic Botanical Building is claimed to be "the
most photographed and painted subject in San Diego."

Botanical Building

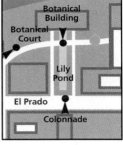

Tip

Use the water. I always look out for a pond or fountain to place in the foreground. It really softens up a building shot. There are two fountains by the Botanical Building— this one (right) is to the west in Botanical Court and the other is by Casa del Prado.

Photographed from Botanical Court.

The Botanical Building is free to enter. Inside are more than 300 species of tropical and subtropical plants including palms, ferns, bamboo and banana trees.

Over twelve miles of redwood laths (thin strips of timber) form a lattice over the steel skeleton, painted to match the redwood. The redwood laths allow filtered sunlight onto the tropical plants and ferns.

The lattice-structured **Botanical Building**, ⏱ gloriously fronted by two reflecting pools, makes for postcard-perfect photographs. It was the largest wood lath structure in the world when it was built in 1915.

In 1911, the president of the San Diego Floral Society, Alfred D. Robinson, proposed a botanical garden and a giant lath palace. Switching to a Persian style, Carleton M. Winslow collaborated with Frank P. Allen, Jr. and Thomas B. Hunter to design a romantic, vaulted building. A dominant central dome over a narrow rectangle is flanked by two barrel vaults on each side. Two Persian-style domes mark the entrances, connected by a white, stucco arcade.

Tip
Although viewable year-round, this shot (below) can only be successfully taken in the summer. Because the Colonnade faces north it is nearly always in shadow, which produces weak color in your shot. The sun is suitably north only between May and August (best in mid-June), at sunrise and sunset.

Stand on the balustrade (a faux-bridge at the north end of the Lily Pond) and use a 50mm lens. When the sun is near to setting, the buildings become a creamy-gold and the long shadows accentuate the rich ornamentation.

The best time is when there's no wind and the three aerating fountains are off. Then the water is calm and produces a peaceful reflection.

The Botanical Building has an open, steel frame, a style popular in late 19th century Exposition work. The most famous example is the Eiffel Tower in Paris. The Botanical Building was never the chassis of a Santa Fe railroad station, as has been alleged.

Fri–Wed 10–4, closed Thur. Free. 619-692-4916.

Lily Pond

This view (below) is one of the prettiest shots of San Diego. The Lily Pond reflects the elegant castle-like towers of the Casa de Balboa (left) and the House of Hospitality (right), joined by the Colonnade.

The Lily Pond is 193 x 43 feet and is home to lilies, lotus, turtles and Japanese Koi fish. The lilies bloom in late spring.

Colonnade ◷
1915 by Frank P. Allen, Jr.

Facing the Botanical Building, the Romanesque Colonnade connects the House of Hospitality to the Casa de Balboa.

The Lily Pond, reflecting the Casa de Balboa and House of Hospitality.

Plaza de Balboa

Reuben H. Fleet Space Theater and Science Center

After the Zoo, the Space Theater is the most attended institution in the park. Built in 1967 and expanded in 1997, the museum has hands-on science exhibits and an interesting store. IMAX® films are shown on a 76-foot, wrap-around dome.
9:30 a.m. to 5 p.m. (9:30p.m. on Fri & Sat). $6.50/$5 or $9/$6.50 with Imax film. Free on the first Tuesday of the month. 619-238-1233.

The fountain makes a good backdrop.

Bea Evenson Fountain 🕐   1972

Surrounded by a 200-foot wide wading pool popular with children, this fountain spurts water up to 60 feet into the air. On windy days, the water pressure is automatically reduced (via a wind regulator on the roof of the Natural History Museum) so that the water doesn't wet people on the perimeter walkway.

The fountain was named in 1981 after Bea Evenson, who spearheaded the "Committee of 100" to protect and rebuild the Spanish style buildings in Balboa Park.

❷

Balboa Park

San Diego Natural History Museum
Bea Evenson Fountain
Plaza de Balboa
Reuben H. Fleet Space Theater and Science Center

San Diego Natural History Museum ⏲

1933 by William Templeton Johnson. Replaced the 1915 Southern California Counties Building / Women's Club Building.

The Natural History Museum exhibits fossils, dinosaur skeletons and rocks. In the entrance is a 43-foot Foucault's Pendulum, which stays still as the earth moves.

The monumental Italianate style building has a mixture of mythological and naturalistic motifs around the entrance and on the parapet.

$6/2, 9:30–4:30, free first Tues. 619-232-3821.

Tip

Use backlighting for fountains. Although most of the time you want light on the front of your subject, there are a few times when light from the back (i.e. you are shooting into the sun) is better. Grass and water often look more interesting when backlit.

With backlighting, the sun highlights the spray and reflects off the water's surface. Like a true Spanish fountain, the Bea Evenson Fountain ⏲ is designed for people to interact with it. Children love to run and splash in the wading pool during the hot summer months.

The Firemen's Ball

In 1925, the predecessor to the Natural History Museum hosted the annual Firemen's Ball. A few hours before the event, the furnace overheated and the building burnt to the ground. Instead of dancing and drinking, the firemen had to spend the night fighting the blaze.

Moreton Bay Fig Tree ⏱

This huge tree has a spread of 120 feet. Imported from Australia, the tree was planted in 1914 as part of a formal garden.

Carousel ⏱ 1910

Built by Herschell-Spillman, this is one of only seven such carousels operating today. It was installed in the Park in 1922. Children can ride a hand-carved sea serpent, giraffe, frog, zebra, ostrich, lion, or horse (with real hair). Grab the elusive brass ring and win a free ride! Summer weekdays 1–5, weekends 11–5:30, winter weekends noon–6. $1.25. 619-460-9000.

Casa del Prado ⏱ 1915

1915 by Carlton Winslow. 1915 Varied Industries & Food Products Building; 1916 Foreign & Domestic Industries Building; 1935 Palace of Food & Beverages. Rebuilt in 1971 as the Casa del Prado.

The south wing of the Casa del Prado has two Baroque façades on the north side of El Prado and one facing Plaza de Balboa. The latter is the most photogenic. Via a colonnade and courtyard, the south wing is connected to the 650-seat Casa del Prado Theater (above), also known as the Junior Theater.

Spanish Village Art Center ⏱ 1935

The Center is an artist's colony where local potters, painters, jewelers and glass-blowers show their wares and teach their skills. Surrounding a painted patio are 36 small studios with red-tiled roofs. Open 11–4, free. 619-233-9050. Adjacent is the Photographic Arts building which is used by several camera clubs.

Balboa Park

A cross **Park Boulevard** from Balboa Plaza, via a pedestrian bridge, are two attractive and serene gardens.

Rose Garden 🕐 1975

The Rose Garden displays over 1,850 rose bushes, representing 156 different varieties. There are several walkways, a fountain and a shady arbor. The Garden is a popular wedding site. The roses are best photographed in the spring.

Cactus Garden 🕐 1977

The Cactus Garden contains over 150 species (1,300 plants) of cacti and other desert plants from North and South America. Peak blooms are between January and March.

Miniature Railroad

A 1/5 scale model of a General Motors "F-3" diesel locomotive can carry 48 passengers around a 2,200-foot track. Operated since 1948. Sat, Sun hols, 11–5, $1.25. 239-4748, operate on weekends, 11–5, $1.

Tip
Pick a detail. You can't photograph all 1,850 roses so select just one. I used a long lens and a simple background for this delicate portrait (above). A wide-angle lens helped emphasize the shape of this plump cactus (right).

Spreckels Organ Pavilion

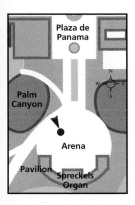

Plaza de Panama

Palm Canyon

Arena

Pavilion

Spreckels Organ

Tip

Find a foreground. Whenever your subject is in the background, such as with the Organ Pavilion, find an interesting foreground for depth and contrast.

Here a couple makes the view romantic. I lucked out with the umbrella—it adds a much-needed splash of color.

The Rolling Stones played a free concert at the Organ Pavilion in 1965.

To the east of the pavilion is the Japanese Friendship Garden, a traditional sand and stone garden that overlooks a wooded canyon. Tue and Fri–Sun 10–4. $2/$1. Free on Tuesdays. 619-232-2780.

Right: Palm Canyon, west of the organ pavilion, has 450 palms of 58 species. It was planted by Fred Bodey, a San Diego horticulturalist.

The Spreckels Organ is the largest outdoor musical instrument in the world. This unique symphonic concert organ contains 73 ranks of 4,445 pipes, from 1-1/2 inches to 32-feet long.

Since pipe organs go out of tune when the air temperature changes, San Diego, with its even climate, is one of the few cities in the world where an outdoor organ is practical.

The organ was built by the Austin Brothers of Hartford, Connecticut and donated to the people of San Diego by Adolph and John D. Spreckels in 1915. Except during WWII, the organ has been played once a week since then.

Flowers decorate the driveway to the Organ Pavilion.

The organ is built into a Neo-Classical pavilion with a curving Corinthian peristyle, designed in 1915 by Harrison Albright. The 2,400-seat arena is criticized for facing north, where the sun shines directly in the faces of the audience, but this keeps the organ out of direct sunlight.

There is a free hour-long recital every Sunday at 2pm. You can take dusks shots during the International Summer Organ Festival (Jul–Aug, Mondays at 8pm).

Aerospace Museum

San Diego Aerospace Museum ⊕
1935 by Walter Dorwin Teague. 1935 Ford Building; 1936 Palace of Transportation.

"A significant example of the futuristic 'Modern' styling of the 1930s."
—Aaron Gallup.

"A giant washing machine."
—James Britton II.

Tip
Use humor. This shot of the Aerospace Museum comes alive due to the plane flying overhead. It's easy to capture as, aptly enough, the museum is under the flight path to San Diego airport.

The A-12 Blackbird reconnaissance plane (precursor to the SR-71 Blackbird) makes a dynamic foreground. Use a wide-angle lens (35mm) to make the Blackbird jump out of the shot.

The Ford Motor Company sponsored this "ultra-modern" circular building for the 1935 fair. The 90-foot tower was designed to look like a gearwheel laid on its side, and the fountain inside the patio was designed to look like the Ford V-8 emblem.

The design was inspired by Albert Kahn's Ford Building at the 1933–34 Chicago Century of Progress.

After the fair, proposed uses included a roller skating rink (1937), library (1937), armory (1938), rifle range (1948), aquatic coliseum (1950), home for the Museum of Man (1957), fallout shelter (1960), and an aerospace museum (1972).

The doughnut-shaped building is packed with original and replica aircraft, from the early days to space flight. Included are replicas of the Red Barron's WWI Fokker Dr. I Triplane and, as a centerpiece, Lindbergh's *Spirit of St. Louis.*

Open: 10–4:30/5:30. $8/$3. Free on the fourth Tuesday of the month. 619-234-8291.

Balboa Park

Charles Lindbergh and the *Spirit of St. Louis*

The *Spirit of St. Louis* was built in San Diego, about a mile west of the museum, near today's Lindbergh

Field airport. It was built by T. Claude Ryan and his company, Ryan Aeronautics.

Ryan was an airmail pilot from Kansas who operated a small fleet of biplanes flying passengers to Los Angeles. He had patented and built the M-1 open-cockpit monoplane which gained fame as a fast airmail plane.

"I shall take the wings of the morning, and fly to the uttermost ends of the sea."
—Charles Lindbergh.

"What a beautiful machine it is, trim and slender gleaming in its silver coat."
—Charles Lindbergh

In 1927, Charles 'Slim' Lindbergh was the chief airmail pilot between St. Louis and Chicago. He wanted to compete for the Ortieg Prize, a $25,000 award for the first non-stop flight from New York to Paris. The were many syndicates competing and time was of the essence.

Impressed with the M-1, Lindbergh raised the money to have a modified version custom built. After an exchange of telegrams, Ryan built the plane in 60 days for $6,000. It was fitted with a Wright Whirlwind J-5C engine.

Lindbergh picked the plane up in San Diego, flew it to New York and then to France. He touched down in Paris on May 21, 1927, after a 33 1/2 hour flight.

Returning to San Diego, Lindbergh was honored with a great dinner at the Hotel del Coronado. Several towns were named after Lindbergh and he became the first *Man of the Year* for Time magazine.

Ryan continued building aircraft. He designed the Ryan ST, a popular training monoplane, and the Ryan X-13 vertical take-off plane.

Pan America Plaza

Tip
Find a complementing foreground. For this shot of the southwestern-style Balboa Park Club, I used the cacti by the Puppet Theater to complement and offset the architecture. Now you could be in Santa Fe rather than San Diego!
To emphasize the cactus, I crouched low and close to the leaves, and used a 28mm lens set to f22 (to keep everything in focus). The tree in the top left helps to frame the shot.

House of Pacific Relations

A cluster of fifteen cottages from the 1935 Exposition represent thirty-one nationality groups. Cottages are open Sunday and first Tuesday of each month, about 12–2. On summer Sundays there are 30-minute displays of native music and dancing on the lawn. Sunday 2–3p.m. summer (Mar–Oct). 619-234-0739.

Balboa Park Club ⊕

1915 by the Rapp Brothers. 1915 New Mexico State Building; 1935 Palace of Education.

A striking Pueblo-Revival style building complete with vigas (wooden tree stumps) that protrude from the walls. It was based on the Church of San Esteban del Rey at Acoma.

Palisades Building ⊕

Adjacent to the Balboa Park Club is the similar Palisades Building which contains a recital hall and the Marie Hitchcock Puppet Theater for children. It was originally known as "The Woman's Palace."

Tel: 619-685-5045.

San Diego Auto-motive Museum
1935 Conference Building.
The museum exhibits over 70 historic automobiles and motorcycles. Look out for the 1948 Tucker "Torpedo," 1932 Rolls Royce, and Steve McQueen's 1934 Packard that he drove with his dog in the rumble seat.
The building is inspired by Mayan temples.
9/10–4:30/5:30 $6/$2. Free fourth Tues. of the month.
619-231-2886.

A 1929 Isotta Franchini, which cost the price of ten Buicks.

Starlight Bowl
1935 Ford Bowl
In the summer, the Starlight Musical Theater and San Diego Civic Light Opera present performances in this 4,324-seat, open-air bowl.
619-544-7800.

Balboa Park Golf Course ⏚
Right: The "19th Hole" clubhouse has a sweeping view of the course's final hole and the San Diego skyline.

San Diego Hall of Champions
1935 Federal Building

A sports museum highlighting the achievements of San Diego County athletes. The building was modeled after the Palace of the Governor in Uxmal, Yucatan, Mexico.

Morley Field ⏚

Occupying the eastern third of Balboa Park is a municipal sports complex. There's a swimming pool, velodrome, archery range, several baseball diamonds, 25 tennis courts, two public golf courses, and a Frisbee golf course. The Field is named after John Morley, from Derbyshire, England, who was the park's superintendent from 1911 to 1939, during both expositions.

Marston House

Nearby

Mission Hills was promoted as an upscale neighborhood and contains several notable houses. Richard Requa's house (1911) is at 4346 Valle Vista; William Templeton Johnson: 4520 Trias Street; Kate Sessions: Montecito and Lark streets.

"Within its spreading mesas and rugged picturesque canyons, there is nothing else like it among the parks of the world."
—Samuel Parsons, Jr.

Balboa Park

Marston House ☻

The George White and Anna Gunn Marston House lies on the north-west corner of Balboa Park.

The 21-room house and 4 1/2 acre estate was the home of George W. Marston (1850-1946), a civic leader and philanthropist. Marston worked at Alonzo Horton's hotel as a clerk before founding a department store. At its height, The Marston Company occupied a five-story building on Fifth Avenue and was the premier place to shop in San Diego. Marston helped develop Balboa Park, founded the San Diego Historical Society, and preserved Presidio Hill.

The house is a fine example of the American Craftsman or Arts & Crafts style and was designed in 1904 by San Diego architects William S. Hebbard and Irving Gill. Inside, the museum contains furnishings and decorations from the Arts and Crafts movement.

3525 7th Avenue. Open Sat and Sun, noon–4:30. One-hour tours. $3 ($4 with gardens)/free. Joint ticket with Villa Montezuma. Tel: 619-298-3142

Tours

Architectural Heritage Tours. First Wednesday of the month. 9:30am from the Visitor Information Center. 619-223-6566.

Balboa Birders Guided Walks. First Thursday of the month. Locations and times vary. 619-232-6566.

Canyoneers Guided Nature Walks. Flora, fauna and geology walks on weekends. 619-232-3821.

House of Pacific Relations Lawn Programs. Each Sunday (March–October) is a display of folk dancing, music and traditional costumes, featuring of one of 31 nations. 619-292-8592.

Offshoot Tours. Saturdays (except December) at 10am, from the Botanical Building. First Saturday of each month: Balboa Park history; second Saturday: palm trees; third Saturday: other trees; fourth Saturday: desert vegetation. 619-235-1122.

Ranger-led Tours. Wednesdays at noon from the Visitor Information Center. History and botany. 619-235-1122.

The 15 Museums of Balboa Park

Most of Balboa Park's museums offer free admission at least one day per month. (Donations may be requested. Admission may be charged for special exhibits.)

Always free:
- Timken Museum of Art
- Centro Cultural de la Raza
- Veterans Memorial Center Museum

First Tuesday:
- San Diego Model Railroad Museum
- San Diego Natural History Museum
- Reuben H. Fleet Science Center

Second Tuesday:
- Museum of Photographic Arts
- San Diego Hall of Champions Sports Museum
- Museum of San Diego History

Third Tuesday:
- San Diego Museum of Art
- San Diego Museum of Man
- Mingei International Museum

Fourth Tuesday:
- San Diego Aerospace Museum
- San Diego Automotive Museum

Not free:
- Marston House Museum

SeaWorld

One of California's most popular tourist attractions, SeaWorld Adventure Park San Diego always makes a very entertaining day out. The big star, literally, is Shamu, a killer whale who stars in one of the park's several acrobatic and amusing shows. Many of the performing animals try their best to soak spectators but the crowds keep coming!

The 150-acre marine-life park also supports research labs and is the only zoological facility in the world to successfully breed emperor penguins. Since 1989, SeaWorld San Diego has rescued more than 3,000 marine animals, including sea lions, harbor seals, dolphins, pelicans, sea otters and gray whales. Many are rehabilitated and reintroduced into the wild.

Opened in 1964, this was the first SeaWorld. Others are in Orlando, San Antonio and Cleveland.

Where

On Mission Bay's south shore at 500 SeaWorld Drive. Take the SeaWorld Drive exit from I-5. Tel: 619-226-3901.

When

Open at 9 in the summer, at 10 rest of year. Closing times vary. Evening entertainment in the summer. This is the busiest attraction in San Diego. There can be long waits in the summer so avoid the weekends and start early.

SeaWorld San Diego
500 Sea World Drive
San Diego CA 92109
Tel: 619-226-3901
www.seaworld.com

Most photos in this section are by Bob Couey, Ken Bohn and Mike Aguilera, copyright © 1998–2003 SeaWorld, Inc. All rights reserved.

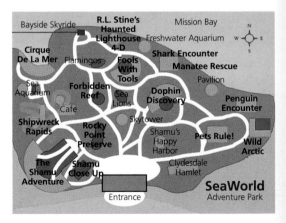

Cost

One-day: $44.95/$35.95. Two-days: $51.95/$41.95. Extra fee for Skytower and Skyride. Parking $7 (car). Prices subject to change. Coupons in publications.

about the Tips

The tips in this section are provided by Bob Couey, Photo Services Manager at SeaWorld San Diego.

SeaWorld

The Shamu Adventure

Photography Notes

Tripods and flash units are permitted. Some of the show areas get very wet so protect your camera equipment and small children from splashes.

Commercial Photography

Guests are encouraged to photograph and videotape SeaWorld for their personal enjoyment. SeaWorld shows, exhibits, and music are copyrighted and guests must have written permission to use photographs or videotape of SeaWorld images for commercial, broadcasting, or publishing purposes. Contact the Public Relations Department at 619-226-3929.

SeaWorld also offers behind-the-scenes guided tours, birthday parties (you and your friends get to wear scary shark hats!) and Camp SeaWorld.

Food is not allowed into the park—there are restaurants and cafes. Pets are not permitted in the park but there is a pet facility for $5.

SeaWorld San Diego is an Anheuser-Busch Adventure Park®.

SeaWorld

The most popular attraction is Shamu and friends—4-ton, black-and-white killer whales who perform amazing acrobatics. The high-energy show lasts for 25 minutes and often fills the 5,500-seat Shamu Stadium to capacity. Expect to get drenched if you sit in the first 14 rows—the 'splash zone.'

The stadium can be approached through two Shamu Skywalks™, which rise 10 feet over the pool area and permit a good view of the whales warming up.

Tip

The best place to photograph the whales is from the western end of the seating area, by the video camera housing. This way you can get the audience in the background to capture their gasps of delight and the thrill of the show.

Try to photograph from water level to emphasize the power and size of the killer whales. Unfortunately, this places you in the first ten rows and well within the splash zone! A heavy-duty plastic bag or waterproof housing is recommended to guard against saltwater. You might position yourself above the slide-out area (center stadium) or extreme sides of the stadium to avoid excess water and salt spray.

Try to include the face of the whale and some reference point, such as the water surface or a trainer. Photograph the whales coming toward you, bowing and breaching for drama. Shots of tail flukes from whales heading away will be uninspiring.

Keeping your composition simple is paramount so try to isolate your subject. Use a long lens and tight close-ups. Long lenses require faster shutter speeds—at least 1/500 is recommended for most shots. Use a tripod or a wall (such as the one near the Skywalk) for support to get sharp images.

Daylight is excellent for every show, providing full-frontal or dramatic side-lighting during morning and later afternoon hours. Side- and back-lighting brings out the water droplets falling from the whales.

Dine with Shamu

Enjoy a behind-the-scenes poolside buffet only feet from Shamu. If you order raw fish, be careful who you show it to!
Lunch is served on weekends and select weekdays, with dinner available in the summer. Reservations required. Tel: 619-226-3601.

Shamu Close Up

(Next page). The large window allows for spectacular shots. Switch your flash off.

killer whales at Shamu Close Up

Skyride^{SM}

A six-minute round-trip ride across Mission Bay. $2.

Southwest Airlines Skytower^{SM}

A five-minute ride takes you straight up, for an aerial view 265 feet above the ground. $2.

Shamu Close Up

Manatee Rescue

SeaWorld is the only U.S. location outside Florida displaying the endangered West Indian manatee with underwater viewing.

Tide Pool

Crabs and starfish reside by the saltwater aquarium.

Forbidden Reef^{SM}

A shallow lagoon where bat rays glide past and take squid from your hands. Venture below water level and see mysterious moray eels in an underwater viewing area.

SeaWorld

Fools With Tools

Fools With Tools

This is SeaWorld's funniest show, featuring the comic antics of sea lions, walruses and river otters.

Tip

Like the Shamu show, this attraction calls for seating down front—eye level action brings the viewer into the scene. The show moves quickly so watch for "peak action" moments. Capturing the humor and spontaneity of this show often requires lightning reflexes, so a few cups of coffee before showtime might help!

The show is staged on one of SeaWorld's more colorful sets. Since the stage is filled with props, separating the subject against a distracting background can be a challenge. You will need to use a wide aperture (f4, f5.6) to throw the background scenery out of focus. Fortunately, such an aperture will allow you to increase your shutter speed and freeze the action.

Cirque de la Mer
A 30-minute show of dazzling watersports, performed in a special 2,800-seat arena that opens into Mission Bay Park. (Summer only).

Wild Arctic

Polar bears play and dive in the Wild Arctic exhibit.

Journey to a desolate land few have seen before—the frozen North Pole. A simulated jet helicopter "flies" you to an arctic research station built around the wrecked hulls of two 19th-century sailing ships, modeled after a real 1845 expedition. Around you swim polar bears, walruses, beluga whales and harbor seals.

Polar bears—earth's largest carnivore—have no natural enemy and swim icy waters in search of food.

Tip

SeaWorld San Diego's Wild Arctic attraction offers some of the most impressive photo opportunities. Polar bears wrestle each other, beluga whales slowly cruise by underwater viewing panels, and walruses hug the glass, inspecting their curious human visitors.

Fortunately, there's sufficient natural light and little or no artificial light is necessary. Such an advantage allows the photographer to concentrate on the action and not on lighting dilemmas. The polar bear's environment closely resembles an arctic landscape so wide shots are as impressive as close-ups.

SeaWorld

Beluga whales

Tip
Water absorbs sunlight so slightly faster film, or a steadier hand, is required.

The underwater viewing panels produce breathtaking underwater shots of beluga whales (above) and a walrus (below). Walruses use their tusks to haul out onto land where they herd for warmth and companionship.

Walrus

Dolphin Discovery

An energy-packed, high-flying show with dolphins and pilot whales performing in the 3,000-seat Dolphin Stadium.

Tip

For those brave enough to tackle rapid-fire action, this show is for you!

The stadium faces south so, for much of the day, the stage and animals are backlit. Look for water highlights and silhouettes to produce dramatic images. For conventional photos, try a late afternoon show and sit in the right-hand portion of the stadium.

Since isolating individual dolphins and dolphin groups is difficult, the slower moving pilot whales make easier subjects to photograph. They bow close to the acrylic panels and look powerful from a low angle.

SeaWorld

Rocky Point Preserve®

Like many SeaWorld attractions, Rocky Point Preserve encourages interaction. This is a good place to photograph the family—a photo of kids with dolphins is hard to beat! Check the signs for feeding times.

You can see more bottlenose dolphins at the Rocky Point Preserve attraction by Shamu Stadium. Feed, touch and interact with 400-pound bottlenose dolphins and view sea otters.

Tip

Unlike trained dolphins, these animals are unpredictable and do not bow or breech on cue. Photographers need to be ready to capture the spontaneity at any moment.

Caribbean flamingo.

Caribbean Flamingo Colony

Flamingos look fantastic with a dark background and back-lighting to enhance the delicate form. This "rim-lighting" is great for other birds too.

A tripod or monopod is recommended for most bird photography. Crop out distracting surroundings and use a fill-flash to put a "catch light" in the birds' eyes.

Since 1975, more than 150 flamingos have hatched at SeaWorld.

Pets Rule!

A zany show where dogs, cats, birds and pigs take charge in a 2,800 seat showplace.

Tip

Be prepared for anything. Use a fast film (such as ISO 400 or 800) to capture the action and allow you to use a long lens. A long lens lets you zoom in tight on the animals. Focus, as always, on the face and eyes.

Animal portraits are readily available. Trainers parade the animals during the show and reintroduce many of them for closer inspection after the show.

Crowned cranes.

Walrus, Seals, Sea Lions and Otters

These animals are generally slow moving and easy to track, giving you a break from active shows and fast film. "Hazy bright" or thin overcast weather conditions will bring out detail and texture in these animals. Frame your subjects tightly. The natural rocky backgrounds enhance pictures.

Above: Alaska sea otter.
Right: Harbor seal.

Penguin Encounter®

More than 350 penguins and tufted puffins swim and waddle in an icy Antarctic environment.

Beached Animal Exhibit

Feed seals and sea lions that have been rescued from local beaches and nursed back to health. The natural rocky backgrounds enhance pictures.

Shark Encounter®

The world's largest display of sandtiger, bonnethead and black- and white-tip sharks. An acrylic viewing tube placed on the floor of the 680,000-gallon aquarium allows you to watch and photograph the sharks underwater.

SeaWorld

Fireworks (nightly during summer) make a great finale to a fun day at SeaWorld.

Tip

A sturdy tripod is essential. Use the 'B' ('bulb') setting on an SLR camera to hold the shutter open to capture a few explosions. Though bracketing (varying) your exposures will help, I find that best results are achieved using f5.6 for about 1-3 seconds. To reduce the effect of street lights, cover the lens with a black card or cloth between bursts.

Use a tungsten film which is color-balanced for artificial light (daylight film will appear green or orange at night). Star filters and soft focus filters can add variety.

Summer Nights

Every evening in the summer, SeaWorld has extra shows and musical bands, capped with colorful fireworks set off over Mission Bay.

Where

The fireworks are best photographed from outside of the park, from the south-east side of Vacation Isle on Mission Bay. Access is free and you can photograph from the parking lot. Exit east off Ingraham Street on Vacation Road.

Photographing SeaWorld

By Bob Couey

Bob Couey is the Manager of Photo Services at SeaWorld San Diego. He has been photographing the animals of the park since 1988.

Couey's work has been published in *People Weekly*, *USA Today*, *Popular Photography*, *Petersen's Photographic*, two "*Day in the Life of*" books, the *New York Times* and the *Los Angeles Times*.

In The Bag

Film:
My colleague, Ken Bohn, and I shoot mostly on Fuji Provia film. We also use Fuji Astia as it is a little "flatter" than Provia and holds detail in dark subjects such as the killer whales.

Cameras:
We use Nikon F4 and F5 cameras with lenses ranging from 15mm to 600mm f4. The "workhorse" lenses are the 20-35mm f2.8 and 80-200 f2.8. Other cameras include a Fuji 6x17 Panoramic, Bronica GS-1 120, and Toyo 4X5 view camera.

Flash:
We use the Nikon SB-26 units (for fill), Norman 400B (for major fill) and a number of Norman 2,000 and Speedotron strobe packs for the big stuff. Radio remotes are Flash Wizard and tripods and monopods are Bogen.

A nimals make fascinating portraits. They are sometimes difficult to photograph but, with a few tips, amateurs can produce exceptional images.

Tight subject cropping is key. Always try to fill the frame as unnecessary background and foreground elements will distract from the animal portrait. Whenever possible, move close to your subject. I often see park visitors fumbling with telephoto lenses when just moving closer to the subject would be sufficient.

Long lenses are indispensable to the wildlife photographer as they help to isolate the subject. Lenses vary in quality and photos taken with well-engineered lenses are superior to those taken with inexpensive equipment. Use a tripod or monopod to reduce camera movement.

Look for 'subject separation.' All too often, an otherwise wonderful animal portrait blends into the background. Move around until you find a background which is simple and a different but complimentary color than the subject. Back-lighting ('rim-lighting') will draw out the form of the animal from its surroundings. If the animal is dark with a bright background, an automatic shot will be too dark so compensate with a bracketed +1 exposure. Use a fill-flash on subjects less than ten feet from you for added lighting.

In the action-packed shows of SeaWorld, the animals move fast so stopping motion is important. Use a shutter speed of 1/500 or faster to freeze the motion. Higher speed films (ISO 400 or more) will allow you to shoot at faster shutter speeds but they have lower picture quality and weaker colors than slow film. With the bright sunlight of San Diego you should have no problem with an ISO 100 film. Accurate focusing is important—a fast auto-focus camera is useful.

Polar bears in the Wild Arctic exhibit.

SeaWorld

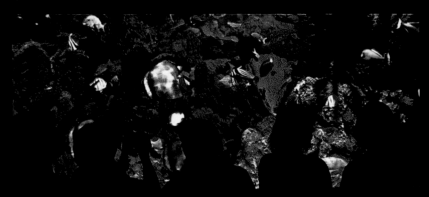

French angelfish

This white card—with a hole cut in the center for the lens—is black on the other side and is used to reduce reflections from the flash.

SeaWorld

How To Photograph An Aquarium

Aquarium photography offers the biggest challenge as the level of ambient light is very low. With a compact camera, use fast film (ISO 400), hold the camera steady near to the glass and switch the flash off (it will only produce glare).

With an SLR camera, a small external, hand-held flash unit solves the problem. Using a long "PC" cord to extend your flash, hold your flash unit at least 18 inches from the camera. Point the flash into the aquarium at a 45 degree angle from the glass surface. If you are photographing a free-standing aquarium, you might hold the flash unit directly above the habitat to simulate natural sunlight. The truly dedicated can use a second external flash, held by an assistant, opposite the main strobe. This will add dimension and produce more even lighting.

Unfortunately, the flash also will light the photographer. UFOs— Unidentified Foto Objects—are all too common in aquarium photographs. To reduce reflections, use a 16" x 20" black card, cut with a hole in the center for your lens. This will eliminate the "flash burn" and produce professional-looking photos. What you lose in mobility, you gain in picture quality.

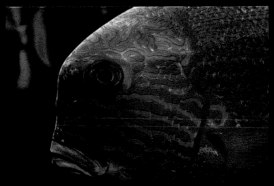

Bluelined sea bream

Quick Tips

- Turn the flash off. It will only reflect off the glass.

- Use fast film (i.e. ISO 400)

- Hold the camera steady to avoid a blurry picture. Rest on a friend's shoulder or use a cloth and put your hand against the glass. Don't let your lens touch the glass as it will scratch the surface.

- Include people for human interest and a sense of scale.

- Concentrate on one animal for impact.

Keep your lens perpendicular to (straight into) the glass. Due to the refraction of water into air, shooting at an angle will distort the subject.

Water softens color and diffuses detail so fish that swim close to the glass will appear clearer and more colorful on film. As always, crop tightly and concentrate on the eyes and mouth of the animals. Patience is important. Good photos happen when the photographer is interested but prepared to wait.

Sea anemone

Downtown

Above: A San Diego Trolley stops at One America Plaza. *Right:* The Hyatt and Marriott hotels.

San Diego has a diverse and thriving downtown area. In 1975, Mayor Pete Wilson announced plans to revitalize the city center. Since then, the area has blossomed with two themed shopping malls, distinctive skyscrapers, and a renovated historical quarter.

The modern skylineh as been described as 'the contents of a toolbox,' with a straight screwdriver (the Hyatt Hotel), a Phillips screwdriver (One America Plaza) and a cluster of Allen keys (Emerald Plaza).

Tip

Nothing beats water. Water nearly always makes a great foreground. It's calming and soft, and the reflections can double the impact of your subject and produce a nice symmetry to the shot.

This shot (right) is from Embarcadero Marina Park East, by the Convention Center, and offsets the boats of the marina with the Hyatt and Marriott hotels.

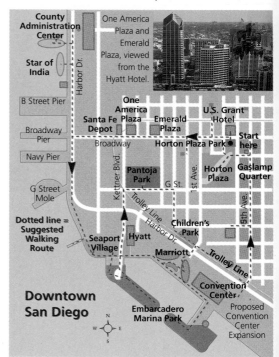

One America Plaza and Emerald Plaza, viewed from the Hyatt Hotel.

Downtown San Diego

County Administration Center
Star of India
B Street Pier
Broadway Pier
Navy Pier
G Street Mole
Harbor Dr.
One America Plaza
Santa Fe Depot
Broadway
Kettner Blvd.
Pantoja Park
G St.
Emerald Plaza
Horton Plaza Park
U.S. Grant Hotel
1st Ave.
Horton Plaza
Gaslamp Quarter
5th Ave.
Start here
Trolley Line
Harbor Dr.
Children's Park
Dotted line = Suggested Walking Route
Seaport Village
Hyatt
Marriott
Trolley Line
Convention Center
Embarcadero Marina Park
Proposed Convention Center Expansion

N W E S

Downtown

A Walk Around Downtown

To see the main sights, follow the paths marked above. I recommend starting at Horton Plaza Park, the official center of San Diego. Located here is the city's Zero Milestone, the point from which all distances to San Diego are measured. But you can start and finish anywhere.

Horton Plaza

Opened: 1985
Designer: Jon Jerde

"I think of architecture as entertainment, and life as entertainment, and I'm not sure where to draw the line."
—Jon Jerde, architect

Where
Broadway and G St., 1st and 4th aves. Parking entrances on 4th at F St. and G at 2nd St. 2 hours free parking with validation. ☎ 619-239-8180.

When
Morning and dusk. Stores are open Mon–Fri 10–9, Sat 10–8, Sun 11–7.

Tip
Although the Palazzo is well-lit during the morning, the most color is produced at dusk. You'll need a tripod so check in at Security first for permission, otherwise the guards will stop you.
Set up on the crosswalk by Mervyn's. You'll need a very wide-angle lens (24mm) to fit in the entire structure. The light is best about 30 minutes after sunset.

A **visual treat** of balconies and toy-town arches, this colorful, outdoor shopping center is justifiably the third-most visited attraction in San Diego.

Horton Plaza was one of the first, and still one of the most successful, malls to use the 'festival marketplace' approach. The whimsical, six-story complex surrounds a crescent-shaped courtyard. Bridges, escalators and stairways defy orientation and make it feel as though "you're walking through an MC Escher drawing."

Conceived by developer Ernest W. Hahn in 1974, at the start of downtown's revitalization. 6 1/2 city blocks were leveled and replaced by a showpiece complex designed by Jon Jerde. Based in Venice, California, Jerde has since created *Universal CityWalk* in Los Angeles and *The Freemont Street Experience* in Las Vegas.

Westfield Shoppingtown Horton Plaza contains 140 stores and restaurants, the Westin Hotel, a performing arts theater, a 14-screen movie theater and a 2,170-space parking area. Horton Plaza mall occupies part of the area first developed by Alonzo Horton in 1867.

Palazzo ②

Right: The classic view of Horton Plaza is of the Palazzo, a triangular façade modeled after the Palazzo building in Venice, Italy. This striking centerpiece is decorated with over a million one-inch Italian tiles.

Note: For safety reasons, tripods require prior approval from the marketing dept., 619-239-8180.

3 4
5 6

The Clock that Grieved

The mechanism of Jessop's Clock was built by Claude Ledger. After working for 27 years, the clock stopped in 1935, on the day Mr. Ledger died. After being restarted, it stopped three days later - the day of his funeral. Entitled "the clock that grieved," the story appeared in Ripley's "Believe It or Not."

324 Horton Plaza
San Diego CA 92101
Tel: 619-239-8180
www.westfield.com

The Obelisk
The Obelisk by Joan Brown is 40 feet high from its base. It is made of copper and decorated with ceramic tiles. Images of fish, jaguar and birds represent the sea, earth and sky.

Jessop's Clock ⏰ 1907

Called "the finest street clock in the US," the 21-foot-high clock has four faces and 20 dials, telling the time all around the world. Built in 1907, it stood outside Jessop's Jewelry Store on Fifth Avenue from 1927–85. The clock was designed and decorated by the Jessop family, using jewels that they mined and cut from native San Diego stones (agate, jade, tourmaline and topaz).

U.S. Grant Hotel ⏰ 1910

This grand, 280-room, 11-story hotel is listed on the National Register of Historic Places. It was built by San Diego businessman Ulysses S. Grant Jr. and named after his father, the Civil War general and U.S. President (who never visited San Diego). The lobby has a glorious marble staircase, Palladian columns and crystal chandeliers.

The Grant replaced the lavish, 100-room Horton House built by Alonzo Horton in 1870 as the centerpiece of his city. 326 Broadway. Tel: 619-232-3121.

The U.S. Grant Hotel, Horton Plaza Park and Broadway Fountain. As photographed from the steps to Planet Hollywood.

7

Alonzo Horton

The "Father" of San Diego

Alonzo Erastus Horton (1813–1909) developed and promoted today's downtown area and is know as the "Father of San Diego."

Born in Union, Connecticut, Horton moved to Wisconsin and founded the town of Hortonville, Wisconsin (pop. 2,000). During the Gold Rush, Horton moved to San Francisco in 1849 and became wealthy selling used furniture.

Horton heard about the small town of San Diego with its magnificent natural harbor and healthy climate. After attending a lecture on West Coast ports in March 1867, he immediately set sail for San Diego.

At this time, San Diego was based by the river at today's Old Town. With the growing importance of shipping over cattle, a competing "New Town" nearer the harbor had been created by William Heath Davis. Davis, another San Francisco merchant, had bought 160 acres by the bay in 1850. With four partners, he had laid out streets, imported houses and built a wharf and warehouse at the foot of today's Market Street. But an economic depression the following year ruined the venture. "New Town" became known as "Davis' Folly" or, for its principal residents, "Rabbitville."

On April 15, 1867, at the age of 54, Alonzo Horton arrived in San Diego on the steamer *Pacific*. He immediately bought 800 acres at a specially-arranged auction. Over the next three years, Horton laid out a square street plan centered on Broadway and 5th Ave.; built a larger wharf at the foot of Fifth Avenue; bought another 160 acres of land; built a theater, bank, and the palatial Horton House Hotel; and gave away 20 free lots for churches and to people who committed to build houses. His city blocks were smaller than normal to give him more higher-priced corners to sell, earning him the nicknames "Corner-lot Horton" and "Short-block Horton."

In 1868, imagining a city as great as New York or San Francisco, Horton campaigned to preserve 1,400

"I could not sleep at night for thinking about San Diego, and at 2 in the morning, I got up and looked on a map to see where San Diego was. And then I went back to bed satisfied. In the morning, I said to my wife, 'I am going to sell my goods and go to San Diego and build a city.'"
—*Alonzo Horton*

""It's the most beautiful place in the world to me, and I had rather have the affection and friendly greetings of the people of San Diego than all the rulers in the world."
—*Alonzo Horton, on his 95th birthday.*

Horton Plaza Park
This small park was the centerpiece of Horton's New Town. The 228 x 108 foot plaza was built in 1870 by Horton so that his guests at the Horton House Hotel had something to look at. Horton sold the plaza to the city in 1894 for $10,000, plus $100 a month until his death.

Broadway Fountain 1910
In the center of Horton Plaza Park is Broadway Fountain, designed by Irving Gill. Built for the opening of the U.S. Grant Hotel, this was the first successful attempt to combine colored lights with flowing water.
Modeled after the monument of Lysicrates in Athens, circa 334 B.C., the fountain has bas reliefs of Cabrillo, Father Serra and Horton.

Nearby
At the corner of 3rd and Broadway is the Times Arts Tix booth where you can buy same-day, half-price theater tickets (cash only). Open Tue–Sat. Call 619-497-5000 for a listing.

acres as a city park—today's Balboa Park.

In 1872, a fire destroyed much of Old Town and many residents (and the civic center) moved to New Town. With the arrival of the transcontinental railroad in 1885, San Diego became a boom-town. The population increased from 2,600 in 1880 to 40,000 in 1887 and Horton made up to $20,000 a day selling land.

In 1888–89, boom became bust. The population dropped to 16,000 and Horton lost his fortune. He remained a supporter of San Diego.

The city's two founders—Davis and Horton—both died almost penniless, in 1909. But their memory lives on in "America's Finest City."

Broadway

One America Plaza ⏱ 1991

The signature building of San Diego, the 34-story One America Plaza anchors and identifies the skyline of San Diego. At 498 feet (24 inches below the FAA's maximum permitted height), it is the tallest building in the city. Designed by Chicago architect Helmut Jahn, the glass-sided tower is tapered to give it the illusion of extra height. At night, white lights illuminate the top.

At the base is an unusual curved trolley stop and the Museum of Contemporary Art, Downtown. This is the auxiliary facility of the main museum in La Jolla. Open Thu–Tue, 11am–5pm, closed Wednesdays. Free admission. 619-234-1001. 1001 Kettner Blvd. at 600 W. Broadway.

ⓘ

San Diego Visitor Information Center
First Ave at F Street, on the west side of Horton Plaza
Open: Mon–Sat 8:30am–5pm.
☎ **619-236-1212.**
www.sandiego.org

Emerald Plaza ⏱

1991
A cluster of eight hexagonal towers, the Plaza is 26-stories high and at night is lit with green neon rings. As well as offices, the Plaza houses the 436-room Wyndham Emerald Plaza Hotel (formerly the Pan Pacific). 400 W Broadway. 619-239-4500.

YMCA ⏱ 1924
Adjacent to Emerald Plaza is the YMCA, noted for its beautiful tiled swimming pool in the basement. 500 W. Broadway.

Spreckels Theater 1912
Built for John D. Spreckels, this respected theater has an exuberant interior and fine acoustics. 121 Broadway.

The YMCA and Emerald Plaza, on Broadway.

Downtown

Light, Water, Rock

Charles Ross, 1986.
Several rainbows appear as water flows down a prismatic wall. Front St. at Broadway.

Fountain of Two Oceans

Sergio Benvenuti, 1984.
The Atlantic and Pacific come together in Wells Fargo Plaza. B Street and 5th.

Bow Fountain ○ Malcolm Leland, 1964.

Symbolizing San Diego's "ship coming in," a prow of a ship cuts through the ocean. In the Civic Center Plaza at 3rd and B Street

Excalibur ○ Beverly Pepper, 1976.

A 60-foot statue of King Arthur's sword. By the Federal Building.

Santa Fe Depot

Left: A tiled tower of the Santa Fe Depot, with the glass-sided First National Bank behind.

Santa Fe Depot 🕐 1915

A railway station constructed for the 1915 Panama-California International Exposition. The twin domes are similar to those of the California Building (San Diego Museum of Man) in Balboa Park. The interior has a vaulted ceiling.

Built on the site of the 1885 Santa Fe railroad station, the Santa Fe depot is an Amtrack station.

1050 Kettner Blvd at Broadway.

One block west is a parking lot called Lane Field, where the Padres played baseball from 1936 to 1957. There are plans to build an opera house and/or aquarium here.

Tip
Shoot in the 'golden hours.' The County Administration Building faces west, and burns a bright gold at sunset. The best view is from across the bay at North Harbor Drive near the Coast Guard Station and San Diego Airport.

County Administration Center   🕐   1938

Designed in the Art Deco style, the County Administration Center is fronted with elegant, slender palm trees and somehow makes San Diego look like Hawaii. The Center was a WPA project and dedicated in 1938 by President Franklin D. Roosevelt. It is considered to be one of the county's most beautiful municipal buildings.

The Center was featured in the TV show "Hawaii Five-0" and looks like Hawaii's Iolani Palace, the only royal palace on U.S. soil.

Guardian of Water   🕐   Donal Hord, 1939

In front of the County Administration Center is this 23-foot-high granite sculpture, representing a pioneer woman shouldering a water jug. It is symbolic of San Diego's role in water conservation.

Star of India

The *Star of India* is best photographed from the corner of Anthony's Fish Grotto (right) or from the Berkeley (above).

Where

On the original dockside area at 1306 N. Harbor Drive on the Embarcadero. All three ships are restored and accessible on one ticket. Open: 9–8/9. $7/$5. 619-234-9153.

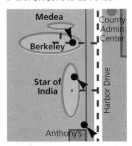

Further south at Navy Pier is the proposed home of the decommissioned aircraft carrier *Midway*.

The *Berkeley*, from the wheel of the *Star of India*.

The **Star of India** is a square-rigged, iron-hulled, merchant tall ship—the world's oldest active such ship afloat. It has survived collision, cyclone, ice and mutiny, and has circled the globe 21 times.

Built in England on the Isle of Man, the ship was launched in 1863 as the *Euterpe*. Her work changed with the times, sailing between England and India with cargo, England and New Zealand/Australia with emigrants, Puget Sound to Australia with timber, and Alaska to California with salmon.

The *Star of India* arrived in San Diego in 1927. After restoration she was opened as a museum in 1961. You can explore the interior, complete with sailors cabins and sailing equipment. In the summer, movies are projected on the sails, in October she becomes 'The Haunted Ship' and in December she is strung with festive lighting.

The *Star* is one of three ships that form the Maritime Museum of San Diego. The other two are:

Ferryboat Berkeley   1898

From 1898 to 1958 this ferry sailed between San Francisco and Oakland. She helped residents escape the fires following the 1906 San Francisco earthquake. Inside is a large collection of model ships, including models of every America's Cup yacht.

Steam Yacht Medea 1904

A luxury steam-powered yacht built in Scotland for a wealthy Englishman.

Seaport Village

The state's most enjoyable waterfront complex.
—Los Angeles Magazine

Overlooking the marina is a 45-foot-high replica of the Mukilteo Lighthouse in Everett, Washington. It houses a cookie store.

Seaport Village is a 14-acre landscaped tourist shopping area recreating a California harbor of a century ago. It is designed as three connecting plazas, individually themed as Old Monterey, Victorian San Francisco and traditional Mexico.

Opened in 1980, the Village was designed by Nobert W. Pieper and given an antiquated look by "authenticators" from Disneyland. There are 75 speciality shops, 13 quick eateries and four restaurants. Four miles of cobblestone pathways wind past ponds, lakes and a fountain, and a quarter-mile of slate boardwalk runs along the bay providing a spectacular view of San Diego's harbor.

Seaport Village is neither a port nor a village. It occupies the site of John Spreckels' old San Diego-Coronado ferry terminal, closed when the San Diego-Coronado Bay Bridge opened in 1969.

Tip

Romantic shots are often dusk shots. Dusk is my favorite time to photograph as city scenes can look even better on film than they do in real life. Shooting from Embarcadero Marina Park put some water in the foreground to reflect the lights of the Mukilteo Lighthouse. I used a long lens (100mm) to emphasize the distant Emerald Shappery Center, with its green hexagonal neon lights.

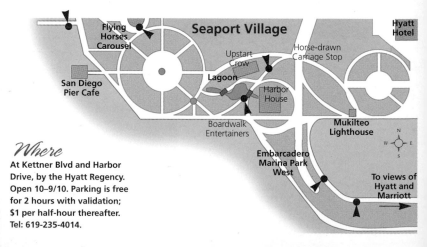

Downtown

Where
At Kettner Blvd and Harbor Drive, by the Hyatt Regency. Open 10–9/10. Parking is free for 2 hours with validation; $1 per half-hour thereafter. Tel: 619-235-4014.

Nearby
The Kansas City Barbeque restaurant was used in the 1986 Tom Cruise movie "Top Gun." 610 W. Market Street.

The carousel contains 46 animals, including dogs, goats and jumping horses with real horsehair tails. Made of poplar wood, they reflect the characteristics of famed master-carver Charles I.D. Looff.

Lagoon ⏲
The lagoon provides several photo opportunities.

Broadway Flying Horses Carousel   1890
An original Charles Looff Carousel, once at Coney Island, New York. Meticulously restored, the carousel is a popular ride for children. If you grab the brass ring you get a free ride!

Born in Schleswig-Holstein, Looff emigrated to New York and became renowned for his classic fairground amusements. He later built Santa Monica Pier. Another Looff carousel stands in Balboa Park and a replica is in Belmont Park in Mission Beach.

Inside is a restored 52-key, 175-pipe Gebruder Bruder Waldkirch Band Organ, built in Germany in 1914.

From Seaport Village you have good views of the aircraft carriers moored at Coronado.

This untitled statue is at the entrance to Embarcadero Marina Park West.

San Diego Pier Cafe ⏲

Supported on stilts, the Cafe offers casual dining over the Bay. Tel 619-239-3968. It is best photographed from the pier just north. Try to include a sail boat for extra effect.

Tip

Look for water. The small lagoon in the center of Seaport Village makes a romantic shot in the afternoon and at dusk. Overflow the bottom of the frame with the water, and include the bridge handrail for that 'village' look.

Pantoja Park

Tucked away in a residential part of downtown, Pantoja Park is a real 'PhotoSecret.' The verdant park has views of One America Plaza and the Emerald Shapery Center.

In the center is a statue, given by Mexico in 1981, of Benito Juárez, the Mexican reformist president.

Pantoja Park is named after Don Juan Pantoja y Arriage, pilot of an ill-fated Spanish surveying party in 1782. The park was the center of Davis' New Town in 1850 and is sometimes referred to as Newtown Park.

This shot is taken from G Street by India Street.

Hyatt Hotel

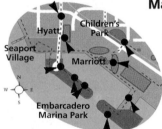

Manchester Grand Hyatt San Diego ⏱ 1992

The West Coast's tallest waterfront hotel, the Hyatt has two towers: the original eaast tower (built in 1992) is 40-stories high, and the new west tower (added 2003) is 34 stories high.

The 1,625-room hotel is the centerpiece of the San Diego skyline. On the top floor of the east tower is a bar and gallery with terrific views of San Diego Bay, Coronado, and downtown San Diego.

One Market Place. Tel: 619-232-1234.

Don't miss this sky-high view of San Diego, from the top floor of the Hyatt.

Marriott Marina

Tip

Look away from the sun at sunset. It's always tempting to just photograph the sun at sunset, but there are often better shots in the other direction. Here the glass-sided Marriott Hotel reflects the sunset's majesty for that picture-postcard quality.

By the entrance to the Marriott is this attractive lagoon (below), in Children's Park (1995). Nearby is the Children's Museum (above), open 1–5, closed Mondays.

San Diego Marriott Hotel and Marina Towers ⊕   1987

One of the most distinctive and attractive buildings in San Diego, the Marriott hotel has twin curving glass towers which look like a large optical lens experiment in progress. Formerly known as the Hotel Inter-Continental San Diego, the Marriott has 1,355 rooms, an outdoor pool with waterfall, and a 446-slip marina.

Both the Marriott and the Hyatt are best photographed from Embarcadero Marina Park.

333 W. Harbor Drive. Tel: 619-234-1500.

Embarcadero

Embarcadero Marina Park

This 22-acre, man-made park extends into the bay and provides great views of the marina. There are pleasant walks on both the west and east portions. In the summer, open-air concerts are staged.

Chart House

The Chart House restaurant was originally the 1899 boathouse of the San Diego Rowing Club.

Breaking the Chains 1995

By the Harbor Club on Martin Luther King Jr. Promenade is a steel sculpture (below). © Melvin Edwards, 1995.

San Diego Convention Center 🕐

To harmonize with its waterfront setting, Arthur Erickson's modern design(below) is said to be inspired by an oceanliner. Huge white 'sails' of Teflon shade an open-air roof area.

The Convention Center is the largest meeting area in San Diego with 760,000-square-feet of space. The complex, built in 1969, includes a large exhibition hall, 32 meeting rooms, a 40,000-square-foot ballroom, a 100,000 square-foot special events area and a bayside amphitheater. On top are six tennis courts.

111 W. Harbor Drive. 619-525-5000.

San Diego Convention Center

The Harbor Club 🕐

Harbor Club condo towers (right) are at 100 Harbor Drive. A resident gained infamy with his habit of taking out the trash while in the nude.

Tip
The lush landscape makes an interesting foreground and the round flower bed contrasts with the square Harbor Club towers. A passing trolley adds a splash of red.

San Diego Trolley 🕐

Established in 1981, the light rail Trolley follows many of the old electric streetcar system (1892 to 1949). The Trolley connects downtown with the Mexican border, Old Town and Qualcomm Stadium.

Downtown

Gaslamp Quarter

The "Historical Heart of San Diego," the Gaslamp Quarter is 16 1/2-block area of restored Victorian buildings dating from 1873 to 1930. The entire 38 acres is on the National Register of Historic Places. Once the haunt of San Diego's founders, as well as gunslinger and gambler Wyatt Earp, the Gaslamp Quarter is now filled with restaurants, galleries, lofts, night clubs, brick sidewalks and, of course, gaslamps.

Left: Gaslamps and the Keating Building.

U.S. Grant Hotel
Broadway
Horton Plaza Park
Louis Bank of Commerce
Keating Building
E St.
Horton Plaza
Gaslamp Quarter National Historic District
4th Ave.
5th Ave.
6th Ave.
William Heath Davis House
Island Ave.
Horton Grand Hotel
N W E S
Harbor Club
Gateway Arch
Convention Center

History

Today's downtown was founded by William Heath Davis in 1850. Alonzo Horton expanded the town in 1867, forming the main business district along 5th Avenue—today's Gaslamp Quarter. One of the area's first houses, the William Heath Davis House, is now a Gaslamp Quarter museum.

After the first railroad arrived in 1885, the town boomed. 5th Avenue became lined with saloons, hotels, bordellos and opium dens. Three gambling halls were run by Wyatt Earp, famous for his 1881 shoot-out at the O.K. Corral in Tombstone, Arizona.

In the bust of the 1890s, businesses and residents moved north of Market Street. The abandoned area became a red light district with 120 bordellos. It was known as the "Stingaree" as visitors were as likely to get stung by merchants in downtown as they were by sting rays in the bay.

Threatened by demolition, the buildings were saved by the Gaslamp Quarter Association, founded in 1974. Ninety-four buildings are now identified as historically or architecturally significant and the area is a National Historic District with development strictly controlled.

Downtown

The most distinctive building in the Gaslamp Quarter is the Louis Bank of Commerce. For this shot, stand at the base of the nearest banner and shoot upwards. Use a wide-angle lens for impact.

Events

There are many events in the Gaslamp Quarter, usually emphasizing the wealth of restaurants. The largest event is "Street Scene" which takes over about 20 city blocks with live bands and tasty food.

ℹ

Gaslamp Quarter Historical Foundation, in the William Heath Davis House Museum
410 Island Avenue
San Diego CA 92101
Tel: 619-233-4692.

The district is named after the gas lamps that lit the streets in the 1880s. Today's versions are simulated but enhance the Victorian ambience.

Gateway Arch ⊕

This entrance to the Gaslamp Quarter (right) is by the Convention Center, at the foot of Fifth Avenue.

Louis Bank of Commerce 🕐 1888

Distinguished by its twin granite towers, this is the most recognizable building in the Gaslamp Quarter. It also has the most colorful history.

Isidor Louis bought the four story building from the Bank of Commerce in 1893. He opened an Oyster Bar which was a favorite of Wyatt Earp. In the 1900s, the upper floors became the Golden Poppy Hotel, a brothel run by Madame Coara. The door to each 'hotel' room was painted with a different color, matching the color of each employee's dress. This way, clients could find the room of the lady they preferred.

Designed by Stannard & Clements, the Baroque Revival building has a granite front with bay windows.

837 5th Avenue. Restored by Don Reeves.

The Keating Building ⏲ 1890

Nicknamed "the widow's building," the Keating Building was finished in 1890 by George Keating's widow, Fannie. The building now houses the popular Croce's Restaurant, operated by the widow of musician Jim Croce, Ingrid Croce.

Ingrid Croce pioneered the revival of the Gaslamp Quarter in 1985. She operates two restaurants and three bars. 802 Fifth Ave. Tel: 619-233-4355.

Croce's Restaurant in the Keating Building.

Tip

Turn the flash off. Although your first reaction may be to use a flash at night, you can get more attractive shots without it. For this shot of the Carriage Stop Café (below) I used a one second exposure and a tripod.

The Carriage Stop Café, under the Keating Building, on F Street at Fifth.

William Heath Davis House ⏱ 1850

The William Heath Davis House is the oldest building in the Gaslamp Quarter and is now a museum operated by the Gaslamp Quarter Historical Foundation. Inside are displays about downtown's two principal founders—William Heath Davis and Alonzo Horton.

The house is the only remaining example of 14 identical houses that Davis had prefabricated in Maine and shipped around the tip of South America to San Diego in 1850. The two-story frame house is in New England "salt box" style. It was originally located at State and Market Streets.

Davis bought and sold this house but it was never his home. Davis' house was identical but no longer remains. The house was, however, the first San Diego home of Alonzo and Sarah Horton. They lived here for a year (1868-69) while their larger house was being built.

410 Island Avenue. Two-hour guided walking tours of the Historic District depart every Saturday at 11am.

Granger Building 1904

The founder of San Diego Zoo, Dr. Harry M. Wegeforth, had an office in this Romanesque building. He was married to Ralph Granger's daughter, Rachel.

964 5th Ave. Architect: William Quayle.

Above: The entrance to the Horton Grand Hotel.

Horton Grand 🕑   1886

A quaint Victorian hotel with an open-air courtyard and interesting bar. It is a combination of two historic hotels—the Horton Grand and the Kahle Saddlery.

The 110-room Horton Grand Hotel is San Diego's oldest Victorian hotel and was designed by Comstock & Trotsche. In 1981, the Horton and the 1886 Kahle Saddlery Hotel, both located at different sites, were slated for demolition. They were carefully disassembled, relocated here, restored, and reopened side-by-side in 1986.

311 Island Ave. Tel: 619-544-1886.

Marston Building   1881

Opposite Croce's is a grand Italianate Victorian style building. For 15 years, this was home to the exclusive Marston's Department Store, owned by George Marston. Marston helped preserve Balboa Park and other San Diego treasures. His store was sold to Broadway Stores, now part of Macy's.

Watts-Robinson Building   1913

Eleven-stories high, this was one of the first Chicago commercial style skyscrapers in San Diego. The steel frame is fronted with cut limestone and granite. Inside are tile floors, marble wainscoting and brass ornamentation. Architects: Leonard Bristow and John Lyman.

Northeast corner of 5th Avenue and E Street.

Villa Montezuma

"The most interesting and imaginatively designed Victorian house still standing in San Diego." —Clare Crane

Where
1925 K St at 20th, just east of I-5. Open Fri, Sat & Sun, 10am–4:30pm. Tel: 619-239-2211. $5/$2. Joint tickets with the Marston House.

Jesse Shepard
1848–1927
Born in Birkenhead, England, Jesse Shepard was brought to America by his parents on the ship *Montezuma*. From 1869–74 he traveled through Europe, entertaining nobility such as the Czar of Russia and Britains's Prince of Wales by playing instantaneous compositions on the piano.
In 1885, while living in Chicago, Shepard met Lawrence Tonner and their relationship lasted over forty years.
Shepard never charged for any of his musical performances and spent his last years in Los Angeles, impoverished and supported by Tonner. Appropriately he died at the keyboard, while playing the last note of a recital.

One mile east of downtown is a fascinating and exuberant Victorian house. Little-known even to locals, it is a real "secret" of San Diego. Built as a cultural showplace at the height of San Diego's boom period, the Villa Montezuma is the unique creation of musical artist Jesse Shepard— the "Psychic Pianist."

Renowned for his musical improvisations and operatic singing, Shepard was a popular guest in the salons of Europe and America. On a tour of California in 1886, he was persuaded to settle in San Diego with the gift of this house. Wealthy rancher brothers, William and John High, had subdivided this area, called Sherman-Heights, and wanted to attract upscale buyers. Impressed with Shephard's cultural influence, the Highs offered Shepard a prime plot of land and funds to build an "entertaining-house" of his own design—a salon in San Diego.

Shepard chose dark redwood and walnut paneling, silvery Lincrusta Walton ceilings, and colorful art glass windows of his artistic idols, including Beethoven and Mozart, Rubens and Raphael, and Shakespeare. The architectural firm of Comstock and Trotsche was paid $19,000 to build the house—a "palace of arts"—which was completed in July 1887.

Shepard, with his life companion Lawrence Waldemar Tonner, lived in the house for about a year. Shepard embarked on a literary career, writing essays for *The Golden Era*, and then traveled to France to publish a book. The book was a success and Shepard returned to San Diego, sold the house in November 1889 for $29,000, and moved to Europe to pursue writing.

The house changed hands several times and was bought in 1970 by the San Diego Historical Society for $26,000. It was restored to its 1887 appearance and is now operated as a museum. Tours are given on the weekend, highlighting the fabulous interior. Cameras are not allowed inside but you can photograph the exterior from the street at any time.

Villa Montezuma ⊕ is capped by an Arabesque dome. Inside is a small stairway leads to the Tower Room which has a 360° view of Point Loma, San Diego Bay, and Mexico. Owner Jesse Shepard placed a revolving chair in the Tower Room so that he could enjoy the view from any side while he wrote.

The house was bought in 1948 by Edward Campbell who believed that Shepard had buried gold in the grounds. After four months digging in the basement, nothing was found and Campbell sold the house.

5 Hotel del Coronado

**On the west side of Corona-
do, 2 1/2 miles from San
Diego. From the bridge, continue on 4th St. and turn left
on Orange Avenue (Rt. 75).
See map on page 152.**

🛈

**1500 Orange Avenue
Coronado CA 92118
Tel: 619-435-6611.
Reservations: 619-522-8000.**

CONTENTS:

Coronado

A fairy-tale American castle, 'The Del,' as it is commonly known, is the largest wooden oceanside hotel on the West Coast. The lavish Victorian dream is the last seaside resort remaining from California's opulent 1880s. It is a National Historic Landmark.

The choice of 14 U.S. Presidents and numerous celebrities, the Del is probably most remembered as the place where Marilyn Monroe frolicked on the beach with Jack Lemmon and Tony Curtis in Billy Wilder's 1959 film, *Some Like it Hot*.

Exploding with turrets, towers and cupolas, all topped with a distinctive red roof, the Hotel del Coronado is a sight to behold, and photograph.

Orange Ave.

Crown Room

Garden Patio

Entrance

Tennis Courts

Beach

Pool

N
W · E
S

Hotel del Coronado

Legends of The Del

"The electrical lighting system was installed and personally supervised by Thomas Edison himself."
No. Edison was not involved and the system was installed by a rival company, Mather Electric, Co.

"Where Prince Edward first met Mrs. Simpson."
Although they may have been first introduced at the hotel, there is no evidence that they became acquainted until 15 years later at her official introduction to the prince in London.

Edward, Prince of Wales and heir to Britain's throne, came to the hotel in April 1920 on a round-the-world cruise. He was the first British royal to visit California. At least two of his functions were also attended by Wallis Spencer, wife of Lieu-tenant Earl W. Spencer, Jr. Mrs. Spencer later divorced and remarried, becoming Mrs. Wallis Warfield Simpson. After becoming King, Edward abdicated the British throne to marry Mrs. Simpson.

The hotel bought Simpson's craftsman-style house and moved it to the hotel grounds, where it is now named the Duchess of Windsor Cottage.

"'Wizard of Oz' was written at the Del."
No. Author L. Frank Baum lived in Coronado only after "Wizard" was written. However, subsequent "Oz" books were written in Coronado. Baum wintered in Coronado for several years, first at the hotel, then at 1101 Star Park Circle in Coronado, the 'Wizard of Oz House' (not open to the public).

Pictures of Marilyn Monroe, presidents and other dignitaries are displayed in the History Gallery.

The ghost of Kate Morgan is said to reside in Room 3312.

History Tours are offered on Thursdays, Fridays and Saturdays at 10 and 11am.

Tip
Look for leading lines. The winding pathway (left) draws the eye into the background. This is a "yellow brick road" shot!

Tip
Use natural light. A camera flash would never light this huge room, so switch the flash off, hold the camera steady, and use natural lighting. Meter off the paneling, or the face of a person in the foreground.

The Garden Patio

The central courtyard (*left*) was originally landscaped by Kate Sessions, now famous for her work in Balboa Park. The gazebo is modeled after Miss Sessions' flower stand, where she made all the flower arrangements for the hotel. It is a popular setting for weddings.

Lobby

The beautiful dark lobby, made from Illinois oak, has a cast-iron bird-cage elevator and a balcony. From the balcony, ladies watched men displaying their day's fishing catch on the marble floor.

Crown Room

The Crown Room (*below*) is the main dining room. It hosted the dinner for Charles Lindbergh to celebrate his flight across the Atlantic.

The arched ceiling, 33-feett-high, is made of natural sugar pine held in place entirely with wooden pegs—there are no nails or pillars. It is hand-polished twice a year. Notice the crown-shaped chandeliers that some say were designed by *Wizard of Oz* author, Frank L. Baum.

Building An American Castle

"We ought to build a hotel, Story, the brightest…smartest hostelry on any coast… We ought to build it on that spot across the bay where we sunburned this morning."
—*Elisha Babcock to Hampton Story, 1885.*

"It was amazing how many rooms were built that were not even planned for at the start of construction."
—*Edward H. Davis, draftsman.*

In 1884, Elisha Spurr Babcock, Jr. moved to San Diego from Indiana and met Hampton L. Story from Chicago. Together they would row to the barren North and South Islands across San Diego Bay to go fishing. In 1885, with San Diego booming and a railroad completed from San Francisco and Los Angeles, Babcock and Story decided to build a hotel. They thought a world-class luxury hotel would raise land prices more than enough to pay for the construction.

In 1885, Babcock and Story formed a syndicate and bought the two islands (today combined as one), a total of 4,185 acres of land, for $110,000. The land was parceled up and sold within three years for $2.2 million. Babcock hired brothers James and Merritt Reid, architects from his hometown of Evansville, to build an Americanized castle.

Ground was broken in March 1887. A small railroad, an iron works, a metal shop, a brick kiln, and a lumber processing plant were all built at the site. Construction was started before the designs were finalized and workmen learned their trade as they built.

The hotel cost a million dollars and opened after 11 months (although construction continued for several years). It opened in 1888 with 399 rooms, each with its own fireplace. The lighting system was completely electric with more than 1,600 lights, making it the largest single installation of incandescent lamps in the nation. The hotel had its own electric power plant which also supplied electricity for the entire city of Coronado from 1888 to 1922.

Shortly after opening however, the real estate boom became a bust. Babcock and Story were unable to pay a $100,000 loan and the hotel was bought by the 24-year-old sugar magnate, John D. Spreckels. Babcock remained as manager but his later business ventures failed and he died virtually bankrupt.

In 1997, the hotel was bought by Lowe Enterprises for a record $330M.

To emphasize the seaside location of the hotel, stand in the ocean and shoot inland.

The best views are of the entrance, on the southeast side. Stand on the far side of the driveway, used for valet parking, and include the main rotunda.

John D. Spreckels
"The Man Who Made San Diego"

Besides owning the Hotel del Coronado, John Diedrich Spreckels (1853–1926) was a major developer of San Diego.

He was born in South Carolina as the eldest son of Claus August Spreckels, the "Sugar King." In the 1860s, Claus Spreckels invested in Hawaii and gained a near-monopoly of sugar on the Pacific coast. John D. Spreckels expanded the business into shipping and moved from Hawaii to San Diego in 1887. He was a frequent guest of the Del.

With his brothers, Adolph and Rudolph, John formed J.D. Spreckels and Bros. At it's peak, besides most of Coronado, the company owned San Diego-Coronado Ferry System, San Diego & Arizona Railway, San Diego Electric Railway (streetcar), two of San Diego's three newspapers (the San Diego Union and the Evening Tribune, now the Union-Tribune Publishing Company) and Belmont Park in Mission Beach.

Coronado

Lights adorn the hotel's exterior during December.

Coronado

"Let Coronado wear her crown as Empress of the Sea; no need she fear her earthly peer will e'er discovered be."
—L. Frank Baum, 1905.

Most of Coronado was purchased in 1889 by John D. Spreckels. The island seceded from San Diego in 1890 and remains a separate city. Spreckels' home is now the Glorietta Bay Inn, and the renowned "Lamb's Players Theatre" performs in the historic Spreckels Building on Orange Avenue.

Coronado Visitor Bureau
1047 B Avenue
Coronado CA 92118
Tel: 619-437-8788.
Open weekdays 9-5, weekends 10-4.

Coronado Historical Museum
1126 Loma Ave, near The Del
Tel: 619-435-7242
Open: Mon–Fri 9–5, Sat 10–5, Sun 11–4. Free ($4 donation requested).

Historical Walking Tour starts from the Glorietta Bay Inn across the street from The Del. Walks are on Tue, Thu and Sat at 11am. $8 for 90 minutes of history and architecture. Tel: 619-435-5993.

Coronado is a charming village with lovely homes and palm-lined avenues. It has more retired admirals than any other city in the country. Over half of Coronado forms North Island Naval Air Station, the "birthplace of Naval Aviation" and home port to three aircraft carriers.

Although called an island, Coronado is technically a peninsular, connected to Imperial Beach by a narrow strip of land called the Silver Strand. It was originally two islands—North Island and South Island—but became one in 1940 when the U.S. Navy filled in the Spanish Bight with dredgings from the bay. The islands were named by Juan Rodríguez Cabrillo in 1542 as the "crowned ones." Coronado is Spanish for "crowned."

Coronado has one of the widest and finest beaches in San Diego, and that too is man-made. In 1945, the Navy dredged San Diego Bay and pumped the sand over Silver Strand and into the ocean. Northerly currents washed it to the shore around Ocean Boulevard. The elite Navy SEALs are based at the nearby Amphibious Base and often run on the beach.

Right: The Boathouse restaurant is built in the same style as the Hotel del Coronado as it was originally the hotel's boathouse.

1701 Strand Way. Tel: 619-435-0155.

The San Diego skyline. Photographed at dusk from Coronado at the foot of Orange Avenue.

Coronado

Coronado

Ferry Landing

Ferry
The ferry operates every day.
Sun–Thur: 9am–9:30pm;
Fri–Sat: 9am–10:30pm. $2
each way. Tel: 619-234-4111.

The Ferry Landing Marketplace ⏱

Some of the best views of the San Diego skyline are from around the Ferry Landing Marketplace on Coronado. A path extends from the ferry pier to a park at the foot of Orange Avenue and provides a variety of photo opportunities.

A fishing pier is used as the dock for the popular ferry from San Diego. The Ferry Landing is near the site of John D. Spreckels' dock for his San Diego-to-Coronado ferry. Spreckels' ferry sailed from today's Seaport Village area; today's ferry sails from the pier at the foot of Broadway.

The Ferry Landing Marketplace is a complex of 33 gift stores and restaurants, located at 1201 First Street in Coronado.

Coronado

Bay Bridge

San Diego-Coronado Bay Bridge 🕐 1969

The 2 3/10-mile-long graceful blue span links downtown San Diego with Coronado. It rises 210 feet above San Diego Bay and has low guardrails that permit an unobstructed view of the San Diego area.

If damaged, the central section is designed to fall away and float. This prevents the harbor from being blocked during a war—a lesson learned from the bombing of Pearl Harbor.

Underneath the bridge on the San Diego side is Chicano Park. Created in 1970, the four-acre park displays colorful murals celebrating Chicano ethnic heritage. (Do not reproduce photographs of murals without the artist's consent.)

Do not take photographs from the bridge. Pedestrians and bicycles are not allowed; it is illegal to stop a car on the bridge; and it is dangerous to take photographs while driving.

Tip

Sunrises are as beautiful as sunsets. If you like sunsets you can double your fun by photographing sunrises too—the atmospheric conditions are similar.
To avoid burning out the image with a bright sun, only photograph when the sun is right on the horizon, or not in the shot at all.

Where

This view of the Bay Bridge over San Diego Bay is taken from Coronado, at the eastern tip of the Municipal Golf Course. Use the solar calendar at the back of this book to predict where the sun will rise.

Coronado

Navy

Aircraft Carriers

Carriers can often be seen docking on the east shore of Coronado. NAS North Island is the command center for all 2,000+ aircraft in the Pacific Fleet.

There are six carriers in the Pacific Fleet. You can identify each carrier by its signage. The 'N' indicates that the ship is nuclear-powered.

CV-63 USS Kitty Hawk
CVN-68 USS Nimitz
CVN-70 USS Carl Vinson
CVN-72 USS Abraham
        Lincoln
CVN-74 USS John C Stennis
CVN-76 USS Ronald
        Reagan

For more information on these carriers, visit http://www.airpac.navy.mil/units/

Marine Corps Air Station Miramar

The "Top Gun" school used to be at Miramar (east of La Jolla), but the famed Navy flight school has since relocated to Fallon, Nevada. Miramar is now home to Marine FA-18 fighter and helicopter squadrons.

San Diego is one of the largest and busiest U.S. Navy ports in the world. 56 vessels are homeported on San Diego Bay, including three aircraft carriers and five submarines. With one of California's largest natural harbors, San Diego is one of the mega-ports for the U.S. Pacific Fleet.

NAS North Island and NAB Coronado Complex

Naval Air Station, North Island (NASNI), on Coronado, is the largest naval aviation military/industrial complex on the West Coast. Although the U.S. Pacific Fleet is headquartered in Hawaii, NASNI is home to Commander, Naval Air Force, U.S. Pacific Fleet, who is responsible for all Pacific Fleet aircraft and carriers.

NASNI is known as the "Birthplace of Naval Aviation" since it was here that Glenn H. Curtiss trained the first naval aviators in 1911. He also opened the first naval flying school and invented the tailhook, allowing aircraft to stop quickly on carriers.

North Island was originally a flat, barren island separate from Coronado. It was sold by John D. Spreckels to the Navy in 1917 and joined to South Island (Coronado) in 1940 when the Navy filled the gap in the Spanish Bight.

South of the Hotel del Coronado, on the Silver Strand, is the Naval Amphibious Base (NAB). NAB is home of the Naval Special Warfare Command, including three SEAL (Sea, Air and Land) teams. No tours are offered but you can often see the SEALs training on the beach by The Del. Together, NASNI and NAB are referred to as "Naval Base Coronado."

Naval Station San Diego

Located in National City, south of San Diego, the Naval Station provides shore support and berthing facilities for 48 ships of the Pacific Fleet.

Navy Tour

There used to be public tours of the station and carriers. But, due to heightened security since 9/11/01, there are currently no public tours of NAS North Island. For updated information visit www.airpac.navy.mil or call 619-437-2735.

From surrounding areas, particularly Cabrillo National Monument, you can aircraft such as:

Jets:
F-14   Tomcat
F/A-18   Hornet
S-3E   Viking

Helicopters:
MH-60   Seahawk
CH-46   Sea Knight

The base is also home to the Navy's only Deep Submergence Rescue Vehicles, Mystic (DSRV1) and Avalon (DSRV2).

The USS Kitty Hawk arrives in San Diego.

The base's first commanding officer, Lt. Cmd. Earl W. Spencer Jr., USN, added a degree of celebrity to North Island. His wife, Wallis, later became the Duchess of Windsor when she married King Edward of England, forcing Edward to renounce the throne in 1936.

Photographing an F-18 on the Navy Tour.

6 Cabrillo Monument

Where
At the end of Cabrillo Memorial Drive (SR209), through the gates of the Naval Ocean Systems Center. Open 9 to 5:15. $5 per vehicle. Bus 26 from Old Town. Tel: 619-557-5450.

The sandstone cliffs are unstable so do not stand near the edge.

Cabrillo National Monument 1800 Cabrillo Memorial Drive, San Diego CA 92106-3601 Tel: 619-557-5450. http://www.nps.gov/cabr/

Point Loma

One of the country's most-visited National Monuments, this memorial to San Diego's 'discoverer' has a great view of the bay and is a can't-miss opportunity for photographers. Nearby are two lighthouses, a whale-watching station, a hiking trail and several tide pools. Over one million visitors a year explore this 144-acre National Park on the tip of Point Loma.

The 14-foot sandstone statue depicts Juan Rodríguez Cabrillo who, in 1542, was the first European to discover San Diego Bay and today's Californian coast. Cabrillo and his men are thought to have landed at Ballast Point, Point Loma, at the end of Guijarros Road in the U.S. Naval Submarine Base.

The statue of the reputedly Portuguese navigator was made in Portugal by the Portuguese sculptor Charters de Almeida. Cabrillo's name is spelt in Portuguese on the base. It was originally designed for San Francisco and the Golden Gate International Exposition of 1939, but was delivered too late and fortunately shipped south to San Diego instead.

The heroic figure holds an explorer's pair of dividers and quadrant in one hand, and a Conquistador's sword in the other. No pictures of Cabrillo survive so the figure is idealized.

The Visitor Center has a good book store and a small but interesting museum. There are exhibits and films of Cabrillo's voyage; films about the tide pools, whales (in winter) and National Parks (in summer); and plaques about the skyline and Navy ships. Monthly bird-watching walks depart from the Center.

On clear days you can see the San Bernadino, Laguna and Cuyamaca Mountains (east), Mount Palomar (northeast), Tijuana and Mexico's Coronado Islands (south) and San Clemente Island (southwest).

When

Unfortunately it's not possible to photograph the monument or lighthouse at dawn or sunset (except in winter) as the 9 a.m. – 5:15 p.m. opening hours are strictly enforced. The surrounding area is controlled by the military and there is a gated access road. The road is closed before 9am and the rangers clear the monument at closing time.

The only time you can get a sunset or dusk shot is around December 21, when the sun sets around 5 p.m.

Note that there are no food concessions on-site or nearby.

Events

The annual Cabrillo Festival is held on the weekend closest to September 28. The festival includes cultural dances, food and a re-enactment of Cabrillo's landing.

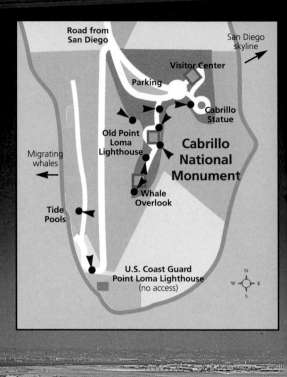

Road from San Diego

San Diego skyline

Visitor Center

Parking

Cabrillo Statue

Old Point Loma Lighthouse

Migrating whales

Cabrillo National Monument

Whale Overlook

Tide Pools

U.S. Coast Guard Point Loma Lighthouse (no access)

Cabrillo

Juan Rodríguez Cabrillo (1498?–1543) was the first European to explore the West Coast of today's United States. His mission was deemed unsuccessful and he died in the process, but Cabrillo has gained immortality as the 'discoverer' of San Diego. With his life spanning the brief Age of Conquistadors, he witnessed much of Spain's conquest of the Aztec and old Mayan empires and reported to the three main explorers—Cortés, Alvarado, and Mendoza.

Conquering the Aztecs

Cabrillo was probably born between 1498 and 1500, in Portugal or possibly Spain. He grew up in Cuba (*Hispaniola*), Spain's first settlement in the New World, and became a skilled soldier and shipbuilder. In 1520, he sailed to Mexico as a crossbowman and joined the army of the famous conquistador, Hernán Cortés. Cortés had recently captured the Aztec capital of Tenochtitlán—a beautiful city surrounded by a vast lake and larger than any European capital of that time. The Spaniards settled in to a life of luxury but they were soon routed in a bloody battle. Cabrillo spent most of the next year building 13 small ships to gain control of the lake. He fought in the final campaign that recaptured, and levelled, the Aztec city.

Cabrillo marched south and spent the next 12 years as a captain for Cortés' second-in-command, Pedro de Alvarado, subduing the tribes of Honduras and Guatamela. Awarded property for his service, Cabrillo became one of the richest citizens in the new capital of Santiago and was able to sail to Spain in 1523 to marry.

Searching the South Seas

Meanwhile, the Age of Discovery was heating up and rivals were emerging. Francisco Pizarro was conquering the Incas in Peru and Cortés was pursuing a route to the Orient. It was thought that the coast of

"On this day, Thursday Sept 28 1542, we discovered a port, closed and very good, which we named San Miguel."
—*Cabrillo's log.*

"We Spanish suffer from a disease of the heart which can only be cured by gold."
—*Hernán Cortés*

Point Loma

California and the Gold of Queen Calafia

The imagination of the conquistadors was fueled by fictional romance novels. One such book was the 1510 *Las Sergas de Esplandián* (The Exploits of Espandián) by Garcia Ordóñez de Montalvo.

The novel told of a fabulous island: "Know that on the right hand of the Indies there is an island called California." There, the author claimed, lived Amazonian women ruled by Queen Calafia. Besides pearl oysters, her empire was a source of gold rivaling that of the Aztecs. Even the swords of her warriors were made of gold, "for in all the island there is no other metal."

The Seven Cities of Cíbola

When the Moors (Islamic Arabs) invaded Iberia (Spain and Portugal) in the 700s, seven Portuguese bishops reportedly escaped. They were said to have sailed west to an island where they each founded a city.

Over the years sailors claimed to have seen the island whose sand was streaked with gold and whose cities streets were paved with gold.

Mexico, or New Spain as it was now called, arched north and west to join Asia—home to the fabulous Spice Islands (Moluccas, or West Indies to the English). The king made Cortés Captain-General of the South Seas (Pacific Ocean) and from 1532–36 Cortés sent several ships north to seek a trade route. One ship crossed the Gulf of California, and the sailors landed on the tip of Baja California, thinking it was the southern part of an island close to Asia. Seeing pearl oysters, they may have named it after a fictional island rich in pearls—California. (In 1539, another Cortés voyage, by Francisco de Ulloa, discovered that Baja lower California not part of Asia but a peninsular of Mexico.)

Competing with Cortés was Alvarado. He had also been given a royal commission to explore the Pacific, as well as the governorship of Guatemala, which made him independent of Cortés. In 1536, he ordered Cabrillo to build an exploration fleet that Alvarado would sail west. But a new objective was to appear that would change the course to a northerly route.

Seeking the Seven Cities

In 1536, the first Spanish adventurer to cross through present-day Texas heard tales of wealthy cities in the north. Rumors quickly spread that these were the fabled Seven Cities of Cíbola. The first viceroy of New Spain, Antonio de Mendoza, immediately dispatched expeditions into the "Northern Mystery" to search for the cities. Francisco Coronado marched overland to present-day New Mexico and Hernando de Alarcon sailed up the Gulf of California to the Colorado River, becoming the first European to stand on present-day California's soil. But they all returned empty handed

Cortés and Alvarado both planned trips north but were both blocked by Mendoza. Cortés sailed to Spain for redress (where he waited in vain for eight years) while Alvarado chose to partner with Mendoza.

By 1540, Cabrillo had built 8 or 9 ships, including

The Strait of Anian

Portugal controlled the route east from Europe to the Spice Islands. But to the Spanish and English, it seemed logical that the Islands could also be reached by sailing west. Somewhere through North America should be a passageway that connected the Atlantic and Pacific, providing a lucrative gateway to the Orient. The English called it the "Northwest Passage"; to the Spanish it was the "Strait of Anian."

"[Cabrillo's fleet] was the largest and best to sail the Mar del Sur [Pacific] up to that time and for many years after."
—Bishop Marroquín

"The lust for gold extends beyond this mortal life and taking a whole world will hardly satisfy it, much less one or two kingdoms."
—Hernán Cortés

"If Cabrillo had not died he would have discovered the great country of spices."
—Francisco de Vargas, crewmember

two for himself, the *Santiago* and the *San Salvador.* He sailed the fleet, combined with other private ships and those of Mendoza, to a new port he discovered, Navidad. But disaster was to strike.

In 1541, just before departure, Alvarado died in an Indian revolt (leaving many debts unpaid), and Santiago was destroyed in a giant mud slide. Both events cost Cabrillo most of his fortune, and made the ships and crew disband.

Mendoza took control of the voyage. He asked Cabrillo to sail north while another group, under Ruy López de Villalobos would sail west. Gathering two or three ships—the *San Salvador, Victoria,* and possibly *San Miguel*—supplies for a two-year trip, and about 160 crew, soldiers and slaves, Cabrillo left Navidad on June 27, 1542.

The Voyage of Cabrillo

Cabrillo's main objective was Asia but he was also to look for the Strait of Anian, the Seven Cities, and any other treasure. Only fifty years since Columbus had landed in the New World, Cabrillo was sailing into *ne plus ultra*— "no more beyond."

Cabrillo arrived at San Diego Bay on September 28, 1542, the eve of the feast day of St. Michael the Archangel, and thereby named the bay *Bahia de San Miguel.* He probably anchored off Ballast Point, a spit of land on Point Loma. He declared the bay, and the Kumeyaay natives he met, to be a possession of the King of Spain.

After six days, the three boats continued their voyage north. They discovered San Pedro Bay (Los Angeles), the Channel Islands, Morro Bay, Monterey Bay, and possibly Point Reyes. They may have traveled as far north as the Russian River before turning south to winter at the Channel Islands.

But Cabrillo was never to complete the voyage. In an unfortunate accident, Cabrillo broke a limb and died a few weeks later on January 3, 1543.

"[San Diego is] a port which must be the best to be found in all the South Sea."
—Vizcaíno's expedition.

"On the twelfth of the said month, which was the day of the glorious San Diego, … mass was said in celebration of the feast of San Diego."
—Vizcaíno's log.

San Diego

San Diego is short for *San Diego de Alcalá*, the Spanish name for Saint Didacus, a fifteenth-century Franciscan.

In sixteenth-century Spain, Prince Carlos was a sick child. He gained a miraculous recovery after sleeping next to the remains of Didacus. The king, grateful for the healing of his son, successfully pursued the canonization of Didacus.

San Diego was also the name of Vizcaíno's flag ship.

Pronunciation notes:
Juan Rodríguez Cabrillo =
hwan rod-REE-gez Ca-BRE-o

Sebastián Vizcaíno =
Se-bas-TEE-an Vee-cay-EE-no

For more information read "Cabrillo" by Nancy Lemke.

After Cabrillo

The ships continued north, under pilot Bartolomé Ferrer, reaching Mendocino or possibly Oregon's Rogue River. But, short on supplies and morale, they returned to Navidad on April 14, 1543.

Although the expedition mapped over 800 miles of coastline, the voyage was considered a failure. Mendoza sent the fleet to Peru but the ships and most of the crew never returned. Most of Cabrillo's property was appropriated and his family was reduced to poverty. There were no more cities of gold to raid and the Age of Conquistadors petered out in the mid-1540s.

Naming San Diego

Offering no gold or route to the Spice Islands, there was no further European exploration of California for 60 years. Spain's attention focused on the lucrative silver-for-spices trade between Manila in the Philippines and Acapulco in Mexico. It was a long voyage and a new port in Alta California was considered.

An unscrupulous merchant, Sebastián Vizcaíno, set sail from Acapulco on May 5, 1602 with three ships. He followed Cabrillo's course almost exactly and arrived in San Miguel in November. Despite strict instructions to the contrary, Vizcaíno renamed most of the places discovered by Cabrillo. Since his crew first said mass on the new land on the feast day of Saint Didacus—San Diego de Alcalá—Vizcaíno renamed the bay *San Diego*.

Vizcaíno recommended Monterey as a port but no action was taken and California remained unscathed by the Spanish for another 167 years.

Old Point Loma Lighthouse

Built: 1853–4
Operational: 1855–91

**Contractors Francis A. Gibbons and Francis X. Kelly, from Baltimore, MD, were hired to build the first eight lighthouses on the Pacific West Coast:
Alcatraz Island, Fort Point, Southeast Farallones Island, Monterey, Point Conception, Point Loma, and Cape Disappointment (Oregon).**

Perched **422 feet** (120m) above the ocean, the Old Point Loma Lighthouse is the highest ocean light in the country. This notability, however, was also the source of its demise, as fog and low clouds often obscured the light. After protecting sailors for 36 years, it was replaced by a new light at the bottom of the hill—the U.S. Coast Guard Point Loma Lighthouse—but the old structure still stands as a romantic museum.

The "Cape-Cod" style building is squat and painted white. The thick walls are made of sandstone, carved from a Point Loma hillside. A brick tower rises from the basement to about six feet above the roof and supports the iron frame of the lens.

Looking down the stairwell.

Tip
Look for abstract designs. Spiral staircases are gifts to photographers as they often make interesting shots.

The interior has been modeled to depict the home of the 19th century lighthousekeeper Captain Robert Israel, his wife Maria and their boys. You can climb the narrow spiral staircase and see the third-order Fresnel lens. The original lens was removed in 1891—today's lens was acquired in 1986. This five-foot high complex of expertly-polished glass was made in Paris, France and shipped all around Cape Horn. In clear weather, the light could be seen for 20 miles.

Today the lighthouse offers dramatic views of San Diego Harbor, the Pacific Ocean and Mexico's Coronado Islands.

Tip

There are good views of the lighthouse from all around. In the morning photograph the entrance (left) which is on the west side. In the late afternoon, shoot from the trail to the **Whale Overlook** (above) and the trail along the sandstone bluffs, to the northwest. Include a mixture of lighthouse and scenery, for a romanntic look.

Whale Overlook

When

Mid-January is the peak of the whale migration, but whales are visible from mid-December to March. Bring binoculars if you can.

The Whale Overlook displays information on the whales. In the winter, the park presents films, speakers and exhibits. Call 619-557-5450.

Swimming several miles off shore, the whales are too distant to be photographed from the mainland.

To see the whales up close, take a whale-watching boat trip. A three-hour cruise (available Dec–Mar) costs around $25/$15.
• H&M Landing
    619-222-1144
• Hornblower Cruises
    619-234-8687
• Harbor Excursions
    619-234-4111

Events

Whale Watch Weekend is held on the third weekend in January. Park rangers help you spot whales and there are special programs about marine life.

Due to its height, Point Loma is one of the best places on land in Southern California to watch migrating whales. Thousands of Pacific gray whales swim past here on their annual winter migration. Bring a good pair of binoculars. As many as 200 whales have been seen on a clear day although the numbers are currently around five per hour.

A permanent Whale Observation Shelter/Overlook is located a short walk from the Old Point Loma Lighthouse. Between December and March, look about a mile or two into the ocean, past the kelp beds (the brown patch of the ocean). Keen eyes can spot the whale's spouts—short bursts of water. The spouts are 8 to 15 feet (3 to 4m) high and formed when the whales

Fire Control Station 1943

Just below the Whale Overlook is a WWII concrete bunker that was used for coast-artillery fire-control. Further along the Bayside Trail—an old army road which now makes a pleasant two-mile nature walk—is a large green box. This housed a 60" searchlight, used to scan the ocean for enemy activity.

Fort Rosecrans was established in 1899 and fortifications were built from 1918 to 1943. During WWII, the harbor entrance was protected by large coast artillery guns. Aiming the guns was determined by soldiers stationed inside these concrete "pill boxes." The soldiers would take readings on the location of a target and relay that information to the gunners, who would then fire onto the target. All the guns were removed in 1947. The old gun emplacements are off-limits to visitors.

During the summer, rangers conduct a 90-minute Military History Walk through the park. A new Military History Museum is planned, focusing on the 19th Coast Artillery stationed at Fort Rosecrans during WWII.

breathe out through their blowholes. The air condenses and mixes with seawater, making the spout white in color. The whales blow three to five spouts, each about 30 to 50 seconds apart, before diving for three to six minutes.

From March to December you won't see whales but you might see dolphins, seals and sea lions.

The Pacific Gray Whale

In September, when the arctic begins to freeze, adult gray whales leave their feeding grounds in the Bering and Chukchi Seas (around Alaska and Russia) and migrate south 6,000 miles (10,000km) to their breeding grounds in Baja California. After giving birth, the whales return along the same route.

The adult whales are up to 46 feet long (12m) and weigh 20–45 tons. The females are larger than the males. Although air-breathing mammals, they can stay underwater for up to 20 minutes.

From 1857–73, whales were hunted in San Diego and other places along the coast. Whale carcasses were dragged onto Ballast Point on Point Loma, their blubber boiled in try-pots to make whale oil (a lamp fuel) and their bones used as corset stays, buggy whips and umbrella stays. The Whaling Bar at La Jolla's La Valencia has a display of artifacts.

The whales were hunted almost to extinction. Today they are protected and their population has grown to about 23,000, probably surpassing their population numbers prior to the 1800s.

Point Loma Kelp Forest

Point Loma Kelp Forest is the largest on the West Coast. Kelp grows, on sunny days, at three feet per day—only bamboo is faster. It has been harvested for use in fertilizer, explosives, cosmetics, medications and ice cream.

Point Loma Lighthouse   1891

Today's operational lighthouse has a pretty setting by the ocean. It is operated by the U.S. Coast Guard and is off-limits to visitors. This view is from the Whale Overlook.

Cabrillo Tide Pools

At the base of Point Loma are several tide pools, home to a variety of specialized creatures. Visit at a low ebb tide and look out for hermit crabs, bat stars, knobby stars, tube snails, giant owl limpets, sand castle worms, sea hares, sea anemones, purple sea urchins and an occasional octopus.

The creatures have all adapted to a specialized existence, baked by sunlight and flooded twice a day by sea water.

Drive, don't walk, to the tide pools. They are best at low ebb tides of fall, winter and spring. Plan in advance by reading the paper and determining the time of low tide. Wear rubber-soled shoes as the rocks are slippery.

Note that this is a federally-protected area and it is strictly illegal to damage or remove anything. Tide pools are interdependent communities. If even one creature is harmed or displaced, a pool's ecological balance can be upset.

Point Loma

Fort Rosecrans, a military reservation established in 1870, is named after General William S. Rosecrans who visited San Diego in 1867.

Tip

Look out for leading lines. Train tracks, straight roads, fences and, in this case, rows of gravestones are visual cues that lead the viewer into the image.

Rule of Thirds. Notice how the main line in this shot (below) is placed one third of the way in to the picture, rather than in the center. Use the 'rule of thirds' to add visual interest. A tree is included on the right for balance and to create a partial frame.

Point Loma Ecological Reserve

Nearly half the Point (640 acres) is protected as the Point Loma Ecological Reserve. A half-mile off the coast is the Point Loma Kelp Forest, the largest on the West Coast.

Fort Rosecrans National Cemetery   1899

The nation's third-largest military cemetery honors over 70,000 military veterans, spouses and children. There are neat rows of white gravestones on a flowing grassy hill. In the center is the "Bennington Monument," a 75-foot obelisk memorial to 66 sailors who died in 1905 when the USS Bennington exploded in San Diego Bay. Victims of the 1846 battle at San Pasqual are also buried here. Please demonstrate respect when visiting the cemetery.

Point Loma

The neon lights of the old Point Loma Theater, now a bookstore, on Rosecrans Street.

Point Loma Nazarene College

With a campus overlooking the Pacific, the college is an undergraduate school affiliated with the Church of the Nazarene. The college has an interesting history, originally having the fabulous name of "The School for the Revival of Lost Mysteries of Antiquity."

The School was founded at the turn-of-the-century by Madam Katherine A. Tingley, leader of the Universal Brotherhood and Theosophical Society. The Society practiced Hindu philosophy and teachings and had several wealthy followers including A. G. Spalding, the sports goods magnate. Spalding House, the administration building, is named after him.

Reading about the healthy climate of San Diego, Madame Tingley bought 132 acres (later expanded to 500 acres) of Point Loma in 1897 and built the Raja Yoga (Royal Union) School in 1900. She erected flamboyant Hindu-inspired buildings, one of which had large onion-shaped domes made of turquoise glass. Lit from the inside, the domes were visible to ships at sea almost as much as the lighthouse.

Madame Tingley was quite a character of her time. In a famous court case she argued that her ex-husband had been reincarnated as her dog Spot. Often dressed in purple she was called "Purple Mother of Lomaland." Upon her death in 1929, the movement dissolved and the property changed hands.

Greek Theater

Built by Madame Tingley in 1901, this was the first Greek theater in America. Others soon followed in Berkeley and Pomona. On the campus of Point Loma Nazarene College.

Shelter Island

This quaint Portuguese chapel is in an old Portuguese fishing neighborhood.

Shelter Island is a T-shaped, man-made peninsula, created in 1950. It was made from dredgings as the Navy deepened the channel into San Diego Harbor. The 'island' is home to the San Diego Yacht Club which held the America's Cup yachting trophy from 1987 to 1995, as well as several marinas, hotels, restaurants and a municipal fishing pier.

Portuguese Chapel ⏱

Fishermen from Portugal settled by the original port of San Diego and started San Diego's tuna industry. The chapel is on Avenida de Portugal.

Tunaman's Memorial

In 1950, San Diego was the country's largest fishing port, bringing in $30m in fish and 40% of the country's tuna. The city once had the largest tuna fleet in the world. There are no more canneries in San Diego.

Three bronze fisherman haul in tuna at the Tunaman's Memorial (1986 Franco Vianello). On Shelter Island by the fishing pier.

Friendship Bell 1960

On the western tip of Shelter Island is the two-and-a-half ton "Friendship Bell." Hanging in an open Buddhist-style building, the bell is a symbol of eternal friendship. It was a gift from San Diego's sister city of Yokohama, Japan.

Old Town

Old Town State Historic Park is a six-block area preserving the first permanent civilian settlement in California. From 1822–1872, during the Mexican and early American period, this was the thriving center of San Diego. The adobe "casas," built for the town's wealthy ranchers and merchants, have been restored and now house museums, restaurants and gifts stores.

History

In 1821, with Mexico's independence from Spain, the Presidio/Mission period ended and the soldiers of San Diego turned to a civilian life. They moved down the hill from the Presidio and, in 1822, formed the town (*pueblo*) of San Diego. The pueblo was centered around a plaza and, by 1835, consisted of several large white-washed adobe houses (*casas*) and about 40 dark brown huts.

The few hundred residents developed a "hide and tallow" industry, using the cattle previously reared by the mission. With Spain's authority gone, the port became open to foreign ships, particularly clippers from England and Boston. Back east, the cattle hides— "California bank notes"—could be turned into shoes and the tallow (fat) made into soap and candles. In return, the residents of San Diego received guns, clothes, jewelry and other exotic goods.

The most important resident of the pueblo was Pio Pico. From 1825–32, Pico was the Governor of California and, during this time, he made San Diego the capital of Mexico's Baja and Alta California.

In 1833 Mexico secularized the missions and the property of San Diego Mission was given away. 3,000 square miles of land, 8,600 cattle and 19,000 sheep made eighteen large *ranchos*, and many wealthy Mexican "dons." With the immense wealth came a period of fiestas, elegant clothing, entertaining, horsemanship, rodeos and bullfights.

The U.S. eyed the rich lands of New Mexico and

Where

Old Town State Historic Park is located four miles north of downtown, by the intersection of I-5 and I-8. Take the Old Town Ave exit from I-5, or the Hotel Circle South exit from I-8.

Tip

This fountain (right) is at the entrance to Bazaar del Mundo. It is a good place to pose your family or friends.

Nearby

Nearby is Presidio Park with foundations of the Spanish *presidio* dating from 1776, and Heritage Park with Victorian houses from the 1880s.

CONTENTS:

Old Town

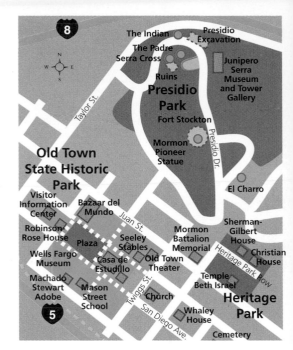

Seeley Stables

This reconstructed barn now houses stagecoaches and covered wagons. It was originally owned, along with the Cosmopolitan Hotel, by Albert Seeley for his Los Angeles to San Diego stagecoach line.
The Stables is currently the Visitor Center, although a new Center is proposed by the northwest entrance of Old Town.
2648 Calhoun Street. Donations requested, 10–5.

Old Town

became worried that England or France may take control of the neglected province. After an offer to buy California and other portions of New Mexico from the Mexican Government was rejected, incidents along Texas' Rio Grande River sparked the Mexican-American War (1846–48).

The "Californios" anguished about a war they could not control and the Americans, led by Commodore Stockton, soon captured San Diego. The Stars and Stripes were raised over the plaza in 1846 by Marines from the USS Cyane. In 1848, Mexico ceded almost half its territory to its imperial neighbor to the north, in exchange for $18 million. California entered the Union in 1850 with San Diego as its first county.

As shipping became more important, two attempts were made to move the town nearer to the bay. Old Town remained active until a fire in 1872, when most residents moved to Horton's "New Town," today's city center.

The Visitor Center is in the Robinson-Rose House. Open: 10am–5pm. There are free guided tours daily at 2pm. Tel: 619-220-5427.

In the Robinson-Rose House is a scale model of Old Town as it appeared in 1872.

The Plaza

Plaza ⏲ 1822

The spiritual heart of Old Town, the Plaza was laid out in the 1820s. It was the scene of bullfights, fiestas, meetings, and executions. The Mexicans called it La Plaza de Las Armas (The Plaza of Arms) and the Americans renamed it "Washington Square." Today the plaza contains a flagpole, two cannons, cork oak trees from Portugal, and eucalyptus trees from Australia.

Above: Making tortillas at the Old Town Mexican Café.

Bazaar Del Mundo ⏲ 1936

The tourist heart of Old Town is Bazaar Del Mundo. Governor Pio Pico had a house on part of this site while he governed Mexico's Alta and Baja California. The present structure is an old motel, the 1936 Casa de Pico motel, artfully redesigned by Diane Powers to house boutiques and restaurants around a courtyard.

Above: Rancho Nopal overlooks the Plaza.

Right: Margaritas around the fountain. At the Casa de Pico restaurant in Bazaar del Mundo.

Bazaar del Mundo

Casa de Machado-Stewart ⏱ 1830s

This restored adobe is described in Richard Henry Dana's classic book, *Two Years Before the Mast*. It was built by Jose Manuel Machado for his daughter, Rosa Machado, who married a shipmate of Dana, John Stewart.

Staff dress in period costume on the first Saturday of the month and every Wednesday.

Casa de Bandini.

Casa de Bandini ⏱ 1827

Built for ranchero Don Juan Bandini, the casa was converted to the *Cosmopolitan Hotel* and is now a restaurant. In 1846, the casa was the war-time headquarters of American Commodore Robert F. Stockton.

La Casa de Estudillo 1827

Facing the top of the plaza, this is the most evocative and largest original adobe casa in Old Town. It has a veranda, courtyard and period furniture. It was built by Captain Jose Maria de Estudillo, a former commandant of the Presidio. The casa is erroneously said to be Ramona's Marriage Place in Helen Hunt Jackson's novel *Ramona*.

4001 Mason St., free with donations. 10–5. $2/1.

El Campo Santo ⏱

1850-78

A Catholic cemetery with about 450 graves.

Old Town

"Of all the dilapidated, miserable-looking places I've ever seen, this was the worst... an altogether dreary, sunblasted point of departure for nowhere."
—Mary Chase Walker, San Diego's first school-teacher, 1865.

The Theatre in Old Town,

In 1968, six blocks of Old Town were made into a State Historic Park with the structures restored or rebuilt. Today, Old Town is a popular destination for residents and visitors alike.

Casa de Pedrorena de Altamirano 1869
Right: An assayer's office with a gem exhibit. Next door to the San Diego Union Printing Office.

Mason Street School ⏰ 1865
This is a one-room frame schoolhouse (above) which served as San Diego's first school from 1865–73.
3966 Mason Street at Congress Street. 10–4.

The Church of the Immaculate Conception ⏲

Built between 1868 and 1918, this catholic church is modeled after Mission San Diego.

Left: A fountain on San Diego Avenue by Arista Street.

Right: Thomas Whaley, a wealthy merchant, built this house with bricks made in his own kiln and walls covered in plaster made from ground seashells.

Wells Fargo Museum   1851

Originally the *Colorado House* hotel (1851), the building has been reconstructed to house Old West artifacts of the Wells Fargo Bank. Inside is a red 1868 Abbot-Downing Concord stagecoach.

San Diego Union Museum   1851

The birthplace, in 1868, of the San Diego Union, the oldest continuously published newspaper in Southern California. The museum now depicts the original editor's office and print room. This prefabricated wood-frame house was built in Maine and shipped around South America. 2626 San Diego Ave.

Robinson-Rose House   1854

The first office building in San Diego. It was originally the law office and house of attorney James W Robinson, and the offices of the San Diego Herald newspaper. It was later bought by Louis Rose and now houses a scale model of Old Town in 1872.

4002 Wallace St.

The Whaley House

The Whaley House ⏲   1956

The oldest brick structure in Southern California. Once San Diego's most luxurious residence, it is now officially haunted, as certified by the U.S. Dept. of Commerce. Inside is a "life mask" of Abraham Lincoln.

2482 San Diego Ave. Wed–Sun, 10–4:30 $3.

Heritage Park

> "[Queen Anne] should have a conical corner tower; it should be built of at least three incongruous materials...; it should represent part of every known and unknown order of architecture; it should be so plastered with ornament as to conceal the theory of its construction; it should be a restless, uncertain, frightful collection of details, giving the effect of a nightmare about to explode!"
> —Gellett Burgess, critic.

Queen Anne

The English Queen Anne style became popular in America around 1876–93, in a time of conspicuous wealth. Houses usually had an asymmetrical floor plan and an exuberant exterior, often with corner towers, tall chimneys, steep roofs, gables, porches, bay windows, and stained glass. Queen Anne was succeeded around 1895 by the more austere Classic Revival style.

O n the east side of Old Town is a 7.8-acre park with six restored Victorian houses from the 1880s. Threatened with destruction, the houses were moved from downtown to this hill-side site and restored.

Christian House 🕐 1889

This graceful Queen Anne-style mansion (above) is home to the Heritage Park Bed and Breakfast Inn. The house is encircled by a veranda and capped with a turret. It was built for Harfield Myrtle Christian.

2470 Heritage Park Row. 619-299-6832.

Temple Beth Israel

🕐

San Diego's first synagogue (above) was built in 1889 by the Congregation Beth Israel. Designed in a simple Classic Revival style, it hosts weddings and bar mitzvahs.

Sherman-Gilbert House 🕐   1887

Right. Notice the "widow's walk" around the tower. Designed by Nelson Comstock and Carl Trotsche in the Stick Eastlake style, this house was first owned by John Sherman. From 1892–1965 it was the home of spinster sisters Bess and Gertrude Gilbert. The sisters held receptions for Yehudi Menuhin and other internationally famous entertainers in this house.

Presidio Park

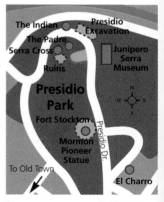

The "Plymouth Rock of the West."

Junípero Serra Museum
2727 Presidio Drive in Presidio Park. Open Fri, Sat & Sun 10am–4:30pm. $5/$4/$2. Tel: 619-297-3258.

Tip

Hyperfocal. You can create dynamic shots of distant subjects by including a very close foreground. Flowers work best. Crouch right over the flowers and get low. Use a wide-angle lens (I used a 28mm lens) and set it to the smallest aperture. At f22, the depth-of-focus can range from a few feet to infinity (the 'hyperfocal distance') so that both foreground and background are in focus. Focus about one-third of the way into the view. You'll probably need a tripod for a sharp image.

Pronunciation notes:
Gaspar de Portolá =
GAS-par day por-tow-LA

Junípero Serra =
hoo-NEEP-pero SAIR-ah

Old Town

T he site of the first European settlement in California, Presidio Park contains the remains of the Spanish fortress ('Presidio') and California's first mission, both established in 1769.

Today's building is not the mission but a museum, built in 1929. The Junípero Serra Museum, operated by the San Diego Historical Society, displays artifacts of the Native American, Spanish and Mexican periods. You can climb the tower for a great panoramic view.

History

In 1769, fearing encroachment in the north by Russian fur traders moving down from Alaska, and English incursions in 'New Spain,' the Spanish resolved to defend their territory. King Carlos III ordered the strengthening and colonization of California with the 'Sacred Expedition of 1769.'

Five exploration and colonization parties—three by sea and two by land— were ordered by General José de Galvez and led by Gaspar de Portolá. The king, eager to spread Christianity through the new lands, required all expeditions to include priests. Portolá's group included five men of the cloth led by Fray (Father) Junípero Serra.

The parties arrived in San Diego between April 11 and July 1. Portolá and 73 men continued north on July 14 to found Monterey while Serra and 39 men, most in ill health, stayed to found San Diego. Serra selected Presidio Hill, with its commanding view of the river and bay, and a brush shelter was built as a church. On July 16, 1769—the feast of Our Lady of Mount

Carmel—Father Serra officially dedicated Mission San Diego de Alcalá, the first in Alta California. A cross was raised and blessed by Serra. The soldiers added defences to the outpost to create a fort (*presidio*).

Although the mission was relocated upstream in 1774, the presidio remained and grew. In 1776–77, a larger adobe citadel was built which, by 1790, was occupied by over 200 soldiers, civilians and children. The presidio was now not just a fort but a colony, with families living around a central courtyard.

"The Indian" and "The Padre" both by Arthur Putnam.

Other presidios were established at Monterey in 1770, San Francisco in 1776, and Santa Barbara in 1782. Although Monterey was the main outpost, the San Diego Presidio had its own administration and was one of the most important military, political and judicial centers in California.

In 1821, Mexico became independent of Spain and the presidio system lost support. The soldiers moved down the hill to present-day 'Old Town' and, by 1835, the presidio was deserted.

Today only the earthen foundations remain, having been slowly excavated since 1965. The walls date anywhere from 1776 to 1828.

Erected in 1913, the 28-foot-high Serra Cross is decorated with tiles salvaged from the Presidio area.

"El Charro" by Juan Fernando Oaquibel. This statue of an expert horseman was a bicentennial gift from Mexico.

Junípero Serra Museum ⏱

Today's structure (far left) is not Spanish but American, built in 1929 above the site of the Presidio and mission. Philanthropist George White Marston (1850–1946) bought the surrounding land for the people of San Diego and funded the building, designed by William Templeton Johnson.

Inside is a museum of the Native American, Mission and Rancho periods. For history after the 1850s, visit the Museum of San Diego History in Balboa Park. You can also view Marston's house, in the northwest corner of Balboa Park.

Fort Stockton   1838

Further up the hill is Fort Stockton Memorial, comprising some earthen walls, a flagpole and a plaque.

The Mexican San Diegans built a fort here in 1838, to protect against an attack from Los Angeles. The fort was taken and renamed in 1847 by American forces led by Commodore Robert F. Stockton. Twelve Spanish guns were used to establish a garrison, but the fort was abandoned in 1848.

Mormon Pioneer Statue ⏱

From July 1846 to January 1847, the Mormon Battalion marched from Fort Leavenworth, Kansas to San Diego, a distance of 2,000 miles. It was the longest march in U.S. military history. The Battalion consisted of 500 soldiers and 81 women and children.

The Mormons arrived too late to join the fighting but instead built civic improvements, including the Court House, the first brick structure in Old Town. While returning to Salt Lake City, some members of the Battalion witnessed the discovery of gold at Sutter's Mill, sparking the Gold Rush.

Left: The Mormon Pioneer Statue, 1969, by Edward Fraughton.

Mission

Founded: 1769
Relocated: 1774
Restored: 1931

Mission Basilica San Diego de Alcalá

"Mother of the Missions"

Where

10818 San Diego Mission Rd. Located in Mission Valley, just east of Qualcomm Stadium. Take I-8 and exit north on Mission Gorge Road. Turn left on Twain Avenue.

CONTENTS:

Mission

Founded on July 16, 1769, Mission Basilica San Diego de Alcalá is the first and oldest of California's chain of 21 missions. It is known as the "Mother of the Missions." Moved to this location in 1774 and rebuilt several times, some parts of the building date from the late 1770s.

Tip
Include the flower bed. The classic shot is taken from the driveway, by the circular bed of flowers. Use a wide-angle lens and put the horizon towards the top of the frame.

The mission faces south so noon is the best time for photography.

Father Junípero Serra established the mission a few weeks after he arrived in Alta California, by raising a cross on present-day Presidio Hill. However, the unruly soldiers harassed the new Indian converts (neophytes)

and the hill proved impractical for farming. So the mission was moved six miles east to the flat, arable land by the river in present-day Mission Valley.

A year later, tragedy struck. Two of the Kumayaay neophytes became unhappy with the rules of the mission and went to the pagan population to incite a riot. As many as 600 Indians attacked the mission. The pastor, Padre Luís Jayme, who had succeeded Serra in San Diego, appealed to the attackers with his usual greeting, "Love God my Children," but he was beaten to death. Jayme became California's first martyr and his body is buried

The camponile and garden of Mission San Diego.

Mexico's Secularization Act of 1833 was "a law stripping [the missions] of all their possessions and confining the priests to their spiritual duties. ... possessions of the missions are given over to be preyed upon by the harpies of the civil power ... who usually end, in a few years, by making themselves fortunes."
—Richard Henry Dana, 1840.

Nearby

Remnants of the Old Mission Dam, completed in 1816, are located in Mission Trails Regional Park. The 5,800 acre park—one of the nation's largest urban parks—is six miles northeast from the mission along Mission Gorge Rd.

beneath today's altar. The two Indians were imprisoned and sent to Mexico but were later freed and returned to their families.

Serra returned to San Diego in 1776 to initiate reconstruction. To thwart the Indian's arrows of fire, the walls were covered in less-flammable adobe and the roof utilized a new feature first devised for Mission San Antonio de Padua—a tiled roof. Red tiled roofs are now a signature feature of Southern California houses.

By 1797, Mission San Diego controlled 50,000 acres of land, 20,000 sheep, 10,000 cattle and 1,250 horses. Crops included barley, corn, wheat and beans, and there were vineyards, orchards and gardens. There were 1,405 neophytes, who were rewarded with parcels of land to live on.

The present structure was started in 1808 and dedicated in 1813. The design incorporated two large buttresses on the front, following damage from an earthquake in 1803. In 1818, a support chapel, Asistencia Santa Ysabel, was built 60 miles to the east.

In 1834, the missions were secularized. Abraham Lincoln returned Mission San Diego to the Roman Catholic Church in 1862, but the building continued in its decline.

"What a mysterious charm this old ruin cast over that placid region, serene in an atmosphere of transcendental silence."
—*Jesse Shepard, 1876.*

Serra's California Missions:

1769: San Diego de Alcalá
1770: San Carlos Barromio de Carmelo
1771: San Antonio de Padua
1771: San Gabriel Archangel
1772: San Lois Obispo de Tolssa
1776: San Francisco de Asis
1776: San Juan Capistrano
1777: Santa Clara de Asis
1782: San Buenaventura

Open: 9am–5pm. $2. Tel: 619-281-8449. Taped tours available at the visitor center.

Tip
The garden is particularly attractive. You have a good view of the camponile (above) and a statue of Saint Francis (right). When photographing something as white as this statue, overexpose by 1/2 a stop to avoid the white statue from appearing gray.

With the support of local citizens and the Hearst Foundation, the Mission was eventually restored in stages from 1915 to 1931. Mission San Diego has had an active parish since 1941 and was made a minor basilica by Pope Paul VI in 1976.

Father Junípero Serra

Father Junípero Serra (1713–84) was the founder of California's chain of missions. Born in Mallorca, Spain, he became a Franciscan at the age of 18 and arrived in the Americas in 1749.

At the age of 55, Serra was chosen to lead the religious contingent of the military exploration party to Alta California in 1769. Serra founded one mission in Baja California—Mission San Fernando Velicatá—before arriving in San Diego on July 1, 1769. He stayed for almost a year, then journeyed to Monterey to establish Mission Carmel.

Serra walked most of the way, covering over 4,500 miles in his journeys despite a chronic leg infection. He had sharp pieces of wire interwoven in his habit next to his skin to atone for his sins.

Serra founded nine missions in Alta California and then returned to Mexico to successfully lobby for their support. He was succeeded by Father Fermín de Lasuén who founded nine more missions before Spain lost control of California in 1821.

A statue of Saint Francis in the garden.

La Jolla

The Jewel of San Diego.

Pronounced in the Spanish style: Lah-HOY-ya

Where

From I-5 south take Ardath Road; from I-5 north take La Jolla Village Drive west, then south on Torrey Pines Road. From both routes turn right on Prospect Street.

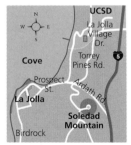

'The jewel' of San Diego, La Jolla is one of California's most scenic and exclusive communities. Rugged cliffs, sculptured caves and intimate beaches line seven miles of serpentine shoreline, and Mediterranean architecture, galleries and restaurants line Prospect Street—the "Rodeo Drive of San Diego."

The quaint "village" area is around La Jolla Cove at the foot of Girard Avenue although the town of La Jolla also includes residential and research centers such as the Salk Institute and the University of California at San Diego (UCSD).

The name 'La Jolla' has two possible meanings in Old Spanish. It most likely means a "hollow, pit or cavity made by water" but the more romantic interpretation is "jewel."

Incorporated in 1850, the town's defining moment came in 1897 when a new resident moved in—newspaper heiress Ellen Browning Scripps.

Tip

Photograph the sunset without the sun. In this shot, the sun has just set outside of the frame, to the left. By photographing away from sun the skylight is more even and produces a smoother backdrop. Remember that any foreground will be silhouetted so use something with an interesting shape, such as these slender palm trees.

This shot is taken from Coast Blvd. facing Ellen Browning Scripps Park. You need a 24mm lens to capture the full length of the nearest palm.

CONTENTS:

La Jolla

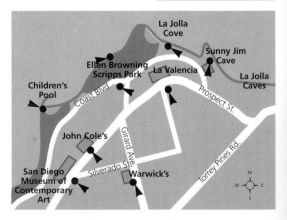

Enjoying the afternoon sun at Ellen Browning Scripps Park.

E.W. Scripps

Edward Wyllis Scripps (1854–1926) was the first of the Scripps to move to San Diego. He was born near Rushville, Illinois. At the age of 24, and with help from his elder brother James, who owned a Detroit newspaper, 'E.W' bought a Cleveland news-paper. E.W. eventually owned 40 newspapers, forming a chain known as the Scripps-Howard News-papers, and developed United Press International (UPI).

In 1890, aged 36, E.W. Scripps moved west to warmer weather. He set-tled in San Diego, buying 2,100 acres that he named "Miramar Ranch," and ran his empire by correspon-dence.

Ellen Browning Scripps

"La Jolla's fairy godmother, who waved her magic wand and made La Jolla the ideal community."

The name of 'Scripps' is indelibly stamped on many parts of La Jolla and San Diego, due to the generosity of syblings E.W. (Ted), Ellen and Virginia Scripps.

Ellen Browning Scripps (1836-1932) was born in London, England and moved to Illinois to join her half-brothers. She worked for the Scripps newspapers and was one of the country's first woman columnists. Having invested wisely she was also a wealthy woman.

Ellen moved to La Jolla in 1895, at the age of 59. In 1897, she built a home on Prospect Street where she lived until her death in 1932. She bought the land around Prospect Street and the coast and donated it to community causes. Thanks to Ellen Browning Scripps we now enjoy: La Jolla Cove, Children's Pool, La Jolla Women's Club; the Bishop's School, Scripps Institution of Oceanography (endowed along with E.W. Scripps), Scripps College in Clairemont, Torrey Pines State Reserve, and the San Diego Zoo.

Ellen Browning Scripps Park is a popular picnic and play area.

A Torrey pine (above) and sandstone cliffs (below) in Ellen Browning Scripps Park.

Ellen Browning Scripps Park

The verdant park is home to several rare Torrey pine trees and encompasses La Jolla Cove.

La Jolla Cove

The spiritual heart of La Jolla is this small and naturally-sheltered cove. The Cove is popular with ocean swimmers who swim to and from the Scripps Memorial Pier about a mile away, as well as snorkelers and scuba divers. The white buoys mark the San Diego-La Jolla Underwater Park, a protected zone of marine life including a kelp forest, reefs and canyons.

Children's Pool

To make a safe playground for children, Ellen Browning Scripps had a breakwater built in 1931. However the beach has become more popular with seals, so perhaps it should be renamed "Seal's Pool."

Children's Pool

La Jolla Cove

 Tip

Use the light. Light is your medium so observe how it illuminates a scene. Here you can sense the opening of the cave without actually seeing it. There's a sense of mystery.

You'll need a steady hand or a tripod as the scene is dimly lit. Also consider a shot looking up the stairs.

Be careful in the caves as you can easily become trapped by the ocean.

Sunny Jim Cave

One of seven caves in La Jolla carved out of the sandstone cliffs by the incessant ocean, Sunny Jim Cave is the most accessible due to a man-made tunnel. The tunnel was dug in 1902–06 by Gustav Schulz, a German mining engineer and artist.

From inside the Cave Shop on Coast Boulevard, 145 steps descend through the rock to a viewing deck. As you look out to the ocean, the cave entrance appears to have the profile of a man's face, with a pointed chin and a tuft of hair. It is similar to a 1900s English cartoon character called "Sunny Jim."

1325 Coast Blvd. 9am–5pm. $3/$2. Tel: 858-459-0746.

The other six caves can be accessed from the beaches at very low tide.

Girard Street

The street, named after American zoologist Charles Girard, is home to Warwick's bookstore (left), boutiques and galleries.

La Jolla

The La Valenica Hotel, inside (above) and out (below).

La Valencia ⏱   1926

Distinguished by its pink walls and palm trees, this Spanish-Colonial landmark was designed by William Templeton Johnson. Built in 1926 and expanded two years later, the hotel has eight floors, six of them below the lobby level. Greta Garbo, Charlie Chaplin, Groucho Marx and Mary Pickford were all frequent guests.

Inside is the Whaling Bar, a favorite of the *Dr. Seuss* author, Theodore Seuss Geisel. Over the bar is a large whaling mural that was recently re-painted to be more politically correct—now the whale is fighting back.

1132 Prospect Street at Herchel Avenue. Tel 858-454-0771.

Above: Mary Star of the Sea, Catholic church. On Girard Ave. *Below:* Saint James by the Sea, Episcopal church. Facing MoCA.

Tip

Tell a story. This shot (right) is almost a car commercial! By including a car and a couple the picture tells a story of people checking into the La Valencia hotel.

La Jolla

John Cole's Book Shop

Irving Gill

With an unadorned Mediterranean style, Irving J. Gill (1870–1936) set the architectural tone of La Jolla. He built houses that were "simple, plain, and substantial as a boulder" and became San Diego's most renowned architect.

Born near Tully, New York, Gill learned architecture in the Chicago office of Louis Sullivan—mentor of Frank Lloyd Wright. After moving to San Diego in 1893, Gill was influenced by the California's simple, Spanish missions.

Gill designed or remodeled more than 200 houses and buildings in San Diego, of which about 75 still exist today. Ellen Browning Scripps commissioned Gill for several La Jolla buildings including the Scripp's Institute (1908), the Woman's Club (1913), and the Bishop's School for Girls (1916).

"Leave the ornamentation to nature, who will tone it with lichens, chisel it with storms, make it gracious and friendly with vines and flower shapes as she does the stone in the meadow." —Irving Gill.

John Cole's Book Shop ⏲ 1905

Originally known as Wisteria Cottage, the house was built in 1904 and bought in 1905 by Ellen Browning Scripps. After being remodeled by Irving Gill, it was used as a guest house by Ellen and her half-sister Virginia. It became John Cole's Book Shop in 1966.

780 Prospect St. Tel: 858-454-4766.

Museum of Contemporary Art ⏲ 1916

Originally the home of Ellen Browning Scripps, the building was designed in 1916 by Irving Gill in the simplified mission style. It was significantly remodeled and opened as an art museum in 1941, and renovated in 1996 by Robert Venturi.

Free admission. Open daily 11am–5pm (until 7pm on Thu). 700 Prospect St. Tel: 858-454-3541.

Museum of Contemporary Art

La Jolla

Tip

Shoot at dawn and sunset for that golden look. The cross is white but for a precious few minutes after sunset it's bathed in gold.

A solitary figure adds a sense of scale and tranquility.

In 1930, Charles Lindbergh's wife, Anne, catapulted off Mount Soledad in a sailplane.

ℹ️

La Jolla Town Council
P.O. Box 1101
La Jolla CA 92038
Tel: 858-454-1444.

Where

On the top of Mount Soledad. Take Hidden Valley Road from the junction of Torrey Pines Road and Ardath Road, or Nautilus Street from La Jolla Boulevard in Windansea.

Mount Soledad Park ⏱

The 43-foot-high Soledad Cross was built in 1954 to honor the nation's war dead. The park affords a magnificent, almost 360-degree view from 822 feet above the ocean. You can usually see La Jolla, Torrey Pines and Del Mar to the north; Miramar air station to the east; and Mission Bay, San Diego Bay, Mexico, and the Coronado Islands in the south.

Birch Aquarium

The Birch Aquarium at Scripps has a spectacular ocean view. This shot is taken from a hiking trail above the aquarium.

Where

Birch Aquarium at Scripps
2300 Expedition Way
From I-5 exit at La Jolla Village Drive and go west.
Open: 9–5. $8.50/$5. Parking $3. Tel: 858-534-3474.

Mailing address:
9500 Gilman Drive
La Jolla 92093-0207
http://aquarium.ucsd.edu

During Jan. and Feb., Whale-Fest at the Aquarium highlights special exhibits about the migrating gray whales.

Golden jacks.

Right: "The Legacy" by Randy Puckett, 1996, is a 40-foot bronze whale sculpture in memory of benefactor Edward W. (Ted) Scripps II.

"[E.W. Scripps] assures us that if we can locate in La Jolla and do something for the scheme that interests him, viz. a popular public aquarium, he will help us."
—*William Ritter, founder, 1903.*

Birch Aquarium at Scripps ⏲ 1992

With 1,500 marine creatures, the Birch Aquarium at Scripps is San Diego's largest aquarium. It is a public education program of the Scripps Institution of Oceanography (SIO), a part of the University of California, San Diego (UCSD).

The aquarium is designed around a central lobby with entrances to three main interpretive areas: the Hall of Fishes with 33 tanks, the most spectacular being a 60,000-gallon kelp forest tank; the Hall of Oceanography, the largest display of oceanographic sciences in the country; and an outdoor plaza with a re-created tide pool.

SIO has maintained a public aquarium since 1907 and the present facility, opened in 1992, was made possible by a donation from the Stephen and Mary Birch Foundation. The hilltop site provides a spectacular overview of the Scripps Institution of Oceanography campus, La Jolla Cove, and the Pacific Ocean.

La Jolla

A tiny garden eel looks nervous.

Gulf grouper.

**Read the SeaWorld section
for tips on photographing
aquariums.**

Scripps Institution of Oceanography 1903

Founded in 1903, the Scripps Institution is the oldest and largest American institution devoted exclusively
to oceanographic research. With a staff of 1,200,
including about 190 graduate students, Scripps operates four research vessels and one research platform,
and its ships log approximately 100,000 nautical miles
each year.

In 1891, Professor William E. Ritter, from the University of California at Berkeley, spent his honeymoon
at the Hotel del Coronado. He became fascinated with
the ocean and started a series of summer lectures. In
1903, Ritter and a group of San Diegans formed the
Marine Biological Association of San Diego to support
the research. Publisher E.W. Scripps, with his half-sister Ellen Browning Scripps, provided financial support
and helped acquire the present site in 1907.

The Association moved into its new facility in 1910
and became part of the University of California in
1912. It was renamed Scripps Institution of Oceanography in 1925 and is now a graduate school of UCSD.

Scripps Crossing 🕐 1993

This unique design, by Frieder Seible, suspends the
bridge from a single pillar and requires no supports
under the bridge. The cable-stayed footbridge crosses
La Jolla Shores Drive by Downwind Way.

La Jolla

Nurse sharks.

Sea nettle.

Facing page:

Upper left: Children enjoy the aquarium's Tide Pool Discovery Station where occasionally they can get up close and personal with local marine life. Nearby is a simulated tide pool.

Upper right: Visitors are awed by the breathtaking giant kelp forest tank teeming with marine life from local Pacific Ocean waters.

Lower left: Black sea bass.

Lower right: California moray eels.

UCSD

The Price Center on UCSD campus.

University of California, San Diego

The largest university in San Diego, UCSD has over 18,000 students and a variety of modern architecture. The 2,000-acre campus includes five liberal arts colleges—Revelle, Muir, Marshall, Warren and Roosevelt, each with its own educational philosophy—plus the UCSD Medical Center, the San Diego Supercomputer Center, the Scripps Institution of Oceanography, and the Graduate School of International Relations and Pacific Studies. The Tony-award winning La Jolla Playhouse, co-founded in 1947 by Gregory Peck, has debuted several Broadway plays.

Geisel Library

The most distinctive building on campus, and the symbol of UCSD, is the Geisel Library (see page 216). The structure is in the shape of an upside-down glass pyramid with huge concrete 'fingers.' Designed by William L. Pereira, the building represents knowledge held aloft by two cupped hands, touching at the wrists.

Previously called the 'Central University Library,' the library was renamed in 1995 after a donation by Audrey Stone Geisel, widow of Theodore Seuss Geisel. Geisel authored the Dr. Seuss "Cat in the Hat" books and was a La Jolla resident.

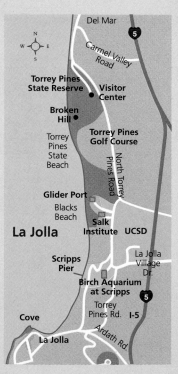

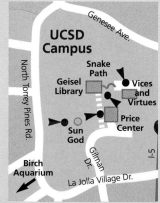

Nearly a mile of neon tubing was used to make Bruce Nauman's "Vices and Virtues.'

"Everyone knows what they are, until they try to write them down."
—Bruce Nauman, on the vices and virtues.

"Sun God" by Niki de Saint-Phalle.

ℹ️

UCSD offers a 90-minute tour. Tel: 858-534-4414. Library: 858-534-7323.

Stuart Collection   1982

Spread around the UCSD campus is an internationally-acclaimed collection of twelve outdoor sculptures. Each artwork is unique and designed for the specific site.

The most recognized artwork is "Sun God" (1983) by Niki de Saint-Phalle, a San Diego resident. A 14-foot-high, colorful Aztec-style bird made of fiberglass stands on a 15-foot concrete arch. "Big Bird," as it has been nicknamed, is near the Mandeville Center. Students have enhanced the statue with sunglasses for "Dudebird", a cap and gown for graduation, a Sony Walkman for "Walkbird," and a headband and machete for "Rambird."

"Snake Path" (1992) by Alexis Smith is a 560-foot-long snake that slithers up a hill to the Geisel Library. Made as a 10-foot-wide pathway with slate tiles for snake scales, Snake Path is best viewed from the top of the library.

Seven-foot tall neon letters form Bruce Nauman's "Vices and Virtues" (1988). Each evening, the seven vices and seven virtues start flashing around the top of the six-story Charles Lee Powell Structural Systems Laboratory. The vices alternate with their respective virtues: Faith/Lust, Hope/Envy, Charity/Sloth, Prudence/Pride, Justice/Avarice, Temperance/Gluttony, and Fortitude/Anger.

La Jolla

Library
Entrance

"To convey the idea that
powerful and permanent
hands are holding aloft
knowledge itself."
—William Pereira,
architect.

The Geisel Library, symbol of UCSD.

Salk Institute

The Theodore Gildred Court at the Salk Institute.

"Hope lies in dreams, in imagination, and in the courage of those who dare to make dreams into reality." —Jonas Salk.

Tip

Look for symmetry. This shot, and the previous library shot, are appealing in their symmetry. While it's generally better to use thirds, the occasional centered image adds variety.

ℹ️

10010 N Torrey Pines Road. Guided architectural tours by appointment, daily at 11am and noon. Closed weekends. Free. 858-453-4100 x1200.

Commercial photographers require permission. Tel: 858-453-4100 x1646.

La Jolla

The Salk Institute for Biological Studies ⊕

Situated on high bluff above the Pacific, this stark design by Louis I. Kahn is considered a modern masterpiece. Kahn called it the "architecture of silence and light." A simple courtyard of travertine marble is bisected by a narrow watercourse. The watercourse is supplied by a small square fountain and seemingly runs into the sky. The courtyard is flanked by symmetrical cubist laboratory blocks, stepped back for a narrowing perspective.

The design was personally chosen by Dr. Jonas Salk. Salk developed the first polio vaccine in 1953 and founded the Salk Institute in 1960 as a "crucible of creativity." The city of San Diego donated the 26-acre site and the building was completed in 1967.

The Salk Institute is one of the world's largest independent biological research facilities. Over 150 M.D. and Ph.D. level full-time scientists study the biology of genes and the brain.

Para Gliders

Torrey Pines Glider Port ⏱

A fascinating sight to watch. People hurl themselves over the 360-foot cliff then rise on a current of air. On windy days, the sea-breeze generated from the ocean, hits the cliffs and creates lift, allowing hand gliders, paragliders and the occasional glider to sail back and forth over the cliff. To see the most para-gliders, come on a windy day in the afternoon.

The glider port is at the end of Torrey Pines Scenic Drive, by the Salk Institute. Tel: 858-452-9858. www.flytorrey.com

Tip
Photograph from high vantage points. It's not obvious but on top of the small cafe is a viewing deck. From this higher vantage point you have commanding views of the launch area.

This is a great place to watch the sunset.

Torrey Pines State Reserve

The view from Yucca Point.

Enter at the north end of North Torrey Pines Road, by Del Mar. See map on page 214. Open 8–sunset; museum 9–5. Weekend nature walks at 11:30 and 1:30. $4 per vehicle. Tel: 858-755-2063.

**c/o California State Parks
9609 Waples Street, Suite 200
San Diego CA 92121
Tel: 858-755-2063.
http://www.torreypine.org**

Torrey Pines State Beach.

Torrey Pines Golf Course

**Adjacent to The Reserve are two public 18-hole championship golf courses. Hole 6 of the North Course has a fabulous view over the ocean and La Jolla Shores. The PGA stops here in February for the Buick Invitational.
11480 Torrey Pines Road. 858-552-1784. Adjacent is the Sheraton Grande Torrey Pines (tel: 858-558-1500).**

The only publicly-accessible reserve for one of the world's rarest trees—the Torrey pine (Pinus torreyana). The only other native stand is on Santa Rosa island, off the Santa Barbara coast 175 miles away, but it is not generally open to the public.

Specially adapted to the sandy soil and infrequent rainfall, the Torrey pine is light and ghostly, often twisted into contortions by the wind. It is distinguished by its clusters of five needles. There are about 4,000 of the protected trees in the 1,750-acre Reserve.

Several pleasant walking trails allow you to explore the Reserve. The largest number of Torrey pines is on the Guy Fleming Trail, while the oldest remaining Torrey pine in the Reserve—130 years old—is on the High Point Trail.

The best photograph is of Broken Hill, with its steep, weathered, textured sides. The hill is the tip of a sandstone promontory, separated from the headland by erosion. It lies at the end of Broken Hill Trail and is best at sunrise.

Yucca Point offers a great coastal view, overlooking the sandstone bluffs. In March through May, colorful wildflowers carpet the ground.

Tip

Plan your shot. To get a rich golden color on the sandstone, arrive before dawn and photograph in the first few minutes of the day.

Right: Torrey pine trees on Broken Hill, at sunrise.
Below: Torrey Pines Golf Course, hole 6 of the North Course.

The Aventine

Stargazer

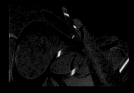

Hyatt Regency La Jolla

Gensia Center

northeast of La Jolla are the areas of University City, Golden Triangle, Miramar and Sorrento Valley. Along with Torrey Pines, the region is known for its bio-tech and communications industries.

Hyatt Regency La Jolla 🕐   1989

Upper left: Renowned modernist architect Michael Graves designed the Avenine complex which consists of a 16-floor, 419-room hotel, a circular athletic center, and a rectangular office block. 3777 La Jolla Village Drive in University City. Tel: 619-552-1066.

Stargazer 🕐   1983

Far left: "Stargazer" (1983) by Alexander Liberman, is a sculpture at the San Diego Tech Center in Sorrento Valley.

Gensia Center 🕐

Lower left: An obelisk rises from a lake at the former headquarters of Gensia Pharmaceuticals. On Towne Centre Drive just north of University Towne Centre mall.

Mormon Temple 🕐

1993 by William Lewis

The Church of Jesus Christ of Latter-Day Saints, San Diego California Temple.

The most distinctive building along I-5 is the Mormon Temple, with its twin 190-foot towers. Although you're welcome to visit the grounds, the Temple is not open to the public and photographing the interior is prohibited. Overlooking I-5 in University City at 7474 Charmant Drive.

Mormom Temple

Beaches

Sand sculpture by Gerry Kirk, from the "Lost City of Atlantis."

Pacific Beach
Grand Ave.
Boardwalk
Mission Blvd.
Mission Bay
Vacation Isle
Mission Beach
Belmont Park
Sea World
Ocean Beach

The boardwalk in Mission Beach.

Beaches

The beach areas of San Diego include Ocean Beach, Mission Beach, Mission Bay and Pacific Beach. Reeling in the Southern California scene, the beach districts are popular for sunbathing, rollerblading, surfing, sailing and people-watching.

Mission Beach—Belmont Park

"A playground dedicated to the people of San Diego."
—John D. Spreckels.

Belmont Park is a restored oceanside amusement park, originally developed by John D. Spreckels in 1925. The highlight is the Giant Dipper, a wooden rollercoaster. The bone-rattling ride includes 2,600 feet of track and 13 hills with a maximum height of 74 feet. Restored in 1991, the Giant Dipper is the only rollercoaster on the National Register of Historic Places and is considered one of the country's best small coasters.

Also in Belmont Park is a replica of a Looff Liberty Carousel, a decorative arch (below) and an indoor swimming pool called The Plunge.

At West Mission Bay Dr. and West Mission Blvd.

Tip

Capture the fear! Photographs of people on rollercoasters are best when you can see the terror in their eyes! The descent at the north side, at the end of the ride, provides the least-obstructed view. Set up beforehand, with a 100mm-200mm lens, and wait for the train to come into view. Use a fast shutter-speed to freeze the action.

The Giant Dipper Rollercoaster
at night.

Where

This view is taken from Mission Bay Park, by the parking
area at Bonita Cove. During
the summer the rollercoaster
operates into the evening
and is lined with flashing
lights. The view is best about
20-30 minutes after sunset.
You can crop the shot afterwards for a panorama.

Sunbathing in Mission Beach.

Hamels, by Belmont Park.

FISHIN CHI
HAMBURGE

CRAB CAKE BURGER 4.95
BEACH BURGER   4.95
HOT DOG/4LB   95
FISH SANDWICH   95
CLAM CHOWDER   50
TERIYAKI CHICKEN 5.95

FRESH FRUIT
Smoothie
ICE CREAM SUNDAE

Beaches

Above: A tranquil view of Vacation Isle and Mission Bay, with the San Diego skyline in the background. This shot is taken from Crown Point in Pacific Beach, on Crown Point Drive.

Above: Mission Bay Park.

Left: Views of Mission Beach and Pacific Beach. *Immediate left:* The San Diego Paradise Point Resort on Vacation Village has a mile of beach and a great view from its observation tower.

Below: Cottages on the Crystal Pier Hotel in Pacific Beach.

Mission Bay Park 🕐

A seven-square-mile (4,600-acre) watersports playground with two islands, many coves and 17 miles of beaches. Mission Bay is popular for sailing, windsurfing, camping, fishing, cycling, kite flying, jet-skis, power boats and water-skiers.

The bay was originally a marshy swamp at the mouth of the San Diego River, named False Bay, *Bahia Falsa,* by Cabrillo in 1542. In the 1950s, the Army Corps of Engineers, funded by the City, separated the mud flats from the river and dredged them, using the sludge to create islands, coves and peninsulas.

Crystal Pier Hotel 🕐

Sleep over the ocean at the only hotel on a pier! A 400-foot pier was opened in 1927 with a large ballroom at the end. In 1936, the ballroom was removed, the pier was extended to 1,000 feet, and cottages were added. A storm in 1983 washed away 300 feet of the pier. The now-700-foot pier has 26 renovated cottages available for rent.

4500 Ocean Blvd. Tel: 858-483-6983.

Pacific Beach

A jogger passes Crystal Pier in Pacific Beach at sunset.

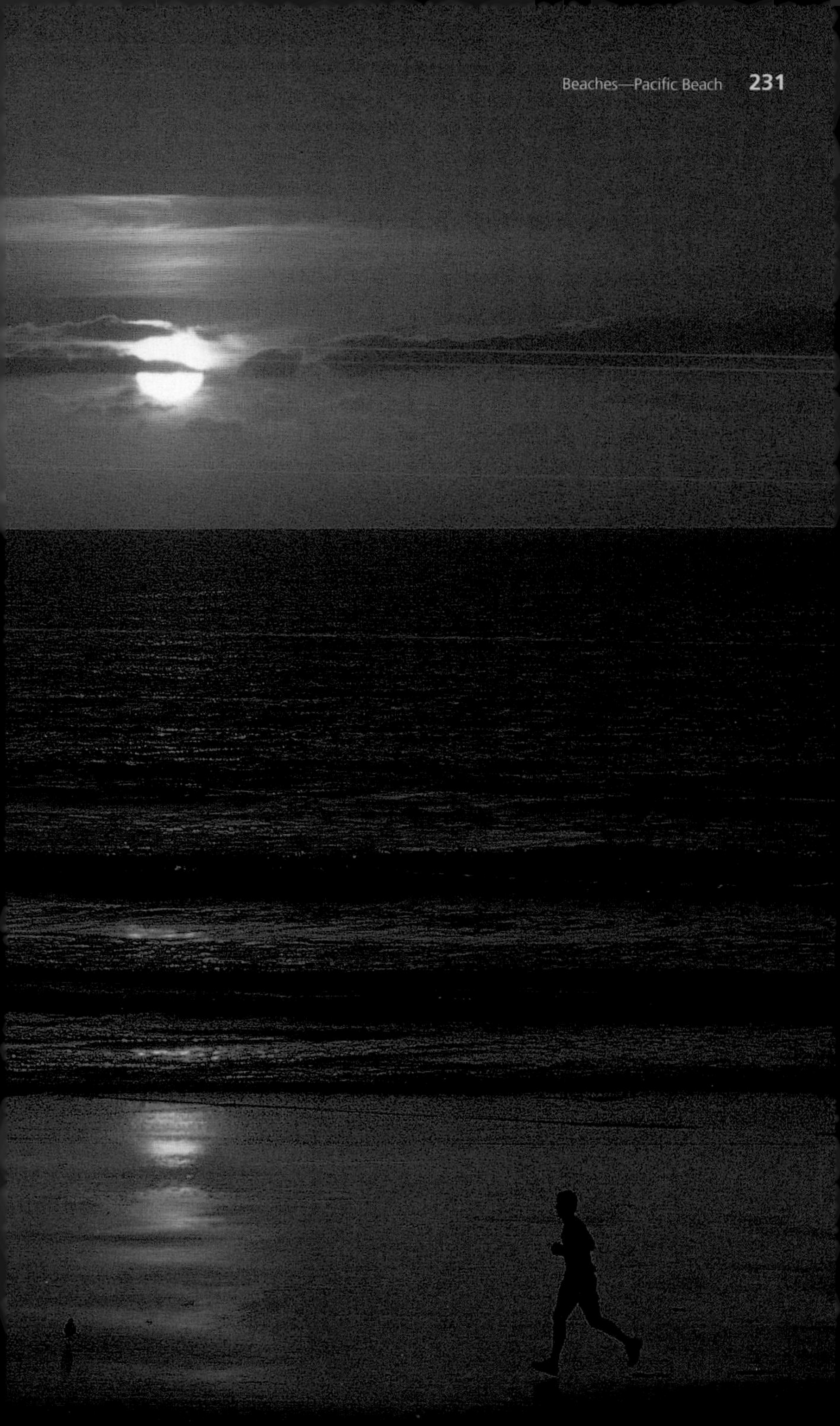

Ocean Beach

Ocean Beach Fishing Pier

This half-mile-long fishing pier stretches far out into the ocean. Nearby are volleyball courts and barbecues, Dog Beach (where dogs run unleashed), and funky bars on Newport Avenue.

PhotoSecrets San Diego

Other Sights

The Classic Skyline

The most beautiful view of San Diego (right) is taken from Point Loma. From here you can see the sail boats of the San Diego Yacht Club, Shelter Island, San Diego Bay, and the downtown skyline anchored by One America Plaza. On a clear day you can also see (distant, behind One America Plaza) Lyons Peak (el. 3,738'), 26 miles away near Jamul, and, to the right, San Miguel Mountain (el. 2,565'), 16 miles away.

Where

This shot is taken from Armada Terrace in Point Loma. The area is residential so don't disturb the residents or their privacy. Just past Harbor View Place is a public stairway and a gap between the houses here affords this postcard-perfect vista.

Lucinda Street, further uphill, has a similar view which includes a large palm tree in the foreground.

When

Late afternoon and dusk are the best times—the shot above was taken about 25 minutes after sunset. Pick a

clear day without haze so that the mountains are visible. Winter provides the clearest days, and brings snow to the mountain tops.

The view is almost exactly on an east-west axis. To get the most sunlight reflected off the buildings (which face west), photograph around March 23 or September 21 when the sun sets due west. The nearest full moon to these days will rise due east, over the skyline.

Photographing Skylines

By James Blank

James Blank is probably the country's most prolific postcard photographer. Over 6,000 of his images appear on North American postcards, and over 3,000 appear in calendars.

Blank's work has been used by Travel and Leisure, Travel-Holiday, Marriott Hotels, Hallmark Cards and Eastman Kodak.

Born in Cedar Rapids, Iowa, Blank is now based in Chula Vista (San Diego). With his wife Marian and daughter Natasha, he operates a stock photography house called 'Scenics of America.' His office is packed with over 200,000 transparencies of U.S. and Canadian cities and scenic areas.

Blank travels constantly, re-shooting each view to keep his images current. He is represented by FPG in New York.

Other

San Diego is my favorite city to photograph. I find the beauty of the landscape here to be mind-boggling, offering so many beautiful and varied places to photograph. My other favorite cities to photograph are San Francisco, Boston, New Orleans, New York, Chicago, Montreal, and Vancouver. Along with San Diego, each of these areas has an ambiance that makes it unique. I have shot these cities over and over again and still look forward to going back and doing it another time.

Tips

I have been asked many times over the years how I get such deep blue skies and clarity in my pictures. The answer is simple: I only shoot on exceptionally clear days with great visibility. As soon as I arrive at a location, I always check the weather forecast for the next few days. I only shoot in good weather—many times I have stayed in a hotel room for several days before the weather was right. I spend part of my time on "bad

Right: From Harbor Island. "I like to include a palm tree—it makes San Diego look tropical."

weather" days looking at postcard racks, skimming picture books, and exploring the area. When the weather breaks, I'm ready to get working.

The one big difference I've observed between an amateur photographer and a professional is this: when both stop and look at a beautiful scene, the amateur will take one picture and move on while the pro, on the other hand, will take many pictures of the same scene at varying times and exposures before moving on. A professional knows that they must get the perfect exposure because their job is riding on it. It's really simple: if a pro doesn't bring back good, usable photography, they won't be asked to shoot again.

Above: From Coronado, at the base of Orange Avenue. "The rose garden is beautiful in the spring."

Above: James Blank's favorite view is from Lucinda Street on Point Loma. "For thirty years I have sold this shot more than any other."

Images that Sell

I usually shoot every good scene in both horizontal and vertical formats. When I first started out, I shot mostly horizontals, and I lost out on a lot of vertical sales. The initial cost of the extra film is more than offset by the increased sales.

Calendar company buyers appreciate photographers who have images representing all four seasons. In putting together their calendars each year, they like to deal with as few photographers as possible.

I've learned that 'size does matter!' In many instances, when given the choice of three images—35mm, 2-1/2, or 4x5—clients will usually take the

Favorite Skylines

Most views are best from 3pm to dusk. At dusk you have the sunlight playing off the glass buildings and also the lights just coming on in the other buildings. I recommend long lenses, from 135mm to 300mm, plus a sturdy tripod.

1. Point Loma

My favorite view of all is a view of the skyline, harbor and the mountains taken from Lucinda Street on Point Loma. This is the quintessential view of San Diego.

2. Harbor Island

There are get great views of the skyline from along the entire length of Harbor Island. I prefer to shoot from the east end where there are palm trees to add foreground interest to the pictures.

3. Harbor Drive

Another fine view can be taken from the boardwalk along Harbor Drive. Here you can get a close view of the downtown skyline with small boats in the foreground.

4. Coronado

Another great view of the skyline is from the end of Orange Avenue in Coronado, looking across the bay to the city. In the spring and summer there are flowers in the park and you can use them as a colorful foreground for your pictures of the San Diego skyline.

Right: The view from Harbor Drive includes sail boats in the foreground.

larger size, regardless of the quality. My advice to 35mm landscape photographers that are just starting out would be to add a medium or large format to their repertoire for increased sales.

Equipment

I've been asked many times by beginning pros if it's necessary to buy expensive (i.e. 'fast') lenses. In the case of landscape photography, I don't think so. Most of your pictures will be taken on a tripod, so a fast lens is not needed. Most of my landscapes are taken at F16, F22, or F32. The only exception is aerial photography where one or two fast lenses can come in handy.

One of the most important items in a photographer's equipment is a tripod. The larger and heavier the

Above: From the top of the Sheraton on Harbor Island. "If you ask nicely, the staff may allow you onto the balcony for this unobstructed view."

IN THE BAG

**Cameras: Pentax 67 (2-1/4")
and Nikon FTN (35mm).** *"I
shoot 90% of the time with
the Pentax 67 and 10% with
my Nikon."*

Film: Fuji Velvia. *"90% of my
photography is with Fuji
Velvia. The color is so vivid."*

camera, the more a tripod is needed. To get great depth-of-field, which is important for landscape photography, a tripod is a "must."

As far as filters go, I use only one—a polarizer. This is really a great filter and, when used properly, increases the color saturation of all the hues in a scene (not just the blue in the sky, as some people think). I have polarizers for all my lenses and take them off only when they aren't needed.

I hope this article will help my fellow photographers get some great pictures of my adopted home town of San Diego. Good shooting!

James Blank
Scenics of America
PO Box J
Chula Vista, CA 91912
Tel/fax: 619-421-0611

Plane View

Landing on the Freeway ⏱

Right: This shot seems to say 'transportation' and has a very 'L.A.' feel. The view is taken from a pedestrian bridge over I-5, near Laurel Street. In the background is a circular Holiday Inn hotel.

Use a long lens (100mm) to make the aircraft appear even closer to the buildings.

Landing on the Roof ⏱

Below: Well someone didn't make it! The staff of Classic Reprographics decided to have fun with their flightpath location and bought a Cessna at an auction. The tailpiece sticks out of the roof and the wings are used for awnings. 1985 Fifth Avenue at Grape Street.

San Diego International Airport (Lindbergh Field)

With the airport located so close to downtown, you get some terrific views when flying in to San Diego. Descending planes appear to almost clip the four-story Laurel Travel Center parking lot (visitors not allowed).

For arrivals, sit on the left side of the aircraft for a good view of downtown. The flight path takes you over Balboa Park and (on the right side of the plane) the open-air Lowell Davies Festival Theater.

Departing the airport, sit on the right-hand side for a great views of Point Loma, Mission Bay and La Jolla.

Other

Other Sights

USD—University of San Diego   1949

Founded in 1949, USD is a Catholic liberal arts university overlooking Mission Bay and Mission Valley. The campus is designed in Spanish Renaissance architecture, inspired by the University of Alcalá de Henares in Spain.

The most distinctive building is the Immaculata Church with a bell tower and dome.

5998 Linda Vista Road. Information at Maher Hall on the east end of the campus. Tel: 619-260-4600.

SDSU—San Diego State University   1897

The oldest institution of higher learning in the city, SDSU was originally founded in 1897 as a teachers college. It was developed by the WPA as a depression-era project.

The Immaculata Church at USD.   The mission-style SDSU.

Other

Left: Spruce Street Bridge is an unusual pedestrian suspension bridge. From Balboa Park follow Spruce Street for six blocks west. The bridge is best photographed from the west side at Brant Street.

The area north of downtown and west of Balboa Park contains some fine Victorian houses. It was originally nicknamed as Banker's Hill or Pill Hill—for the bankers and doctors that lived there. At 2408 First Avenue is the Long-Waterman House (1889), an ornate Victorian once owned by a governor of California, Robert Waterman.

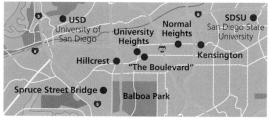

North of Balboa Park are several attractive neighborhoods. Many sport large street signs in their business district.

Exploring San Diego County

South

Imperial Beach Municipal Pier

Imperial Beach is the most southwesterly city in the continental U.S. The 1,500-foot-long pier is at the base of Evergreen Avenue. Take I-5 south and exit west on Palm Avenue (75), then left onto Seacoast Drive for six blocks.

Every July or August, Imperial Beach hosts the U.S. Open Sandcastle contest—the longest-running annual sand castle building competition in the world.

Del Mar

Chairs at the Del Mar Plaza.

Del Mar Plaza ⏲

Right: Designed by the architect of Horton Plaza, Jon Jerde, this romantic open-air complex is at Del Mar Heights Road and 15th Street.

Del Mar Fairgrounds and Racetrack

Where the turf meets the surf. Famous for its county fair and thoroughbred racing, the 350-acre grounds host over 100 events each year. Bing Crosby and Jimmy Durante started the racetrack in 1937.

2260 Jimmy Durante Blvd. Tel: 858-755-1141.

Hot Air Balloons ⏲

On calm days, hot air balloons rise over Del Mar, Rancho Santa Fe, and the San Dieguito River Valley.

Del Mar Fairgrounds Events

- **Del Mar Horse Show** Apr/May. 619-792-4288.
- **Arabian Horse Show.** May. 760-722-4843.
- **San Diego County Fair.** Jun/Jul. 858-755-1161.
- **Hot Air Balloon Classic.** July 4. 858-481-6800.
- **Del Mar Horse Racing.** Mid–July to early September. Six days weekly (no racing Tuesdays). Post time is often 2pm for the nine race program. Tel: 858-792-4242.
- **Holiday of Lights** Dec. 858-793-5555.

North

Encinitas

Swami's 🕐

This is one of San Diego's most famous surfing spots. This view is from the parking lot.

Self Realization Fellowship 🕐 1937

Founded by Yogi Paramahansa Yoganada in 1937, the SRF has gold lotus domes and a public Meditation Garden. 216 K Street. Tel: 760-753-1811.

North

Quail Botanical Gardens 🕐

Displaying over 3,000 species of plants in 30-acres, Quail Botanical Gardens is one of the world's most diverse plant collections.

Open: 9–5 daily. Guided tours Sat 10am. East of I-5 on Encinitas Blvd at 230 Quail Gardens Dr. $8/3. Tel: 760-436-3036.

Nearby is San Elijo Lagoon Ecological Reserve, a 1,000-acre sanctuary with over 250 bird species. 760-694-3030.

Boat Houses 🕐 1929

Looking like a fleet of boats run aground, these unusual houses were designed by Mile M. Kellogg. Each boat is 15 feet high and 20 feet long and has 19 portholes. Inside is a galley and a pilothouse, complete with a steering wheel. These are private homes so do not trespass.

726-732 Third Street at G Street. Tel: 760-753-6041.

Balloon Companies

A Skysurfer Balloon Co.
858-481-6800
California Dreamin'
800-373-3359
Del Mar Balloons
858-481-4100
Great American
909-927-2593
Panorama
800-455-3592
Sky's The Limit
800-558-5828
Skysurfer Balloon Co.
800-660-6809

Rancho Santa Fe

This exclusive hillside residential community is a California Historical Landmark. Lilian Rice, one of California's first successful women architects, supervised the development and designed many of the original homes in Spanish Colonial Revival.

In the 1880s, almost all of the 9,000-acre Rancho San Dieguito was bought by the Santa Fe Railroad and renamed Rancho Santa Fe. 4,000 acres of Australian eucalyptus trees were planted for railroad ties.

In the 1920s, Rancho Santa Fe was subdivided as a residential community, with homes bought by Bing Crosby, Douglas Fairbanks and Mary Pickford.

Vista

Around the city of Vista are two interesting adobes:

Rancho Guajome Adobe 🕐 1853

This adobe is one of the finest examples remaining of the traditional Spanish-Mexican one-story haciendas. Ysidora Bandini acquired the house and its 2,219-acre cattle ranch on her marriage to Col. Cave Johnson Couts.

The adobe is three miles north of Vista at 2210 N Santa Fe Ave. Open for weekend tours at 11am, 12:30pm and 2pm. $5/$1. Tel: 760-724-4082.

The adobe is located in the 579-acre Guajome Regional Park, Vista. Also in the park is the Antique Gas and Steam Engine Museum. 2040 N Santa Fe Ave. 10–4. $3/$2. Tel: 760-941-1791.

Rancho Buena Vista Adobe 🕐

After the missions were secularized, Governor Pio Pico deeded the 1,184-acre Rancho Buena Vista to American Indian Felipe Subria. This 4,000-square foot ranch house can be viewed on a 45-minute walking tour. In Vista, at 651 East Vista Way. Wed.–Sun., 10–3. $3/$0.50. Tel: 760-639-6164.

Carlsbad

The "Village by the Sea."

Carlsbad

San Diego

Once a popular spa-resort, the town of Carlsbad was named for its mineral water.

The town was originally called Frazier's Station, after Captain John A. Frazier who initiated a railroad development. In 1882, Frazier sank a well and found mineral water. The mineral content was claimed to be similar to that from a famous spa in the present-day Czech Republic—Karlvy Kary (Karlsbad).

Train Station   1887

Now the Carlsbad Visitors Bureau, the original train station has served as a telegraph station, Wells Fargo stagecoach depot, post office and a general store.
400 Carlsbad Village Drive at Elm St. 760-434-6093.

Neiman's Restaurant

An 1887 house that was originally one of a pair. They were remodeled as hotel in 1914. Only one remains and it is now a restaurant.
2978 Carlsbad Blvd.

Batiquitos Lagoon

A wetlands restoration, visited by migrating birds such as the great blue heron, snowy egret and American avocet.

Legoland

Southern California's newest theme park was opened in 1999 by Danish toy maker Lego. The park contains replicas of five U.S. cities and a medieval castle, all made from 30 million plastic bricks. Hours vary, opening at 10am and closing between 5pm and 8pm. $41.95/$34.95.
Exit I-5 at Cannon. Tel: 760-918-5346.

Alt Karlsbad Hane Haus

Frazier's well is preserved along with the original spa house and a statue of Frazier. 2802 A Carlsbad Blvd. Tel: 760-434-1887.

North

Flower Fields of Carlsbad

Tip

The Fields are so large that it's difficult to know what to photograph! A popular technique is to photograph a friend or relative standing at the side of a field with the flowers behind. Including a person (see over) certainly adds human interest. Also try concentrating on a few flowers (above).

Nearby to the west is Andersen's Windmill, a Danish-style windmill attached to Andersen's Holiday Inn. You can include this in your shot either as a backdrop by shooting from the top of the flowered hill, or as a foreground by photographing from west side of the freeway and using a long lens.

One of the most spectacular sights of North County occurs in the spring. Each March and April, over 50 acres of fields explode in color with ranunculus blooms. Arranged in ribbon-like bands of color and open to the public, this is a "can't-miss" sight for anyone with a camera.

At the peak, there are over eight million vibrant Tecolote® Giant Ranunculus blossoms. Yet the blooms are merely a by-product of the business. Only two percent of the flowers are sold—the flowers are grown for their bulbs. The Flower Fields boast one of the largest ranunculus bulb production operations in the world and the only one open to the public.

Ranunculus blossoms have decorated this Carlsbad Ranch hillside every spring for more than thirty years. They thrive with a mild winter climate, dry summers, and well-drained sandy soil. Edwin Frazee started growing the flowers in San Diego County in 1933 and moved his operations to this hill in 1965.

The Flower Fields are easy to find. Take I-5 to Carlsbad and exit onto Palomar Airport Road. Go east two blocks, then turn left on Paseo del Norte. Open only around March and April (closed rest of the year). 9am–5pm, or 6pm after daylight savings. Entrance: $7/$4. Free parking. Tel: 760-431-0352.

To capture the expanse of flowers, shoot from the base of the hill and use a wide-angle lens. Place the horizon high in the frame to emphasize the flowers. Include people on the pathway (left) for a sense of scale.

North

Oceanside Municipal Pier

At 1,942 feet, this is the longest overwater pier in Southern California. It's so long that a golf cart is used to take people from one end to another. At the end is Ruby's Diner. Originally built in the 1890s, the pier was rebuilt and restored in 1987.

I used this pair of palm trees to provide some foreground interest and frame the shot. Notice how everything except for the sky is silhouetted. Look for a day with high whispy clouds that will reflect the setting sun.

Oceanside Harbor has a fake but photogenic lighthouse.

Heritage Park Village and Museum

A self-guided walk takes you past houses by Irving Gill and Julia Morgan. Get a map from the Oceanside Visitor Information Center at 928 N Hill Street. Tel: 760-721-1101.

Camp Pendelton Marine Corps Base

Separating San Diego County from Orange County and Los Angeles is Camp Pendelton, the country's largest Marine Corps amphibious training base.

There are self-guiding tours which include the Amphibious Vehicle Museum. Driver's license, vehicle registration and verification of automobile insurance are required.

The land was previously the 133,340-acre Rancho Santa Margarita. It was bought by the military in 1942 and named for Major General Joseph H. Pendelton who established the first marine base on North Island in 1914.

Oceanside Municipal Pier. Photographed from the
steps off Pacific Street at Mission Avenue.

Oceanside Mission

"King of the Missions."

ℹ️

4050 Mission Avenue, four miles east of Oceanside off SR 76. Open daily 10am–4:30pm. $4.
Tel: 760-757-3651.
www.sanluisrey.org

Tip
Try photographing the altar from the choir loft.

In the courtyard, use the branches of the pepper tree to frame a shot of the retreat center.

Mission San Luis Rey de Francia 🕐　1798

Known as the 'King of the Missions,' this is the largest mission in California. It was used in the Zoro films by Walt Disney.

This was the ninth and last mission founded by Father Fermín de Lasuén, successor to Father Junipéro Serra. Founded on June 13, 1798 Mission San Luis Rey de Francia was the 18th in the chain of 21 missions and was the most successful. Up to 3,000 Indian converts worked here, raising cattle, growing fruit and making soap.

The mission is named for St. Louis IX, King of France (1215–70). It is substantially rebuilt and only the walls of the church, dating from 1811, are original.

The grounds contain: the oldest pepper tree in California (from Peru in 1830); the oldest cemetery in North San Diego County; and a lavandería (laundry area) which was supplied by aqueducts.

Where

Asistencia de San Antonio de Pala is on Pala Mission Road, in the town of Pala, off SR 76. Open: 10–3. $2. Tel: 760-742-3317.

Asistencia Las Flores

Founded in 1823 by Father Antonio Peyri, this asistencia to Mission San Luis del Rey was a tile-roofed adobe chapel and hostel. The asistencia no longer remains and is marked by a plaque in Camp Pendelton Marine Base, 0.6 miles southeast of Las Pulgas gate.

Asistencia de San Antonio de Pala 1816

Built as an asistencia (satellite mission) to Mission San Luis Rey de Francia, this is the only original mission still serving Native Americans. It is on the Pala Indian Reservation. The asistencia was founded in 1816 by the popular Father Antonio Peyri, and was restored in 1903 and 1959.

The bell tower is unusual in that it is separate from the church. Father Peyri is reputed to have planted a tiny cactus on the top of the tower to symbolize that Christ would conquer the desert, not only of Southern California but also of the human soul.

Grape Day Park, Escondido

The park includes a Santa Fe Depot and Pullman railroad car, and Heritage Walk—a collection of the city's Victorian buildings. Bordering the park is the California Center for the Arts, with a 1,524-seat concert hall, and the Escondido Civic Center City Hall, with a 60-foot latticed rotunda entrance and fountain.
On Broadway between Washington and Valley Pkwy.

North

Tip
Use the fountain. At Mission San Luis Rey de Francia there are few foreground possibilities other than the fountain. To create this lake-like image, I leant over the fountain and overflowed the bottom of the frame with the water.

"We found before us, on an elevated piece of land, the superb structure of Mission San Luis, the glittering whiteness of which flashed back to us by the first rays of the day. At the distance in which we were and in the still uncertain light of dawn, this edifice, very beautifully modeled and supported by numerous pillars, had the aspect of a palace."
—Auguste Duhaut-Cilly, a French traveler, 1827.

Wild Animal Park®

Where

The Wild Animal Park is 32 miles north of downtown San Diego, just east of Escondido. Take I-15 and exit east on Via Rancho Parkway. Follow the signs six miles east to the Wild Animal Park.

When

9–8 summer, 9–4 rest of year.

Cost

$26.50/19.50. Parking $6. Two-park ticket available with the San Diego Zoo. Join the Zoological Society of San Diego and receive free admission for one year to the Zoo and Wild Animal Park.

East

San Diego Wild Animal Park

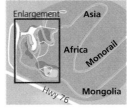

A "second campus" of the San Diego Zoo, the San Diego Wild Animal Park provides over 2,200 acres where large animals can roam in entire herds and flocks. This time the animals are free while you're enclosed!

The Park contains over 3,200 rare and endangered animals representing 121 species of mammals and 285 species of birds. You can see and photograph the largest captive rhino population in the world plus giraffe, zebra, elephants and tigers.

ⓘ

San Diego Wild Animal Park
15500 San Pasqual Valley Rd.
Escondido, CA 92027

Tel: 760-747-8702
www.sandiegozoo.org

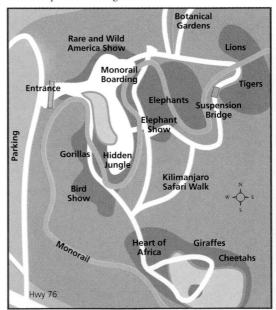

Above: A calf and mother southern white rhinoceros. The Wild Animal Park is a sanctuary for 51 endangered animals species, 41 of which have successfully reproduced here. Over 400 animals are born or hatched in the Park each year.

Below: Hartmann's mountain zebras blend into the background.

The lagoon and Congo Fishing River Bridge in Nairobi Village.

Waterfall in the Botanical Center.

Roar and Snore

For that true safari experience, camp overnight amidst the animals. Includes al fresco dining and a roaring campfire. Fridays, Saturdays and some Sundays, from mid-April through October. Tel: 1-800-934-CAMP.

Getting Around

The main guest area, Nairobi Village, is based around a lagoon. There are restaurants, gift shops, a camera shop, lockers, and stroller and wheelchair rentals. You can visit the aviaries and three shows—Rare and Wild America, a bird show, and an elephant show.

To see the main animal preserves, take the Wgasa Bush Line Monorail, a 5 mile, 55-minute ride on an electric tram.

Kupanda Falls Botanical Center ⏰

To the north is a pleasant 1 1/4-mile walk through numerous gardens.

Kilimanjaro Safari Walk ⏰

To get close to the tigers, lions, rhinos, elephants and cheetahs, take this 1 3/4-mile walking trail. There are lookout points and a picnic area.

Heart of Africa℠ ⏰

The newest exhibit is this 30-acre themed experience showing the diversity of Africa. It is claimed to be the largest and most diverse safari experience in the Western Hemisphere. Walk through flourishing wetlands, sprawling savannahs and open plains.

The 3/4-mile loop trail includes floating footbridges and panoramic overlooks. You can see more than 30 species of birds and mammals in natural settings, including Thomson's gazelles, impala, wildebeest, oryx, okapi, giraffe, herds of antelope, cheetahs, rhinos, Colobus monkeys, and wattled cranes. There's also an area where you can feed the giraffes.

East

Waterbuck.

Bird-eating spider.

Picture credits this section:

© 1998–2003 Zoological Society of San Diego: Ron Gordon Garrison: 264, 26 (lion), 267 (lorikeets and leopard), 269 (giraffes); Ken Kelley 267 (spider); Craig Racicot 267 (butterfly).

© 1998–2003 Photo Tour Books, Inc.: Andrew Hudson: 265 (2), 266 (lower four), 267 (deer), 268 (2), 269 (rhinos).

Dryadula phaetusa.

Rainbow lorikeets in Lorikeet Landing.

Cheetah in Heart of Africa.

Photo Caravan

Tip

Come prepared with both a wide-angle lens (28mm) and a long zoom lens (100–300mm). Use the wide-angle for the rhinos and giraffes as they're being fed. Include people to show how fun it is. Use the long lens for all the other animals you'll see. There's lots to photograph so be ready to change lenses and bring some spare film.

Ivan the giraffe inspects visitors for signs of biscuits.

Want to get some really great shots? Take the Wild Animal Park's Photo Caravan. An open-top Safari truck drives you not *around* the enclosures but *through* them, so you can get up close and personal with the locals. It's the only way to travel!

You're accompanied by an enthusiastic safari guide who provides anecdotes and information about each animal you encounter. The groups are limited in size and the trucks vary their routes depending upon animal patterns. Stephen Spielberg took this tour before filming *Jurassic Park*. You can see the influence it made as you enter the enclosure through the double gates. Although you see many animals, the highlight is being able to feed giraffes with biscuits, and rhinos with apples. With their long necks, the giraffes swoop down and become very interested in a good biscuit.

Gainda, a 5,000-pound female Indian rhino doesn't mind being patted, as long as you have an apple to offer.

Tours

Photo Caravan Tour #1:
East Africa and Asian Plains. In East Africa: Baringo giraffes, white-bearded gnu, Kenya impalas, Roosevelt's gazelles, Cape buffalos, vultures, flamingos, and herons. In the Asian Plains: Indian rhinoceroses, Malayan sambar deer, axis deer, Persian goitered gazelles, and Indian gaurs. 1 3/4 hours. $59 for members; $65 for non-members.

Photo Caravan Tour #2:
South Africa and Asian Waterhole. South Africa: southern white rhinoceroses, reticulated giraffes, Hartman's mountain zebras, sable antelope, gemsbok, eland, and ostrich. Asian Waterhole: water buffalo, Formosan sika deer, and Indian sambar deer. 1 3/4 hours. $59 for members; $65 for non-members.

Photo Caravan Tour #3:
Covers tours 1 and 2 combined. 3 1/2 hours. $81 for members; $89 for non-members.

Prices subject to change.

Reservations are highly recommended. Tours can be booked for several weeks so plan ahead. Children under 12 are not permitted. Do not touch the giraffes—they like people but don't enjoy being touched. For reservations, call 619-738-5022.

Palomar Observatory

East

More than a mile above sea level is America's largest telescope—the 200 inch Hale Telescope—housed in an enormous white dome. Both the dome and the telescope move as the earth rotates.

Inside the 12-story, 135-foot dome is a stairway leading to a viewing area where you can see the massive 530-ton telescope. The telescope is a giant camera, using a 20-ton glass disk to reflect light onto a photographic plate. It has a range of over one billion light years.

Palomar Observatory was opened in 1948. It is operated by CalTech in Pasadena and funded by an agency of the Rockerfeller Foundation. By the parking lot is the Greenway Museum showing galactic photographs and a 45-minute video.

Palomar is Spanish for "pigeon roost."

When

At 5,598 feet above sea level, the mountain sees snow in winter. The Observatory is open July and Aug 9am–4pm, rest of the year on weekends only. It is located 11 miles north of SR 76. Tel: 760-742-2119.

Julian

Julian makes a pleasant lunch stop on the road to Anza-Borrego Desert.

www.julianca.com
Tel: 760-765-1857

Right: The Julian Hotel is the most photogenic building in Julian. I crouched low over the flowers for a colorful foreground. 28mm lens.

Santa Ysabel Chapel.

The old gold mining mountain town of Julian is famous for its apple harvest and fall foliage. It lies 4,234 feet above sea level and makes a pleasant stop while visiting San Diego's backcountry.

Following the discovery of placer gold in a creek in 1869, 50 claims were made and the valley became a thriving commercial center. The town was established in 1870 by Drury D. Batley on his farmland, and named after his cousin, Michael S. Julian. In the early 1870s, Julian had eight saloons and two hotels.

The gold was buried in quartz and 18 hard-rock mines removed $5 million of gold in ten years. The gold played out by 1906.

Eagle Mining Company

Two of the original hard-rock mined are preserved—the Eagle and the High Peak. One hour tours are offered of the tunnels. At the north end of C Street. 10am–2:30pm. $8/$4. 760-765-0036.

Julian Hotel   1897

Thought to be the oldest continually operating hotel in San Diego County, the Julian Hotel (right) was built by Albert Robinson, an ex-slave from Missouri.

Witch Creek School   1888

Ten miles west of Julian is an old school house, now a library. In Witch Creek at 2133 4th Avenue.

Santa Ysabel Chapel   1818 site, 1924 building

Mass was first celebrated on this site in 1818 and by 1822 Asistencia Santa Ysabel had been established. An extension of Mission San Diego de Alcalá, the asistencia served about 450 neophytes.

The present white stucco chapel was built in 1924 although continuous religious service is claimed since 1818.

Eight miles northwest of Julian and 1.4 miles north of Santa Ysabel on SR 79. 760-765-0810.

East

Anza-Borrego Desert

Above: Wildflowers carpet the desert floor in spring time.
Right: Fan palm trees in Southwest Grove.

ℹ️

**Anza-Borrego Desert State Park, Visitor Center
200 Palm Canyon Drive
Borrego Springs, CA
Tel: 760-767-5311.**

http://www.anzaborrego.
statepark.org
http://www.desertusa.com

Occupying over 600,000 acres, Anza-Borrego Desert State Park is the largest state park in the contiguous United States. The dry, mainly flat region is a great valley or bowl, surrounded by rocky mountains. The Park contains more than 600 species of plants, 500 miles of dirt roads, and 12 wilderness areas. Photographers can capture wildflowers, palm groves, cacti, eroded landscapes and sweeping views.

The Park is named after Captain Juan Bautista de Anza, who established the first overland trail though the desert, and the bighorn sheep —"borrego" is a Spanish word for sheep.

Wildflowers

The most photogenic time to visit is in the spring, when the desert explodes with color from the blooms of wildflowers. The spectacular show lasts only a few weeks, between late February and early April. It is best after heavy rains in winter but may not appear at all in dry years.

Call the park headquarters' wildflower hotline at 760-767-4684 to learn exactly where and when the best show is. The blooms start on the desert floor, at

Desert

Where

The Park occupies much of the eastern portion of San Diego County. The Visitor Center is about an 80-mile drive from San Diego. The prettiest route starts from I-8. Follow Highway 79 through Cuyamaca Rancho State Park, or S1 through the Laguna Mountain Recreation Area. Both roads crest at about a mile in elevation (4740' and 5900' respectively) before dropping almost to sea level into the valley.

When

Open: Oct–May 9–5; rest of year weekends only 9–5.

Visitor Center

Start your tour at the Visitor Center, just west of Borrego Springs off S-22. The building is cunningly designed to blend in with the scenery. It is paved with local stone and built partly underground. Inside are helpful rangers, exhibits on geography and wildlife, and a wide selection of books. There's also an information slide show.

Weather

Spring, fall and winter are pleasantly warm and dry, at around 70–85°F. The summer becomes scorchingly hot, often over 100°F. Bring lots of water and drink it!

the base of Coyote Mountain in Borrego Valley, sweeping up to higher elevations as spring progresses. Early March is often the best but if you arrive late, go to the higher elevations such as Blair Valley or Culp Valley.

The most prominent flower is the spindly ocotillo with a brilliant red blossom. Also on display are desert sunflower, desert lily, white dune evening primrose, yellow desert dandelions, golden poppies, purple sand verbena and blue phacelia.

You can ask the rangers to send you a card about two weeks before the expected peak. Send a stamped, self-addressed postcard in an envelope to:

Wildflowers, Anza-Borrego Desert State Park,
200 Palm Canyon Dr., Borrego Springs CA 92004
On the Internet, check out www.desertusa.com.

Fan palms at the trailhead to Borrego Palm Canyon.

Borrego Palm Canyon

About a mile from the Visitor Center is a trailhead to Borrego Palm Canyon. By the parking area are a few palms (left) and the Palm Canyon Nature Trail.

A moderate hike of less than two miles goes uphill about 350 feet to a small grove of fan palms. During the spring a waterfall appears, making this the most idyllic place in the desert. Past the waterfall area is a larger grove of over 800 fan palms.

Big Horn Sheep

The most famed animal in the Park is the peninsular big horn sheep, often called the desert bighorn.

The bighorn is an endangered animal native only to the deserts of Southern California. Small in number and very elusive, they reward only the occasional, patient photographer.

Bighorn sheep are best photographed in mating season, June–November. They can sometimes be seen high on the mountains near Montezuma Grade or Yaqui Pass Road. Rangers at the Visitor Center keep a log of all sightings.

The bighorn sheep lives in the Santa Rosa Mountains on the north edge near the Visitor Center. The Santa Rosa is the highest mountain range in the Park and contains the only year-round watercourse in the desert.

History

Native Americans lived in this area around 8,000 B.C., as evidenced by pictographs around Blair Valley. The first European to pass through was Pedro Fages in 1772.

The first overland trail through the desert was established by Spanish explorer Captain Juan Bautista de Anza. In 1774, de Anza left Sonora, Mexico with 23 soldiers and priests and crossed the desert to Monterey. He repeated the trip in 1775–76 with 240 soldiers and settlers to found San Francisco.

The Anza Trail, also known as the Sonora Road, became the basis of the 1824 Southern Emigrant Trail. The trail became popular in the gold rush for Mexicans heading towards the gold fields. In 1846, the Mormon Battalion marched 2,000 miles from Iowa to San Diego through the desert. From 1858 to 1861, the trail was used for the Butterfield Overland Stageline and Mail Route, a 2,600-mile route connecting St. Louis with San Francisco.

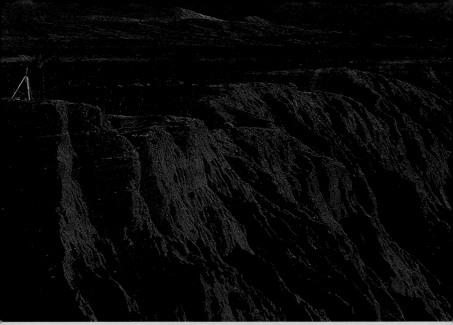

A photographer at Font's Point at sunrise.   Jerry Schad.

Animals

The best places to watch for wildlife is at the water holes, at Coyote Creek (the only year-round stream), Palm Canyon, Rattlesnake Spring and Seventeen Palms Oasis. There are over 50 species of snakes and lizards in the Park.
Birders should head for Octillo Flat, Lower Willows (both closed in the summer) or Yaqui Well (open all year).

Font's Point

The most dramatic view of the desert is from Font's Point at dawn. The morning light picks out the rugged, golden cliffs. From the Point you have a clear panoramic view over the Borrego Valley to the west, and the sharp ridges and deep gullies of the Borrego Badlands to the south, 300 feet below. This is one of the most breathtaking views in all the southwest deserts.

Font's Point is named for Father Font, a priest in Juan Bautista de Anza's second 1776 expedition through the region.

The only access is via a soft and rutted road and a 4WD vehicle is required. Take County Road S-22 then turn south for four miles along a sandy, dirt road.

Southwest Grove

There's a small grove of California fan palms at Southwest Grove (previous page). During the spring a small stream may form through the rocky canyon. The grove is reached by a short uphill hike and you have a good view east over the desert and Carrizo Badlands.

Off S2 by Mountain Palm Springs Campground.

Borrego Badlands, photographed from Font's Point.   Jerry Schad.

California Poppies

In March poppies adorn the well fertilized cow pastures in the higher areas near the Palomar observatory all the way down to Culp Valley in Anza Borrego.

Driving to Borrego Springs.

Tarantulas

From October to early December you can get up close and personal with wild Tarantulas. They start hunting for a mate and are easily seen on roads near Split Mountain and the Elephant Tree hike. It takes about 10 years for the spiders to reach sexual maturity but they're generally harmless and make an eye-catching picture.

Borrego Badlands

The Borrego Badlands (above) is a forbidding and dramatic landscape with stark gorges and jagged hills. It was created by rainfall runoff from the Santa Rosa Mountains to the north. The land is colored in red, yellow, pink and green from iron in the soil.

A 4WD vehicle is required to reach the best viewpoint—Font's Point.

Carrizo Badlands

Carrizo Badlands (next page) is more accessible than Borrego Badlands since it can be easily viewed from a well-marked overlook just off S2. Over a million years ago the area was a lake and mastodons, sabertooth tigers, zebras, camels, and llamas roamed this region.

Indian Pictographs

For signs of ancient Indian life, park at the Blair Valley Campground off S2 and take a short hike east. You'll see pictographs and morteros—small holes in rocks used for grinding seeds. Do not touch.

There are more morteros and some caves by Mine Canyon, off Hwy 78 east of S3.

Ghost flowers.

Split Mountain ☽

On the east side of the Park is a natural canyon, 600 feet high and only a few feet wide. Nearby are some wind caves.

Take Split Mountain Road from Hwy 78 at Ocotillo Wells.

Box Canyon

The wagon trains of the Old West left trail markings which you can explore around Box Canyon. In 1847, the Mormon Battalion cut a passage by hand through the rocky canyon walls for their wagons. There's a marker for the Butterfield Stage Route and you can see ruts made by wagon wheels.

On S2, 8.6 miles south of Hwy 78.

Carrizo Badlands, from the overlook on S2. The eroded landscape is rich in fossils.

Buckwheat and cholla cactus.

Vallecito Stage Station ☽

In Vallecito Stage Station County Park is a 1934 reconstruction of an 1852 stagecoach station. The Station was used by the "Jackass" San Diego-San Antonio mail line (1857–59), emigrants, and the Butterfield Overland Stage Line. The Station is on S2.

Goat Canyon Trestle at Carrizo Gorge

Crossing Carrizo Gorge is an impressive curved wooden bridge. The Goat Canyon Trestle is six hundred feet long and two hundred feet high. This was part of the "impossible railroad"—the San Diego and Arizona (1906–1919)—built by John D. Spreckels.

Due to age and storm damage the trestle is no longer in use and may be torn down. View the trestle only from afar—it is illegal to walk on the tracks and the rickety bridge is structurally unsound and dangerous.

Jerry Schad

Anza-Borrego Desert State Park, as viewed from Mount Laguna.

Our Lady of the Pines ⏲

This red Catholic Church in the Laguna Mountains is best photographed in the morning.

Tip

Find a subject. Although amazing in real life, the desert can lose its power in photographs. Look out for a suitable foreground subject to give your photo meaning and reference. Try to use the desert as a backdrop rather than a subject.

It's easier to see the model at the San Diego Railroad Museum in Balboa Park.

Access is via Mortero Canyon Road. Talk to the Camp Host at Box Willow Campground for information.

Nearby

Mount Laguna ⏲

Escape the heat of summer at Mount Laguna—6,200 feet above sea level with expansive meadows and cool summer breezes. In the spring, colorful wildflowers and three crystal-clear lakes appear.

Sunrise Highway offers several panoramic views of the desert below. The most obvious is from a nature trail by the picnic area near the peak, but a less-obstructed view can be photographed from the parking area outside of FAA Mount Laguna Station. This is reached via an unmarked road, 100 yards north of the picnic ground.

SDSU's Mount Laguna Observatory is open to the public most Friday and Saturday nights at sunset, from May to August. Free. 619-594-6182.

Desert Tower ⏲   1922

Just off I-8 at In-Ko-Pah Desert Outlook is a stone tower with views over the Anza-Borrego Desert. Access is not permitted when the tower is closed.

Afoot and Afield

Jerry Schad is the author of 12 books including *Afoot and Afield in San Diego County*, the best-selling guidebook to the county's wilderness areas.

Schad also pens a weekly outdoor column, "Roam-O-Rama," in the *San Diego Reader* and hosts a television series, "Afoot and Afield in San Diego," on KPBS-TV.

Schad specializes in photography of sunlit landscapes by day and moonlit scenes by night. His stock photographs are represented by Photo Researchers, Inc. in New York.

East

Cross-country skiing on Laguna Meadow.

A thin stream of icy vapor rises from the lake, gets caught on a puff of wind, and interposes itself between a back-lit Jeffrey pine and my hand-held camera. I'm on cross-country skis, having arrived at this spot in the Laguna Mountains after only 40 minutes of driving from my home just outside San Diego, plus another 40 minutes of easy kicking and gliding over a freshly-fallen blanket of snow. A radial pattern of sunrays appears around the tree, waxing and waning in intensity as the breeze shapes the vapor steam like a diaphanous curtain. With numb fingers barely manipulating knurled knobs, I bracket exposures and keep shooting into the glinting sun, hoping for a least one perfect shot.

Later that day, I lie face-down in the warm afternoon sunshine on the brink of a barren cliff, my camera at the edge and tilted downward to capture a pseudo-aerial shot of the Borrego Badlands. A maze of sunlit razorback ridges and gloomy sand-drowned ravines fills the viewfinder. I squeeze off shots at my leisure as the shadows lengthen. I drive home that evening after a rewarding day of exploration and photographic adventure, never having left San Diego's "big back yard."

After twenty-five years of photographing and writing about greater San Diego's natural landscapes, I'm con-

Buckhorn cholla cactus, Anza-Borrego.

vinced there's no other place offering a comparable mix of contrasting natural scenery. Connecticut-sized San Diego County contains mountains topping 6,000 feet in elevation, a desert region of fascinating geologic interest and lethal summer-time temperatures, and canyons harboring hidden waterfalls.

The sun-drenched, balmy coastline and coastal strip, where the vast majority of San Diego County residents live, encompasses only about one-tenth of the county's land area. The rest, however, remains largely in a natural state. San Diego County contains more than 1,500 square miles of lands open to public recreation—about one-third of its total area.

Jerry's Tips

The better scenic shots of San Diego County landscapes include a foreground element or elements. Include a blooming cactus, for example, with the surrounding sky added to give perspective. For compositions such as these, a 24mm or 28mm lens is invaluable.

When it is preferable to isolate a single subject, I like using a longer lens affixed with the camera to a stable tripod. Stopping the lens down increases the field depth, but at the expense of a slow shutter, which can be gently triggered with the addition of a cable release.

Distant landscapes are best shot under low-angle sunlight, or sometimes during sunrise or sunset itself. Here, again, a lightweight tripod is valuable, as light levels are often much lower than during the bright midday hours.

Top left: Kitchen Creek Falls, Laguna Mountain.
Above: Cuyamaca Lake at dawn.
Below: Santa Ysabel Valley.

Sunset on the Laguna Mountains.

East

The sharply contrasting landforms, climates, and geologic regimes of San Diego have resulted in a remarkable diversity of plants and wild animals. Biological surveys have revealed some 2,000 native plant species on San Diego County lands—more than in any other county in the United States. The county is also recognized as the nation's leader in counts of migrant and resident bird species.

Nature and landscape photography in San Diego County poses some unique challenges. Most surprising is the fact that winters are decidedly much better for photography than summers. Hazy skies shroud the area during much of late spring through summer, thickening near the coast to a low, often persistent overcast known as "June gloom." Fall and winter, on the other hand, bring dry Santa Ana winds from the northeast, which scrub the atmosphere clean and usher in surrealistically clear, blue skies. Most rain in San Diego County arrives in intermittent spurts during the winter. Such rainy episodes are often followed by a string of warm, sunny days, perfect for outdoor photography.

San Diego County, which looks rather dry and

Jerry Schad carries two 35-mm camera bodies, wide-angle lenses (typically 24mm and 35mm) and sometimes a medium tele-photo, such as a 100mm. He uses a small but fully-functioning tripod, cable releases, and warming fil-ters (for open shade).

"I use slow, fine-grained films such as Kodachrome 64 and Fuji Velvia (which I push-process one stop to ISO 100) for most daylight work."

Left center: Desert sunflowers, Anza-Borrego Desert State Park.

Left lower: Barrel, hedgehog, and cholla cacti, Anza-Borrego Desert State Park.

All photos in this section © 1998 Jerry Schad.

brown in summer and fall, can turn green almost overnight with the onset of late fall rain. By March, the accumulated rainfall and warmer temperatures trigger a wildflower bloom, which starts in the lower elevations of the coastal and desert regions of the county and moves upward into the mountains by May. Wildflower displays in the desert usually peak in mid-March, with an intensity that depends on the amount and timing of the winter rains.

Although there is no strong tradition of leaf-peeping here, autumn color in the higher mountains—Cuya-maca, Laguna, and Palomar—can be stunning in late October and early November. This is largely due to the deciduous black oak, whose yellowed leaves literally glow when illuminated by backlight.

Perhaps the most effective single nugget of advice I can give to nature and landscape photographers is this: *Get there early.* That way, you'll take advantage of some of the purest light you can find anywhere.

Dawn over Lake Cuyamaca.

PhotoSecrets San Diego

Resources

Photography

Photography is the perfect companion to travel. It encourages us—as travelers—to discover an area; it provides tangible memories of the trip; and it is an enjoyable way to express ourselves in art.

A camera is really an excuse to delve deeper into a place than we otherwise would. Looking for a good shot forces us to seek out the unique features and scenic beauty of a location, to explore further, and to interact with our surroundings. When you press the shutter release, you're making a personal connection to the place and it's people. You are *there*.

Photographs preserve the memories of our trip. We can show others the exciting places we've been to, the wonderful scenery, and the fun people we met. Our minds are triggered by images and reviewing our photographs helps everyone on the trip relive it's adventures and misadventures.

Taking pictures is also a very accessible artform. With a little thought and effort, you can create captivating images of your own creation and interpretation.

The Secret of Photography

Fortunately, taking good photographs has little to do with owning expensive equipment and knowing technical data. The secret is in seeing. Ask yourself: "What do I look at, and how do I see it?" A good photograph has qualities that display the skill, art, interests and personality of the photographer.

What Makes a Good Photograph?

A photograph is a message. It conveys a statement ("Here we are in ..."), an impression ("This is what ... looks like"), or an emotion. You are an author trying to convey this message in a clear, concise and effective way. But how?

Like any message, you first need a subject. This may be your traveling companions, a building, a natural vista, or some abstract form. The subject is the central point of interest and is usually placed in the foreground of the shot (towards the viewer). Now compose the message by including a second element, a context, which is often the background. The context gives the subject relevance, location, or other interest. It is the combination of the two elements—subject and context, foreground and background—that tells the message.

Just as important as knowing what to include, is knowing what to exclude. Anything that isn't part of the subject or it's context is only a distraction, cluttering up the image and diluting the message. So eliminate extraneous surroundings, usually by moving closer to the subject, and make a clear, tidy shot. A painter creates art by addition—adding more paint—whereas a photographer creates art by subtraction—removing unnecessary elements.

The recipe for a good photograph is: "A foreground, a background, and nothing else."

What Makes a Great Photograph?

A great travel photograph is a piece of art. It captures the spirit of a subject and evokes emotion. Bob Krist calls it: "The Spirit of Place." You are an artist that can use subtle tricks to appeal to your viewer's senses. Let's see how.

A picture is a playground, with places for our eyes to wander and investigate, plus spaces for them to rest and relax.

When we first see something, we are defensive. Our eyes instinctively find light, bright areas, and look for people, particularly their eyes and mouth. Do we know the people in the picture? What are they feeling, and how does this relate to us? Are they drawing attention to something? If so, do we recognize it (a building, a landmark) and what does it look like? What is this picture about? What is the main subject or objective? How big is the subject?

We determine scale by comparing elements to something of known size, such as a person, animal, or car. Once we've checked for people, we turn our attention to more abstract features.

We first notice the subject's color or tone. Firey red, calming blue, natural green, foreboding black. Then we see shape. Soft curves, hard edges, sweeping lines. How the light strikes the subject gives subtle hints to it's three-dimensional form. As a photographer, you can manipulate this by searching for shades and shadows, shifting intensities of tone and hues.

The way the elements are arranged and affected by the same light makes us consider their qualities and interrelation. Balance draws our eye from one element to another, investigating their unity, contrast, and detail, each item adding pleasure to the next. What is the relevance of everything?

The overall composition, the proportions of layout, denotes importance of the elements. As the artist, you can decide which features appeal to you, and how best to emphasize them.

Ten Tips

"The [35mm] camera is for life and for people, the swift and intense moments of life."
—*Ansel Adams.*

Include people

Magazine picture editors always like people in the shot. It gives the viewer a human connection, a sense of being there, and a sense of scale.

Photographs evoke emotion and empathy comes with someone's face. Avoid crowds and simplify the shot down to one person. The young and old are preferred subjects, with, respectively, their innocent expressions and weather-worn faces. People make your shots warm, friendly and personable. Just like you are.

Have you ever got your photos back only to discover that something that looked awe-inspiring at the time looks dull on paper? This is because your eye needs some reference point to judge scale. Add a person, car or something of known size to indicate the magnitude of the scenery.

1. Hold It Steady

A problem with many photographs is that they're blurry. Avoid 'camera shake' by holding the camera steady. Use both hands, resting your elbows on your chest, or use a wall for support. Relax: don't tense up. You're a marksman/woman holding a gun and it must be steady to shoot.

2. Put The Sun Behind You

A photograph is all about light so always think of how the light is striking your subject. The best bet is to move around so that the sun is behind you and to one side. This front-lighting brings out color and shades, and the slight angle (side-lighting) produces some shadow to indicate texture and form.

3. Get Closer

The best shots are simple so move closer and remove any clutter from the picture. If you look at most 'people' shots they don't show the whole body so you don't need to either. Move close, fill the frame with just the face, or even overflow it. Give your shot some impact. Use a zoom to crop the image tighter.

4. Choose A Format

Which way you hold the camera affects what is emphasized in your shot. Use a vertical format to emphasize height, for a tall tree or building. Use a horizontal format to show the dramatic sweep of some mountains.

5. Include People

Photographs solely of landscape and buildings are enjoyable to take but often dull to look at. Include some of your friends, companions, family or even people passing by to add human interest. If there's no one around, include yourself with the self-timer.

Depth

Always include some pointer about depth. A photograph is two-dimensional but we want it to appear three-dimensional. If you're shooting a background (mountains) include a strong foreground (people).

Use a wide-angle lens for exaggerated depth. With a 20mm to 28mm lens, get just a few feet from your subject and, with a small aperture (large f-number), include an in-focus deep background too. This exaggerated 'hyperfocal' perspective is used in a lot of magazine shots. What impact!

Alternatively you can remove all depth by using a long, telephoto lens. This compresses or compacts the image, making your 3-D subject appear flat.

Always centering your subject can get dull. Use the 'rule of thirds' to add variety and interest.

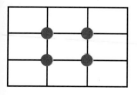

● **= suggested placement of subject in frame.**

6. Consider Variety

You may take the greatest shots but if they're all the same type or style, they may be dull to look at. Spice up your collection by adding variety. Include landscapes and people shots, close ups and wide angles, good weather and bad weather. Take personal shots that remember the 'being there'—friends that you meet, your hotel/campsite, transportation, street or hiking signposts.

7. Add Depth

Depth is an important quality of good photographs. We want the viewer to think that they're not looking at a flat picture, but through a window, into a three-dimensional world. Add pointers to assist the eye. If your subject is a distant mountain, add a person or a tree in the foreground. A wide angle lens can exaggerate this perspective.

8. Use Proportion

The beauty of an image is often in it's proportions. A popular technique with artists is called the 'rule of thirds' or the 'golden mean.' Imagine the frame divided into thirds, both horizontally and vertically, like a Tic-Tac-Toe board. Now place your subject on one of the lines or intersections.

9. Search For Details

It's always tempting to use a wide angle lens and 'get everything in.' However this can be too much and you may loose the impact. Instead zoom in with a longer lens and find some representative detail. A shot of an entire Sequoia tree just looks like a tree. But a shot of just the wide base, with a person for scale, is more powerful.

10. Position The Horizon

Where you place the horizon in your shot affects what is emphasized. To show the land, use a high horizon. To show the sky, use a low horizon. Be creative.

Advanced Tips

"Emphasis on technique is justified only so far as it will simplify and clarify the statement of the photographer's concept."
—Ansel Adams

Simple Clean Layout

A good shot focuses your attention on the subject by using a sparse background and a simple but interesting composition. Always remove clutter from the picture—this is a real skill. Like a musician, it's always difficult to make things look easy. Zoom in, get close, get to eye level, find a simple backdrop, look for balance.

Bold Solid Colors

'Stock-quality' images make great use of color. Look for solid primary colors: bright 'sports-car' red, emerald green, lightning yellow, and ocean blue. Use a polarizer to bring out the colors. Avoid patterns—keep it simple. Bright afternoon sunlight will add warmth. Alternatively, look for 'color harmony'—scenes restricted to similar tones and colors, or even a single color. This presents a calm, restful image where the eye plays with the differing shades and intensities. Look for pastels, cream, or delicate shades.

1. Use a Narrow Tonal Range

Photographic film can't handle a wide tonal range. When you photograph very bright things and very dark things together—sunlight in water and shadows in trees—the film will lose all the detail and you'll end up with stark, overexposed white and total underexposed black. Instead, look for mid-tones with little difference between the brightest and darkest highlights. Flowers, trees and people are often best photographed on overcast days as the dispersed light fills in shadows.

Your eye can handle a difference in brightness (a 'dynamic range') of about 2,000:1 (11 camera 'stops'). Print film is limited to no more than 64:1 (5 stops) and slide film is even worse, at 8:1 (3 stops). Ansel Adams' 'Zone System' divided light levels into 11 'zones' and advised using a narrow zone (or tonal) range.

2. Work The Subject, Baby!

As film directors say, film is cheap (although it's not always their money!). Work the subject and take different shots from different angles. The more you take, the more likely you are to get a good one. Don't be afraid to take five shots and throw four away. Find different, unusual viewpoints. Shoot from high and from low. It's often said that the only difference between a professional photographer and an amateur photographer is that the professional throws more shots away. I use about 4 shots from each roll of 36. *National Geographic* magazine uses only 1 out of every 1,000 shots taken.

3. Hyperfocal

A popular 'pro' technique is capture great depth by combining a close foreground and deep background. Use a wide angle lens (20-28mm), get a few inches from the foreground (often flowers), put the horizon high in the frame. Using a small aperture (f22) keeps everything in focus ('hyperfocal'). Use a hyperfocal chart to correspond distance with aperture, or just use the smallest aperture (highest f-number) possible.

Dramatic Lighting

Photographs that win competitions are often ones that make interesting use of light. Look out for beams of light shining through clouds, trees or windows, long shadows, and the effect of side- and backlighting. Shoot in the warm golden 'magic hours' of early morning and late afternoon.

Preparation

A great shot takes time. Scout out the area, make mental notes of important features, unusual and interesting angles, and changing crowd levels. Take time to prepare the shot. Get there before the best time of day, clean your lenses, set up a tripod or mini-tripod, add a cable release, try out different filters, wait for a good foreground, and talk with people who may be in the shot so that they're comfortable and will pose well.

"Chance favors the prepared mind."
—Louis Pasteur.

4. Expose For Highlights

When a scene has a mixture of very bright and very dark areas, the light meter in your camera will have difficulty finding the right exposure. In such high-contrast shots, try to expose for the highlights. To do this, walk up to, zoom in to, or spot meter on the most important bright area (a face, the sky, some architectural detail) and half-depress the shutter release button to hold the exposure (exposure lock). Then recompose and take the shot. To be on the safe side, take several 'bracketed' shots (see below).

5. Under- (over-) Expose for Deeper Colors
SLR only

On slide film, a slightly underexposed image (on print film, a slightly overexposed image) can give deeper, more saturated colors. The deeper color also makes the subject appear heavier. To underexpose on a manual SLR camera, select the next shutter speed up (for example 1/250 when 1/125 is recommended by the meter). On an automatic camera, set the exposure compensation dial to -1/2 or -1. Similarly, you can underexpose for paler, lighter images.

The effect is dependent upon your camera and film so try some test runs to find the best combination. On my camera—a Minolta X-700 with Fuji Velvia film—the recommended exposure works best and underexposure just loses detail.

6. Bracketing   *SLR only*

When in doubt about the correct exposure, take several 'bracketed' shots. You 'bracket' around a shot by taking one regular shot, then a second shot slightly darker (-1 stop) and a third shot slightly lighter (+1 stop). Slide film is more sensitive than print film and you can detect exposure differences down to a third of a stop. Professionals therefore often bracket at +/- 1/2 stop. Some cameras offer bracketing as an automatic feature.

Photographing People

There are **several factors** to consider when photographing people:

Location

The first thing to do is find your location. Choose a spot with a simple, medium-toned background. Tree foliage, grass or the ocean works well. For dark skin, look for a similarly dark background to keep the highlight (and thus the camera's exposure) on the face.

Minimize patterns, shapes and colors. Keep the background simple, or include a famous landmark for 'location.'

Lighting

Get the sun behind you and to one side. If it's bright, put people in the shade (harsh, direct sunlight washes out the face). Use the fill-flash feature to brighten up the face.

The best time is the late afternoon as it gives a nice, warm, golden glow. At other times you can simulate this glow with an 81B or C filter.

A 'pro' technique is to put the sun behind your subject, so that the sun shines through their hair. This shows the outline of the head and draws the face out of the background. Use a strong fill-flash to lighten up the face. A good light meter is useful to get the correct exposure. Bring a small reflector or white card to reflect sunlight into the harsh shadow areas.

If you're shooting indoors with an SLR, 'bounce' the flash off a light-colored wall or ceiling for more natural lighting.

Lens

If you have an SLR, use a 135mm or similar lens for the most pleasing perspective. Use the widest aperture (e.g. f4.5) to blur the background and highlight the face for a movie-like look. If the background is important, use a small aperture (e.g. f22) to get everything in focus.

Positioning

Get close. Don't include the full body but zoom straight in to the face. For close ups, crop out the top of the head and overfill the frame. Being at eye level usually works best so, for children, kneel down.

Proportion

Generally try to keep the eyes—not necessarily the head—in the center of the frame. If the person is looking slightly to one side, add extra space in the frame to that side for balance.

If your subject is to one side, your camera may misread the exposure and/or focusing. Take a 'spot' reading off the face by filling the frame with the face and pressing the 'exposure lock' or 'focus lock' button. Keep this button pressed down while you recompose and take the shot.

Relax Your Subject

Get your subject relaxed and happy. For friends or family, remind them of a silly event. With children, give them something to play with. For local people, ask them about the location, their job or skill, or complement their clothes. People hate waiting while you adjust your camera so always plan the shot and adjust your camera first, before asking people to pose.

Don't Forget You!

The problem with being the photographer is that you end up not being in your own photographs! Remind the viewer what you look like and ask someone else to take a shot. You can arrange a photograph by propping the camera on a small tripod or wall (use stones, paper or coins for adjustment) and using the self timer.

Fun Shots

To add fun and action to a shot, hold the camera at an angle such as 30 degrees with the right side up. It looks as though the photographer was caught off guard, emphasizing danger and action, and is great for parties.

Stage a joke shot by pretending to interact with a statue, or use a wide-angle lens to distort the face.

Action

If your subject is moving, deliberately blur the background to emphasize speed, excitement and urgency. Track the subject with your camera and use a medium or slow shutter speed (1/60s). This will blur the background and, optionally, also your subject. Using the flash (particularly a 'rear-curtain sync' feature, if your camera has one) helps freeze the subject in a moving background.

Equipment

Compact Cameras

A 'compact' or 'point-and-shoot' automatic camera makes life very easy as it's small and simple to operate. They're even preferable over more expensive 'SLR' cameras in some circumstances, such as when you need something less noticeable and intimidating (for photographing people) or something small and light (when walking around town or hiking).

Some models have one fixed lens (usually a 30mm wide angle) which is the lens you'd use most on a more expensive camera. Other models also offer a second, telephoto lens, or a single zoom lens to help you capture details and make good portraits of people.

Look for a model that feels good in your hands and that you can understand how to operate. I like a very wide angle lens (28mm) to capture buildings and make big, punchy shots. A 'fill-flash' feature is very useful to brighten people's faces. Other useful features include lockable autofocus (to focus on subjects which aren't in the center of the frame), a self-timer, and a panoramic mode.

1. Lenses

Most people start with a medium zoom lens, such as 35-80mm or 80–135mm, then a telephoto 100–210mm. The lens I use the most is a 24–35mm as you can do so much with it. Many professionals like a 20mm lens. The exaggerated perspective adds great punch and depth to their shots.

A popular 'long' lens is 80–210mm. I prefer a 100–300mm telephoto as that extra 90mm seems to go a long way. You can use a 2x convertor to double the length but there are drawbacks. The convertor adds one or two precious f-stops resulting in a slower shutter speed, and decreases the optical quality by 10-20%. With such a long focal length you'll need a tripod.

2. Cases, Caps and Straps

Lenses are fragile and expensive so protect them with front and rear lens caps. Adding a UV or Skylight filter to each lens serves as extra protection. If you're like me and prone to dropping things, it's cheaper to replace a damaged filter than a broken lens.

A strap can be useful for carrying the camera. It keeps your hands free while keeping the camera primed for action. A nice wide strap spreads the load. Personally, however, I prefer not to use a strap as it just gets in the way. Instead I carry the camera in a padded case.

Choose a camera case that carries all your kit and is well padded. Adjustable compartments and pockets are useful. Shoulder bags are popular but carrying the weight on one side all day can get uncomfortable. I prefer a backpack as it frees up both hands and makes it easier to travel.

Many professionals prefer a bag that also fits around the waist. This way, they have ready access to a range of lenses.

3. Filters

Your choice of filters, as with everything else, is one of personal preference. The most useful filter, and the

SLR Cameras

The 35mm camera of choice for experienced photographers is the SLR—Single-Lens Reflex. This type of camera contains an angled mirror and prism to show you exactly the scene viewed by the lens. This is a benefit over the simple point-and-shoot camera (which has a separate viewfinder lens) as it allows you to better monitor the image.

The greatest benefits of using an SLR camera is your ability to change lenses according to the situation, and to have manual control over focus, aperture and shutter-speeds. SLRs are typically more cumbersome, expensive, and technically demanding than a compact camera, but you are rewarded with increased flexibility and control.

Look for a model that feels comfortable and that you understand how to operate. I like a built-in flash, auto-focus capability, and aperture-priority mode (where you set the aperture and the camera determines the corresponding shutter speed). A light-weight design is valuable when you're traveling.

only one you ought to have, is a 'polarizer.' Rotating this filter gives deep blue skies and strengthens colors by removing glare and reflections. Many of the shots in this book benefit from a polarizer.

In general, don't use a filter unless you require a specific effect.

4. Extra Film

Always carry extra film as you never know when something interesting may happen. I like to carry 2-5 spare rolls. Consider carrying a fast film (400 ISO) for interiors and night shots, and a good slide film in case you find something suitable to win a competition! Use a sealable 'zip-lock' bag for storage.

5. Camera Care

Dirty lenses or filters produce low-contrast images and washed-out colors. Keep things clean with a soft lint-free cloth, special dust-free tissues, lens-cleaning fluid and a blower brush. A pair of tweezers is useful if sand or dirt gets lodged inside the camera. A small screwdriver can tighten up any screws that come loose, particularly on long lenses which don't like the vibrations of traveling.

6. Flash

A flash is useful for brightening people's faces on overcast days, and for indoor shots. Many cameras today include a built-in flash which is suitable for most purposes. If you're keen on interiors, consider a hand-held flash to brighten dark areas while the shutter remains open. Remember that many museums prohibit flash units as they can damage the exhibits.

7. Second Camera

If you have one, also take a compact or a disposable camera. This is great for fun shots in restaurants and quick snaps of unsuspecting friends in embarrassing situations. Many professionals carry a second SLR in case one jams or they're shooting with two different films. But that's a little extreme.

Filters

Color Polarizer: Adds blue or yellow to areas (Cokin #173 Blue/Yellow).

Color Enhancer: Enhances reds, but leaves a cold blue/violet cast and is expensive.

Color Correcting: Enhances particular colors—green is good to enhance foliage. For example, a CC20G adds 20% green by reducing other colors by 80%.

FL-D: Used for dusk shots to color balance the green fluorescent light from office buildings. Adds a pink tint.

Single Color: Add an overall blue, orange or sepia, etc. cast to your shot.

81A, 81B or 81C: Simulates late afternoon light by adding an orange/brown cast. 'A' is light, 'B' medium, and 'C' strong.

Haze 1 or Skylight 1A: Can reduce haze at high altitude. Skylight 1A adds a slight pink 'warming' cast. Often used just to protect lens.

Neutral Density and Split-Field Neutral Density: Reduces the brightness of a scene, for better control of aperture. A Split-Field Neutral Density reduces a bright neutral density sky to match a shaded foreground.

Red or Yellow: Increases tonal contrast in black and white photographs.

8. Tripods

A full-size tripod is essential for steady, top-quality shots, but is too cumbersome for most travelers. Instead carry a mono pod, or a mini-tripod—coupled with a wall or table, they're almost as good.

If you have a tripod, you'll also need a cable release to avoid camera movement when you take the shot. Alternatively use the self-timer feature.

A carrying strap is very useful for hiking between views.

9. Notepad and Pen

A notepad and pen is useful for remembering good locations, details about your subjects, and addresses of people you meet. If you're considering submitting shots for competitions, you'll need to note your camera settings.

10. Batteries

It's easy to avoid buying spare batteries but there's nothing more infuriating than getting somewhere fabulous and finding out that your camera won't power up. As Gary Larsen (almost) said, just when you find the Loch Ness Monster, Bigfoot, and Elvis, all sitting together, your batteries die.

The Magic Hours

How To Get Deep Colors

1. Use a polarizer filter
2. Shoot in the late afternoon
3. Use 'saturated' slide film
4. Use a narrow tonal range
5. Keep your lenses clean
6. Underexpose slightly (for slide film, overexpose print film)

Bad Weather

Bad weather doesn't mean bad photographs, it just changes your options. Overcast skies reduce contrast and are preferred for shots of trees and foliage. Colors may appear cool and blueish so add an 81A, B, or C filter to warm up the image. If the sky is boring, disguise it with an overhanging tree, or exclude it completely by raising the horizon in your frame. When low clouds or rain reduce color saturation, try black and white film to emphasize the range of gray tones. You may need a faster film since there's less light. Storms and heavy rain add drama and power to an image. Dusk shots are improved with reflections of neon lights in puddles. Clouds create moving patterns of interesting highlights, particularly when a storm is clearing.

The most important element to many great photographs is the lighting. Warmth, depth, texture, form, contrast and color are all dramatically affected by the angle of the sunlight, and thus the time of day. Shooting at the optimum time is often the biggest difference between an 'amateur' and a 'professional' shot.

In the early morning and late afternoon, when the sun is low, the light is gold and orange, giving your shot the warmth of a log fire. Professional photographers call these the 'magic hours' and most movies and magazine shots are made during this brief time. It takes extra planning, but saving your photography for one hour after sunrise, or one to two hours before sunset, will add stunning warmth to your shots.

Plan Your Day

Assuming a sunrise at 6 a.m. and sunset at 7 p.m., and that your spouse/kids/friends suddenly give you the reverence and servility you so obviously deserve, a good day might be:

5am: Pre-dawn: A pink, ethereal light and dreamy mist for lakes, rivers and landscapes.

6–7am: Dawn: Crisp, golden light for east-facing subjects.

7am–10am: Early morning: The city comes to life.

10–2pm: Midday: The sun is too harsh for landscapes and people, but perfect for monuments, buildings and streets with tall buildings.

2pm–4pm: Afternoon: Deep blue skies with a polarizer.

4pm–6:45pm: Late Afternoon: Terrific warm, golden light on west-facing subjects. Best time for landscapes and people, particularly one hour before sunset.

6:45 – 7:30pm: Sunset: Great skies 10–30 minutes before and 10–30 minutes after sunset.

7 – 7:45pm: Dusk is great for skylines, while there's still a purple color to the sky.

9pm: Go to bed—you've got to be up early tomorrow!

Film

There's a surprisingly large range of film available. For 35mm alone there are over 120 films. Generally, a good medium speed print film is recommended.

Size

The easiest decision you have is format, as your camera will only accept one size. The most common format is 35mm. This number represents the width of the film (actually 36mm x24mm—a 3:2 aspect ratio). 35mm film gives excellent results and can be enlarged to about 20"x30" before the resolution, or 'grain,' becomes too noticeable.

APS film ('Advanced Photo System,' called *Advantix* by Kodak) is a competitor to 35mm film. The film is smaller (at 24mm—70% the size of 35mm) but yields pictures almost as good as 35mm. APS cameras are generally smaller and lighter than 35mm cameras, and offer additional features such as easier film loading, selectable print formats, and data encoding. However, printing is currently more expensive and few labs do one-hour developing.

Larger formats are available if you wish to produce higher quality and more detailed images. The cameras are so large and heavy that most professional travel photographers stay with 35mm.

Slide vs. Print

Should I use slide or print film? The quick answer is: Use print film, unless you have a specific reason otherwise (such as competitions or magazine/book printing).

Print film (also called 'negative' film as it records the inverse, complementary colors) is the most popular choice. The resulting prints are easier to store, view and show to people. They are also cheaper to enlarge, and the film is more forgiving (less picky about it's exposure). Over 90% of the film sold worldwide is for color prints.

If you're looking for the best quality enlargements however (for use in a magazine, to hang on a wall, or to submit in competitions), go for slide film as it captures greater detail, and deeper, truer colors (it's more 'saturated'). All the shots in this book for example were taken on Fuji Velvia (ISO 50) slide film, famous for it's rich blacks, deep blues and vibrant greens. Kodak Ektachrome E100S and E100SW are also popular saturated slide films. Note that slide film is much more picky about exposure (it has less 'latitude') than the more forgiving print film, so correct exposure and the use of a narrow tonal range is more important.

X-Rays

You may be wary of X-ray machines. Depending upon their strength and duration, X-rays can cause fogging on camera film. Generally you're OK with carry-on scanners but don't put your film in your main checked luggage.

The new CTX5000 machines, used to scan checked luggage, does damage film so don't place film in baggage. Carry-on (hand-luggage) scanners are less powerful and do not noticeably damage standard camera film. To rest peacefully, put your films in a clear plastic bag and drop them in the hand inspection bucket with your wallet or purse.

Storage

Always keep film out of direct sunlight and heat, and preferably in a moisture-resistant bag in a refrigerator. Popular bags are Slide-Loc™ from Ziploc® and OneZip™ from Hefty®.

Black and White

With its emphasis on tonal contrast, this powerful medium can evoke mood and atmosphere, and has a loyal group of supporters. Black and white film is far easier than color to develop and a lot of the appeal is in manipulating the image in a home darkroom, through selective exposure and choice of paper. Much of Ansel Adams' artistry was in the darkroom developing his prints, rather than in the field taking the shots.

Speed

The 'speed' of a film (100, 200, 400, etc) represents how quickly the film reacts to light. 200 is the most popular. If your pictures come out blurry (you're prone to camera shake), use a 'faster' film such as 400 or 800. Most disposable cameras contain 800 or 1000 film for this reason. If you're looking for quality (entering a competition or enlarging photos), use 100, 64, 50, 32 or even 25 film as the 'grain' or resolution is finer. Pros generally use slow film. Slow films however can end up costing you more as, due to the longer exposure, you're more likely to need a lot of sunlight, faster lenses (ones with low f-numbers - they're expensive), and a tripod. With normal 6" x 4" prints you won't notice any grain improvement with films slower than 100.

Generally 'slow' film (100) is suggested for bright days and 'fast' film (400, 800) for overcast days.

Getting Technical

The F-Stops Here

Acamera is your media, so the better you understand the media, the better your pictures are likely to be. The two most useful controls are:

1. Focal Length (the zoom of your lens), which affects how much of the view is included in the shot, and;

2. Depth-of-Field (the f-stop of your lens), which affects how much of the foreground and background is in focus.

To use these techniques effectively, you need to understand lenses and exposure.

Lenses

The first thing to play with on most cameras is the lens. A long lens (say 210mm), allows you to zoom in to your subject, to get close to it. A short lens (say 35mm), is often called a wide-angle lens because it allows you to zoom out and get a wider view.

Select a lens based on what you want included in the shot, and how you want to portray depth. A short lens exaggerates depth, combining a close foreground with a deep background. Use a short lens for impact. A long lens contracts the image, giving it narrow depth. This is useful to create a flat image, or to emphasize the scale of your background relative to your foreground.

Film

Camera film is a strip of material coated with chemicals. When exposed to light (*photos-* in Greek), the chemicals react and produce a defined image (*-graph*). Unlike our eyes which can see under a variety of conditions, film chemicals are acutely particular about how much light they react to—the exposure. Too much light—overexposed—and the image will be pale and washed out; too little light—underexposed—and the image will be dark and indistinct.

Due to the film sensitivity, the correct exposure is vital. Your camera has controls to obtain the correct exposure.

Exposure—The Four Factors

A camera is essentially a box with a hole in it. The correct exposure is determined by four factors:

1. How large the hole is (the aperture);
2. How long it stays open for (the shutter speed);
3. How quickly the film reacts (the film speed), and;
4. How much light is reflected off the subject (the light level).

Fortunately, most cameras are automatic and will make all these decisions for you. However, higher-end cameras allow you to intervene to create particular effects. It's useful to understand how these four factors interact so that you can use them to your creative advantage.

Let's review each factor in turn (in order of usefulness) and see how it can improve your photography.

1. Aperture

Inside the lens is an adjustable device, the diaphragm, which alters the size of the opening—the 'aperture.' Changing the aperture is useful as it has a handy side-effect. A very small aperture makes everything (background and foreground) in focus. A large aperture makes only the subject you're focused on in focus. Try squinting your eyes (everything is in focus) and then opening them wide (some things are blurry).

This zone of acceptably sharp focus extends both in front of, and behind of, the point of focus. It's called the 'depth-of-field.' With landscapes, we usually want a wide depth-of-field to get both the background (hills or mountains) and the foreground (a flower or people) in focus. With portraits, we want to emphasize the foreground (a person's face) so we make the background blurry by using a narrow depth-of-field.

How can you tell how much of the image is going to be in focus? The depth-of-field is affected by three things: the size of the aperture; the focal length of the lens; and the distance to the subject you're focused on (the focal distance). To make things easier, the first two items are combined to give us a field number, or 'f-number.' The depth-of-field is set by the f-number. The bigger the f-number (say f11 or f22), the bigger the depth-of-field (i.e. the wider the zone of focus).

2. Shutter Speed

Inside the camera is a mechanism—a shutter—which controls how long light is allowed to act on the film. When you take a photograph (by pressing the shutter release), the shutter opens and then closes a fraction of a second later. How quickly this is done is called the 'shutter speed' and is measured in seconds (shortened to 's'). A fast shutter speed (say 1/500th of a second) is good for action shots as it freezes movement. A slow shutter speed (say 1/60s) blurs moving objects, which is useful when you want to emphasize movement and speed.

Most of the time, you select a shutter speed based on your lens size. This is because when you hold a camera, you introduce unwanted movement, called 'camera shake,' and how much shake is noticeable on the photograph depends upon how much you are zoomed in.

A good rule of thumb says that you're safe with a shutter speed equal to, or faster than, the length of your lens. For example, with a wide lens of 35mm, you're fine with a shutter speed of 1/60s. But when zoomed in to 210mm, you need a faster shutter speed of 1/250s.

3. Light level

In outdoor photography, the amount of light is usually set by mother nature. Generally, the brighter a view is, the better the photograph.

If someone is in the shade, you can add light to their face by using a flash unit. This is called 'fill-flash' because it fills in some light. You can do the same thing with a reflective surface, such as white card or a purpose-made reflector.

If a sky is too bright, you can reduce the amount of light with a filter (such as a gradiented neutral-density filter).

So What is an "F-Stop"?

In photography, a "stop" is a unit of measurement. It is a halving of one of the four four factors which affect exposure. By using a term common to all four factors we can better juggle the camera controls necessary for a correct exposure.

The term "stop" comes from the aperture ring on a lens. As you turn the ring you reduce the aperture (the diameter of the lens). The ring is notched so that you can stop turning each time the aperture is halved. Since aperture is measured in f-numbers, each halving is one "f-stop."

The term is useful when you consider the other factors of exposure. Changing from f8 to f16—going "down a stop"— halves the aperture. To maintain the same exposure you need to double the shutter-speed—going "up a stop" say from 1/500s to 1/250s. Alternatively, a studio photographer could double the amount of light ("up a stop") or use a film which was twice as fast, say ISO 200 instead of ISO 100 (also "up a stop").

4. Film Speed

How quickly the film's chemicals react to the light is known as the 'film speed.' A rating system was developed by the International Standards Organization (ISO) so that a film rated 200 ISO is a 'faster' film (i.e. it reacts twice as quickly) than a 100 ISO film. (You may have also heard of ASA or DIN—these were two other standards which were replaced by the ISO.)

There is a trade-off between speed and resolution, or 'grain.' Generally it is preferable to use a slower film (say 100 ISO) as it gives a sharper image (a finer grain). But when there isn't enough light (indoors or at night), you'll need a faster film (say 400 or 1600 ISO) and will have to suffer its less-distinct image (coarser grain).

Combining the Four Factors

To get the optimum exposure, you must consider all four factors—aperture, shutter speed, light level, and film speed. Remember that these four factors are all interrelated—when you set one, you must juggle the others to get the right exposure.

For example, say you're shooting a landscape with a 100mm lens set to f5.6. When you activate the light meter in your camera, based on the light level and the film speed, it recommends a shutter speed of 1/125s. So your four factors are: f5.6, 1/125s, a fixed light level, and your film speed.

Now lets say that you want both the background and the foreground elements to be in focus. To get a wider depth-of-field you need a larger f-number. The next f-number from f5.6 is f8 (up a "stop"). This halves the aperture so, to compensate, you need to double the shutter-speed, from 1/125s to 1/60s (down a stop). You have successfully juggled your factors.

Summary

You can take more creative photographs when you understand how aperture, shutter speed, light levels and film speed affect both focusing and exposure.

Making a Journal

Keeping A Journal

Decide beforehand how you're going to organize the journal (usually by date) and stock up with enough books or paper to last the trip. Try to write something each day, particularly funny stories and irreverent remarks people made. Include the date and location. Ask your companions to contribute notes every now and then.

Don't Forget The Fun

Many of the fun times occur between sights so capture these with 'ordinary' shots—in a car, waiting at a bus stop or train station, in the hotel room, eating at a restaurant, and with the people you meet. Tell a story with your photography and create a visual variety of views, people shots, and fun stuff.

Planning Your Trip

Before you leave home, decide where you want to visit. Review this book, other guide books, magazines, tourist information literature, brochures, and other ground information and find out what you can't miss. Then draw up a preliminary itinerary.

Test your camera and polish your skills by setting yourself some practice assignments. Use the preceding tips section for techniques to work on. Try different lenses (you can borrow from friends or rent from a good camera store) to find out which ones you need. Try out different film types to determine which best suits your style and budget. Then stock up on rolls of film—twice the amount you think you'll use.

While You're Traveling

Start with the end in mind. Always think how your photos will look when you show them to your friends. You'll be narrating a story at the time so take shots for 'chapter headings,' ones designed to introduce locations and sections. Look out for signs of place names and directions.

Collect memorabilia of the trip. Tickets stubs, timetables, postcards, restaurant receipts, napkins with logos, and hotel brochures. You can use these later to liven up your album or journal. Make notes of your travels and sketch a map showing your route. If you might enter some of your shots in photography competitions, keep a note of the camera settings you use (f-stop, shutter speed, film type and lens size).

When You Get Home

After you've recovered from the trip, put your films in for developing (don't leave them for months as the quality will slowly degrade). Ask for a second set of prints if you want to send copies to other people.

Assign a free evening and edit your shots. Don't be afraid to throw the weak ones out—the more you edit, the higher the average quality will be.

Enlargements

A great way to remember your trip, and to let people admire your photographic skills, is to get enlargements made of the best shots. They come in standard sizes (5x7, 8x10, 11x14). A good tip for some revisionist improvements is to enlarge your shot to one size larger, then crop the print down (use a sharp knife and a metal edge) for an even tighter shot. Or ask your local film processor if they can crop it for you at the development stage. It takes extra time, cost and effort but enlargements are the most admired result of your skill and art.

Newsletters

Use your shots to illustrate a newsletter of your trip to your friends and family. Cut up spare prints, stick them on paper and make photocopies (black and white, or color). Alternatively get them scanned into a computer and use a word processor or page layout program for a professional presentation. You could also make your own posters, key rings, refrigerator magnets, note cards and seasonal cards.

Storage

Keep negatives in the sleeves they came in, or transfer them to special acid-free paper sleeves in a ring binder. Store photos, negatives and slides in a cool, dry place, and don't subject them to pressure with heavy items on top of them. If you're going to send slides away for competitions or magazines, make duplicate copies first so that you keep the original.

Making An Album

Buy a good quality album, with refillable pages and thick paper. You'll need to know your print size (usually 4 inches x 6 inches).

As you install the prints, consider each spread as a single story or subject. Paste in postcards, brochures and other memorabilia to highlight the story. Don't be afraid to crop some photographs by cutting out unnecessary elements, or trimming around a figure.

The Digital Domain

There are an increasing number of options to use your photographs with computer applications. Generally you'll need to scan in the shots. You can buy a scanner or use a service bureau to scan prints. For top quality, get the negatives or slides scanned into Photo CD format. Use an image editing program, such as Adobe Photoshop, to sharpen the scan and save it to the correct format.

There are several file formats to consider. World Wide Web (Internet) pages use JPEG (best), PING and and CompuServe GIF formats. For four-color printing in books, magazines or flyers, use TIFF or EPS formats. All the pictures in this book were saved as EPS files.

Slide Presentations

There's not a more fun re-union of travel companions than a slide show. The golden rule is to keep it short—less than one hour or else people will drift off. Tightly edit your shots to the best ones (resist showing everything) and arrange them to tell a narrative story. Test out the projector and the focus before the show, and keep the pace moving along. Get in the drinks and food and make an evening out of it, remembering the escapades.

Photography Law

By Dianne Brinson

Dianne Brinson, a copyright attorney, received her law degree from Yale Law School and her B.A. from Duke University. A former law professor, Dianne currently teaches Law for Internet Users at San Jose State University's Professional Development Center.

For more information, read the book Multimedia Law and Business Handbook, by J. Dianne Brinson and Mark F. Radcliffe (available from Ladera Press for $44.95 plus shipping (telephone: 800-523-3721).

If you're **photographing** for anything more than personal snapshots (e.g. for publishing in a magazine, on the Internet, or to sell as stock photography), you need to be aware of photography law. You may need permission for the following: Photographing buildings, works of art, or other copyrighted items; photographing people; photographing on public or private property. In this short article, attorney Dianne Brinson briefly discusses when permission may be required.

Copyright

Under current U.S. law, copyright protection arises automatically when an "original work of authorship" is "fixed in a tangible medium of expression." A work is "original" in the copyright sense if it owes its origin to the author. For example, a photograph of San Diego's skyline is original so long as it was created by the photographer, even if it's the zillionth photo to be taken of that scene. Only minimal creativity is required to meet the originality requirement, no artistic merit or beauty is required.

Works of art—sculptures, paintings, and even toys—are protectable by copyright. Furthermore, buildings created on or after December 1, 1990 are protected by copyright. A copyright owner has the exclusive right to reproduce a copyrighted work, and photographing a copyrighted work is considered a way of reproducing it. Thus, you may need permission to photograph a building or an art work.

Here are some guidelines:

Buildings

Only buildings created after December 1, 1990 are protected by copyright. Fortunately for photographers, the copyright in an architectural work does not include the right to prevent others from making and distributing photos of the constructed building, if the building is located in a public place or is visible from a public place. So you don't need permission to stand on a public street and photograph a public building. You don't need permission to photograph a public building from inside the building (although you may need permission to photograph separately-owned decorative objects in the building, such as a statue). You don't need permission to stand on a public street and photograph a private building such as a church or a house.

This "photographer's exception" to the copyright-owner's rights applies only to buildings, a category which includes houses, office buildings, churches, gazebos, and garden pavilions. The exception does not apply to monuments (protectable as "sculptural works") or other copyrighted works, such as statues and paintings.

Art

You may need permission to photograph a copyrighted work of art, for example, a statue in a public park, or a painting in a private collection or art museum. Getting permission can be tricky, because, according to copyright law, you need permission from the copyright owner, not from the owner of the work of art itself. In copyright law, ownership of the copyright in a work is distinct from ownership of the work (the tangible item).

For example, suppose that you are taking photographs of a painting in an art collector's private home collection. The art collector probably does not own the copyright in the painting, the artist does. Unless your photograph of the painting is "fair use" (discussed later) you need permission from the artist.

When You Don't Need Permission

You don't need permission to photograph a work that is not protected by copyright (in "the public domain"). Works fall into the public domain for several reasons, one of which is expiration of the copyright term. In 1998, works created before January 1, 1923 are in the public domain. Also, works created by federal government officers and employees as part of their official duties are not protected by copyright. (This rule does not apply to works created by state or local government officers and employees).

You don't need permission to use a copyrighted work in two circumstances: (1) if you are only copying facts or ideas from the work; or (2) if your use is "fair use."

You are free to copy facts or ideas from a protected work. The copyright on a work does not extend to the work's facts. This is because copyright protection is limited to original works of authorship, and no one can claim originality or authorship for facts. Anyone can use ideas.

Fair Use

It may be that your photograph is "fair use" of the art works you photograph. If so, you don't need permission. Whether a use of a copyrighted work is fair use is decided on a case-by-case basis by considering the purpose and character of the use, the nature of the copyrighted work, the amount and substantiality of the portion used, and the effect on the potential market for, or value of, the protected work.

There is no simple rule to determine when an unauthorized use is "fair use." You are more likely to be able to rely on fair use if your work serves a traditional fair use purpose (educational, research, news reporting, criticism, or public interest). Fair use is always subject to interpretation.

Publicity and Privacy Rights of individuals

You may need permission to photograph people due to state laws giving individuals privacy and publicity rights.

Most states in the U.S. recognize that individuals have a right of privacy. The right of privacy gives an individual a legal claim against someone who intrudes on the individual's physical solitude or seclusion, and against those who publicly disclose private facts. Unless you have permission, avoid publishing or distributing any photo of an individual that reveals private facts

Permits

If you are going to shoot commercial photographs on public property, you may need to get a permit from the appropriate government authority (usually a local or state film commission). Permission is generally not required for taking the usual "tourist type" photos (although you should obey any "no entry" signs you see).

If you are going to shoot on private property, get permission to enter and use the location for shooting and to show the premises in your work, in order to avoid trespass and invasion of privacy claims by the property owner.

about the individual (particularly if revealing those private facts might embarrass the individual).

Almost half the states in the U.S. recognize that individuals have a right of publicity. The right of publicity gives an individual a legal claim against one who uses the individual's name, face, image, or voice for commercial benefit without obtaining permission. In case you are wondering how the news media handle this, newspapers and news magazines have a "fair use" privilege to publish names or images in connection with reporting a newsworthy event.

Be particularly careful about celebrities. Using a photograph of a celebrity for your own commercial gain—for example, posting a photo you took of Clint Eastwood on your business's marketing material or web site—is asking for a lawsuit, even if you took the photograph when you ran into Clint on a public street.

Commercial photographers avoid right of publicity/privacy lawsuits by obtaining photographic releases from people shown in their shots. If you are considering selling your photos or using them on your web site, you may want to do the same. The Multimedia Law and Business Handbook contains a sample release. Experienced performers and models are accustomed to signing these releases.

The Internet

The laws and rules described in this article apply to photos used on the Internet. Copyright law and other laws do apply to the Internet, and posting a photo on the Internet exposes your photos to the eyes of the whole world.

Camera Stores

Camera Stores

Nelson Photo Supplies   619-234-6621
  1909 India, Little Italy.
  Nearest store to downtown.

George's Camera   619-297-3544
  3837 30th Street.
  Northeast of Balboa Park.

Bob Davis Camera   858-459-7355
  7720 Fay Ave, La Jolla

Point Loma Camera   619-224-2719
  1310 Rosecrans, nr Shelter Island

Camera Mart   619-283-7321
  3311 Adams Ave, North Park

3-D Discount Photo   619-449-9991
  9745 Mission Gorge Rd. Off I-8.

Camera Repair

Kurt's Camera Repair   619-286-1810
  7811 Mission Gorge Road

Professional Photo   858-277-3700
  7910 Raytheon Rd, Kearny Mesa

Nolan's Camera Clinic 858-581-3777
  4454 Ingraham, Pacific Beach

Professional Developing (E6)

Chrome (2 stores)   619-233-3456
  2345 Kettner, Little Italy
  6150 Lusk Blvd, Sorrento Valley

Chromacolor   619-232-9900
  1953 India Street, Little Italy

Masters Developing   858-558-4546
  9833 Pacific Height Blvd

Film Express   619-574-1875
  1268 University Ave, Hillcrest

Point Loma Camera   619-224-2719
  1310 Rosecrans, nr Shelter Island

Color Craft   619-234-4668
  636 7th Ave downtown

Photo Express   619-296-3385
  3572 Hancock Street, Point Loma

Ruff's Fast Foto   858-552-0072
  10920 Roselle St., Sorrento Valley

Pacific Coast Photo   858-454-9137
  5661 La Jolla Blvd, Birdrock

Professional Enlargements

Award Photo Imaging   858-549-3900
  7686 Miramar Road, Mira Mesa

Digital n Beyond   858-565-0556
  4820 Mercury Street

Mesa Photo X   858-271-1950
  9530 Padgett Street

Photographix   858-693-1892
  9889 Hibert Street

Photodyne   858-292-0140
  7012 Convoy Court

Museums

MoPA   619-238-7559
  Museum of Photographic Arts
  1649 El Prado, Balboa Park

Publications

"California Photographer" newsletter.
Tel: 760-324-7499   www.calphoto.com

Camera Clubs

Escondido Camera Club 760-749-1421
Joslyn Senior Center, Escondido

Fallbrook Camera Club 760-728-0654
Silvergate Retirement Residence

Rancho Bernado C.C. 760-749-1421
3rd floor, Pomerado Hospital

Sierra Club Photo Sect. 619-299-1744
Tierrasanta Rec. Center ext 2070

Underwater Photo Soc. 858-566-6170
Scripps Instit'n of Oceanography

Vista Camera Club 760-438-3170
Green Valley Mobile Home Park

The following clubs meet in Balboa
Park in the Photographic Arts Building,
by the Spanish Village Art Center:

Darkroomers	619-280-2221
Photo Arts	760-753-7391
Poly Photo	619-279-9726
Stereo (3D)	619-262-2940
Showette	619-295-1587
Daytime	619-422-3995
Photo Naturalists	619-286-3288
Movie Makers	619-444-1262
Tuesday Workshop	619-464-1744

Associations

The Professional Photographers of San
Diego County meets at the Four Points
Sheraton. 619-743-4130.

The Southern California Association of
Camera Clubs (SCACC). Represents
the 14 clubs listed above. 619-232-
1321 (evenings only, when building is
occupied by a club).

Other Information

**San Diego International
Visitor Information Center**
11 Horton Plaza (1st Ave & F Street),
San Diego, CA 92101.
Tel: 619-236-1212.
Hours: Mon–Sat., 8:30am–5pm;
(Sun 11–5, Jun–Aug)

**Mission Bay
Visitor Information Center**
2688 E Mission Bay Drive,
San Diego, CA 92109.
Tel: 619-276-8200.
Hours: 9am–sunset.

Information Centers

San Diego Convention and	
Visitors Bureau	619-236-1212
Gaslamp Quarter	619-233-5227
Balboa Park	619-239-0512
Coronado	619-437-8788
Carlsbad	760-434-6093
Chula Vista	619-425-4444
Oceanside	800-350-7873
North County	800-848-3336
Tijuana	619-428-1422
Travelers Aid Society	619-232-7991
Bus and Trolley	619-234-1060
Spotlight SD (events)	858-551-6464
Discovering San Diego	619-232-8538
International Info. Ctr.	619-232-8583

Weather	619-289-1212
Time	619-853-1212
Police	619-531-2000
Beach Report	619-221-8884
Directory Assistance	411

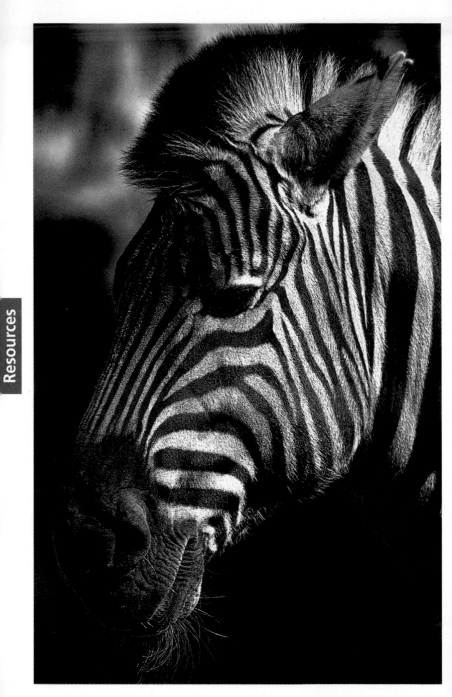

Weather

California: "blessed with a climate, than which there can be no better in the world; free from all manner of diseases."
—Richard Henry Dana, Two Years Before the Mast, 1840.

San Diego has an almost perfect climate, probably the most pleasant of any city in North America. Averaging 70°F, the temperature rarely requires you to wear more than a T-shirt and shorts and the sky is usually clear and blue.

The climate is 'Mediterranean' or 'dry subtropical' with low rainfall and low humidity. Coastal temperatures are regulated by the ocean, keeping winter in the mid 60s, and summer in the mid 70s. Further inland, winter brings snow to the mountains (above 5,000 feet) and summer roasts the Anza-Borrego Desert over 100°F.

May is often the worst time as the marine layer of low clouds, "June gloom," envelopes the coast for several weeks. January has the clearest skies and August is the warmest month.

Santa Anas are hot, dry winds that blow in over the desert during late summer and fall.

For current weather conditions, call 619-289-1212.

Climate

	Jan	Feb	Mar	Apr	May	June	July	Aug	Sept	Oct	Nov	Dec
Temperature: High (°F)	65	66	66	68	69	71	76	78	77	75	70	66
Temperature: Low (°F)	48	50	52	55	58	61	65	67	65	60	54	49
Sunshine average (%)	72	72	70	67	59	58	68	70	69	68	75	73
Rainfall average (inches)	2.1	1.4	1.6	0.8	0.2	0.1	0.0	0.1	0.2	0.3	1.1	1.4
Average humidity (%)	63	66	67	67	70	74	74	74	72	70	65	64

Source: National Weather Service

Dates To Be Wary Of

You're asking for traffic jams, expensive airline tickets and fully-booked hotels if you have to travel on these popular weekends:

Memorial Day	Last monday of May
Independence Day	July 4
Labor Day	First Monday of September
Thanksgiving	Fourth Thursday of November
Christmas Day	December 25

Festivals and Events

Resources

America's Finest City has some attractive festivals and events. Don't let your camera miss the Desert Wildflowers (February), the Carlsbad Flower Fields (March) or the U.S. Open Sandcastle Competition (July or August).

For an up-to-date list, contact:

San Diego Internat'l Visitor Information Center
11 Horton Plaza (1st ave & F Street),
San Diego, CA 92101
http://www.sandiego.org
Tel: 619-236-1212   sdinfo@sandiego.org

For more detailed information, consult the *Night & Day* (thursdays) section of the *San Diego Union Tribune*, or the *San Diego Reader* (weekly, free, available on thursdays). Events, dates and details are subject to change. This list may be incomplete. Information courtesy of the San Diego Convention and Visitors Bureau.

Note that, at the time of publication, the 619 area was due to be split into three unidentified area codes.

January

California gray whales swim along the coast on their annual migration. Mid-December to Feb.

San Diego Union-Tribune New Year's Day Race. Boat regatta on Shelter Island. 619-221-8400.

Whalefest. All you want to know about whales, at the Birch Aquarium. 619-534-FISH

San Diego Boat Show. Power boats and yachts, indoors and out. Convention Center. 619-274-9924.

Martin Luther King Day Parade. County Admin Bldg to Seaport Village. 619-264-0542.

Whale Watch Weekend. Films, speakers and presentations at Cabrillo Nat'l Monument. 619-557-5450

Imperial Beach Birdfest. Birdwatching, seminars and nature walks at Veteran's Park. 619-282-8687.

San Diego Marathon. Along the coast in Carlsbad. 619-792-2900.

February

Wildflowers Bloom in the Desert. Colorful wildflowers appear almost magically in the Anza-Borrego Desert. Dependent upon winter rains; dates vary by year. 760-767-4684.

Buick Invitational (PGA Tour). Golf at Torrey Pines. 619-281-4653.

Mardi Gras in the Gaslamp Quarter. Street parade. 619-233-5227.

Imperial Beach Bird Fest. 619-282-8687.

March

Flower Fields of Carlsbad. Spectacular display of flowers. March and April. 760-431-0352.

Ocean Beach Kite Festival. Kite flying competitions. 619-224-0189.

St. Patrick's Day Parade. Starts at 6th & Juniper Streets. 619-299-7812.

Sham Rock. Irish block party in the Gaslamp Quarter. 619-233-4692.

April

Buds 'n Blooms—A Floral Fiesta. Horticultural celebration in Balboa Park. 619-239-0512.

Auto Show. New cars at the Convention Center. 800-345-1487.

Festival of Animation. *Wallace & Gromit* and *South Park* were introduced here. Museum of Contemporary Art, La Jolla. 619-459-8707.

Santa Fe Market. Arts, crafts and cultures of the American Southwest. Old Town State Park. 619-296-3161.

San Diego Crew Classic. Rowing competition with over 3,000 rowers. Mission Bay. 619-488-0700.

America's Schooner Cup. Large yachts race past Shelter Island. 619-223-3138.

Old Town Spring Bonnet Competition. Children in colorful hats. Old Town. 619-291-4903.

La Jolla Easter Hat Promenade. More hats in La Jolla. 619-454-2600.

Borrego Springs Grapefruit Festival. Celebrates the Borrego ruby red grapefruit. 760-767-5555.

Coronado Flower Show. The largest flower show under a tent in Southern California. 619-437-8788.

Encinitas Street Fair. Over 300 arts and crafts vendors. 760-943-1950.

Lakeside Western Days & Rodeo. Lakeside. 619-561-1031.

Chicano Park Celebration. Aztec dancing, music and food. Chicano Park. 619-563-4661.

Ramona Pageant. Outdoor play at Ramona Bowl, Hemet. 800-645-4465.

Fallbrook Avocado Festival. 760-728-5845.

Day at the Docks. Sportfishing festival on Harbor Drive. 800-994-FISH.

Del Mar National Horse Show. Dressage and jumping. Del Mar Fairgrounds. 619-792-4288.

Temecula Valley Balloon and Wine Festival. Balloon launches at Lake Skinner. 909-676-4713.

San Diego Historical Society's Annual Showcase. Tour an historical house. 619-533-7355.

Adams Avenue Roots Festival. Blues and jazz. 619-282-7833.

Hanamatsuri Bazaar. Japanese art, flower arranging. Vista. 760-941-8800.

La Jolla Half Marathon. Del Mar to La Jolla Cove. 619-454-1262.

Art Walk Festival. Downtown. 619-481-1168.

Wings over Gillespie. Over 50 WWII vintage aircraft. 888-215-7000.

May

Cinco de Mayo. Celebrated in Borrego Springs, Encinitas, Oceanside, Old Town and Calexico.

Maytime Band Review. Competition of marching bands in National City. 619-475-6124.

Cupa Days Celebration. Native-American dancing, handgames and art. Pala Indian Reservation. 760-742-1590.

Spring Village Faire. Largest one-day street fair in California. Carlsbad. 760-434-8887.

Pacific Beach Block Party. Live music on Garnet Ave. 619-641-5823.

Sicilian Festival. Music and dancing in Little Italy. 619-233-0595.

Ramona Round-Up Rodeo. One of the country's top full-scale professional rodeos. Ramona. 760-789-1484.

Armed Forces Day Festival. Aircraft displays at Miramar. 619-537-6365.

Imperial Beach Chili and Jazz Festival. Cool music and hot food. 619-423-6581.

Oceanside Off-Shore Grand Prix. Powerboat racing. 888-313-0004.

American Indian Cultural Days. Traditional dancing and food. Balboa Park 619-281-5964.

Santa Ysabel Art Festival. 760-765-1676.

Avenue of the Arts. Gaslamp Quarter. 619-239-1143.

Chula Vista Lemon Festival. 619-422-1982.

Escondido Street Faire. 760-745-2125.

Portuguese Fiesta. Parade, pageantry and food. Point Loma. 619-223-5880.

Ethnic Food Fair. Balboa Park. 619-239-0512.

Mainly Mozart Festival. 619-239-0100.

June

SeaWorld's "Summer Nights." From June through August, entertainment and fireworks nightly. 619-226-3901.

Nighttime Zoo. San Diego Zoo stays open until 9pm with nocturnals animals and lights.

Park at Dark. Wild Animal Park. 619-234-6541.

Fiesta del Sol. Surfing contest and music. Solana Beach. 619-755-4775.

Deer Park Spring Concours d'Elegance. Classic cars and wine. Escondido. 760-749-1666.

Del Mar Fair. County fair with carnival rides, music, art and jewelry. 760-749-1666.

ESPN X Games. Gen-X extreme Olympics, mainly at Mariner's Point, Mission Bay. 619-523-7800.

Ocean Beach Street Fair. 619-226-2193.

San Diego Scottish Highland Games. Bagpipes and dancing in San Marcos. 619-645-8080.

Grunion Festival. Pacific Beach. 619-274-1326.

San Diego Grand Prix. Indy car racing downtown. 619-297-8418.

Indian Fair. American Indians from around the U.S. gather in Balboa Park. 619-239-2001.

Rock 'n Roll Marathon. 26 mile race with live bands. Balboa Park to downtown. 619-450-0819.

July

San Diego's biggest July 4 fireworks are from SeaWorld. Other displays from Coronado (Murietta Bay), La Jolla (Cove), Vista (Brengle Terrace Park).

Coronado Independence Day Celebration. Parade in the morning, US Navy aircraft demonstration in the afternoon, and fireworks in the evening. 619-437-8788.

Old Town Fourth of July Celebration. Flag raising, pony rides and pie-eating. 619-293-0117.

Hot Air Balloon Classic. Del Mar Racetrack. 619-481-6800.

Pacific Islander Festival. Embarcadero Marina Park. 619-445-8567.

Festival of the Bells. Anniversary celebration of the founding of California's first mission. Mission San Diego de Alcala. 619-283-7319.

Underwater Photo Festival. Slides and lectures of marine life. UCSD. 619-534-6467.

Over-the-Line Tournament. Beach softball on Fiesta Island, Mission Bay. 619-688-0817.

U.S. Open Sandcastle Competition. Stunning creations on Imperial Beach. 619-424-6663.

Coronado Sports Fiesta. Golf, diving, and a triathlon. 619-437-8788.

Julian Gold Rush PRCA Rodeo. Full-scale rodeo. 760-765-1857.

August

Del Mar Racing. Nine races everyday except Tuesdays. 619-755-1141.

A Taste of National City. Heritage Square, National City. 619-477-9339.

Mission San Luis Rey Fiesta. Birthday celebration. Oceanside. 760-757-3651.

Toshiba Tennis Classic. Top stars play at La Costa Resort & Spa. 760-438-9220.

Latin American Festival. Bazaar del Mundo, Old Town. 619-296-3266.

Hillcrest Street Fair. Live music, food and beer garden. 619-299-3330.

Body Surfing Contest. More than 300 surfers in Carlsbad. 760-434-2989.

World Body Surfing Championships. Boardless surfers compete in Oceanside. 760-966-4535.

Fleet Week. Parade of ships and fly-over by the Blue Angels. 619-544-1362.

America's Finest City Half Marathon From Cabrillo National Monument, through downtown, to Balboa Park.

619-297-3901.

Miramar Air Show. Air display with the Blue Angels. 619-537-6365.

Midnight Madness Fun Bicycle Ride. Twenty mile bike ride from Seaport Village. 619-338-9983.

Off-the-Wall Street Dance. La Jolla. 619-534-1503.

September

Traditional Gathering and Pow-Wow. Sycuan Indian Reservation, El Cajon. 619-445-7776.

Barona Pow Wow. Indian dancing. Barona Indian Reservation, Lakeside. 619-443-6612.

Chula Vista Bay Fair. Hydroplane racing boats. 619-426-2882.

Oceanside Rough Water Swim. 760-966-4545

Street Scene. California's largest urban food and music festival, in the Gaslamp Quarter. 619-557-8490.

La Jolla Rough Water Swim. The largest rough-water competition in the U.S. 619-456-2100.

Dia Del Independencia. Old Town celebrate the Mexican day of Independence. 619-291-4903.

Thunderboat Races. The world's fastest boats compete loudly on Mission Bay. 619-268-1250.

Mexican Independence Fiesta. Calexico. 760-357-1166.

Oceanside Harbor Days. 760-722-1534.

Chula Vista Harbor Days Festival. 619-420-6602.

Cabrillo Festival. Re-enactment and festival of Cabrillo's landing at San Diego. 619-557-5450.

Adams Avenue Street Fair. Outdoor music stages. Kensington. 619-282-7329.

California American Indian Days Celebration. Balboa Park. 619-281-5964.

Art Festival in the Village of La Jolla. Artwork and music. 619-645-8484.

Poway PRCA Rodeo. 760-736-0594.

Rosarito-Ensenada 50 Mile Bicycle Race. Attracts over 8,000 riders. 619-583-3001.

October

AIDS Walk San Diego. More than 13,000 participants walk 5k in Balboa Park. 619-291-9255.

Zoo Founder's Day. Free entry on October 5.

LEGO Construction Zone. Design competition in Horton Plaza. 619-238-1596.

Columbus Day Parade. Celebrate the discovery of America along Harbor Drive. 619-698-0545.

Julian Fall Apple Harvest. Apple cider and pie amidst autumn foliage. 760-765-1857.

Oktoberfest. German celebration in Carlsbad, Encinitas and El Cajon.

Children's Month at the San Diego Zoo. If you're under 11, you get in free. 619-234-3153.

Frightmare on Market Street. 619-231-3611.

Borrego Springs Desert Festival. 760-767-5555.

Underwater Pumpkin Carving Contest. Scuba divers carve Halloween pumpkins in the ocean off La Jolla Cove. 619-565-6054.

Encinitas Halloween Festival. 619-943-1950.

November

Fall Village Fair. Largest one-day street fair in California, with over 800 exhibitors. Carlsbad. 760-434-8887.

Mum Festival at the Wild Animal Park.

Veteran's Day Parade. From the County Admin bldg to Seaport Village. 619-239-2300.

Score Baja 1,000. Off-road race for cars, trucks and motorcycles. Baja California. 818-583-8068.

Holiday Avenue of the Arts. Gaslamp Quarter. 619-239-1143.

Mother Goose Parade. Floats, clowns, bands and equestrians. El Cajon. 619-444-8712.

Thanksgiving Dixieland Jazz Festival. Town & Country Hotel. 619-297-5277.

Holiday of Lights. 200+ lighted holiday displays at Del Mar Fairgrounds. 619-793-5555.

December

Giant Poinsettia Star. Carlsbad Flower Fields. 760-431-0352.

Holiday Bowl & Parade. College football at Qualcomm Stadium and marching bands downtown. 619-283-5808.

Coronado Christmas Open House and Parade. Parade along Orange Ave and fireworks. 619-437-8788.

Christmas on the Prado. Balboa Park. Free entry to zoo and museums after 5pm. 619-239-0512.

Starlight Yule Parade. Drill teams, floats and marching bands in Chula Vista. 619-422-1982.

Mission Christmas Faire. Mission San Luis Rey in Oceanside. 760-722-1534.

Poinsettia Street Festival. Encinitas. 760-943-1950.

Holiday Homes Tour. Rancho Buena Vista Adobe decorated for Christmas. 760-631-5000.

Re-enactment of the Battle of San Pasqual. Recreates the 1846 battle. 760-489-0076.

Old Town's Las Posadas and Luminarias. Recreates the birth of Christ. 619-297-1183.

Old Town Holiday in the Park. Candlelight tours of historic homes and museums. 619-220-5422.

Wild Animal Park Festival of Lights.

Holiday Parades. In Vista, Encinitas, North Park, La Jolla, Ocean Beach, Oceanside, Escondido, Calexico, Coronado.

Mission Bay Christmas Boat Parade of Lights. Sail boats and electric lights. 619-488-0501.

San Diego Harbor Parade of Lights. Colorfully lit boats sail around the bay.

Sunrise/Sunset Times

Day	Rise A.M.	☼	Set P.M.	☼
January				
1	6:51	118	4:53	242
2	6:51	118	4:54	242
3	6:51	118	4:55	242
4	6:51	118	4:56	242
5	6:52	117	4:56	243
6	6:52	117	4:57	243
7	6:52	117	4:58	243
8	6:52	117	4:59	243
9	6:52	117	5:00	243
10	6:52	117	5:01	243
11	6:52	116	5:02	244
12	6:52	116	5:02	244
13	6:51	116	5:03	244
14	6:51	116	5:04	244
15	6:51	116	5:05	244
16	6:51	115	5:06	245
17	6:51	115	5:07	245
18	6:50	115	5:08	245
19	6:50	115	5:09	245
20	6:50	114	5:10	246
21	6:49	114	5:11	246
22	6:49	114	5:12	246
23	6:49	114	5:13	246
24	6:48	114	5:13	246
25	6:48	113	5:14	247
26	6:47	113	5:15	247
27	6:47	113	5:16	247
28	6:46	112	5:17	248
29	6:45	112	5:18	248
30	6:45	112	5:19	248
31	6:44	111	5:20	249

Notes:
2–4 **Perihelion**—Earth is nearest to the sun.
8 Latest sunrise of the year.

Day	Rise A.M.	☼	Set P.M.	☼
February				
1	6:44	110	5:21	250
2	6:43	110	5:22	250
3	6:42	110	5:23	250
4	6:41	110	5:24	250
5	6:41	110	5:25	250
6	6:40	109	5:26	251
7	6:39	109	5:27	251
8	6:38	109	5:28	251
9	6:37	108	5:28	252
10	6:37	108	5:29	252
11	6:36	108	5:30	252
12	6:35	107	5:31	253
13	6:34	107	5:32	253
14	6:33	106	5:33	254
15	6:32	106	5:34	254
16	6:31	105	5:35	255
17	6:30	105	5:36	255
18	6:29	105	5:37	255
19	6:28	104	5:37	256
20	6:27	104	5:38	256
21	6:26	103	5:39	257
22	6:25	103	5:40	257
23	6:24	103	5:41	257
24	6:22	102	5:42	258
25	6:21	102	5:42	258
26	6:20	101	5:43	259
27	6:19	101	5:44	259
28	6:18	100	5:45	260
29	6:18	100	5:45	260

Notes:
29 Leap year (in the years 2000, 2004, 2008,…)

Day	Rise A.M.	☼	Set P.M.	☼
March				
1	6:17	100	5:46	260
2	6:15	100	5:46	260
3	6:14	99	5:47	261
4	6:13	99	5:48	261
5	6:12	98	5:49	262
6	6:11	98	5:50	262
7	6:09	97	5:50	263
8	6:08	97	5:51	263
9	6:07	96	5:52	264
10	6:06	96	5:53	264
11	6:04	95	5:53	265
12	6:03	95	5:54	265
13	6:02	94	5:55	266
14	6:00	94	5:56	266
15	5:59	93	5:56	267
16	5:58	93	5:57	267
17	5:57	92	5:58	268
18	5:55	92	5:59	268
19	5:54	92	5:59	268
20	5:53	91	6:00	269
21	5:51	91	6:01	269
22	5:50	90	6:01	270
23	5:49	90	6:02	270
24	5:47	89	6:03	271
25	5:46	89	6:04	271
26	5:45	88	6:04	272
27	5:44	88	6:05	272
28	5:42	87	6:06	273
29	5:41	87	6:06	273
30	5:40	86	6:07	274
31	5:38	86	6:08	274

Notes:
20 **Spring Equinox** Day and night are the same length.
22–23 Sun sets due west.

Full Moon Nights (Lunar Calendar)

Year	Jan	Feb	Mar	Apr	May	June	July	Aug	Sept	Oct	Nov	Dec
1999	2,31	-	2,31	30	30	28	28	26	25	24	23	22
2000	21	19	20	18	18	16	16	15	13	13	11	11
2001	9	8	9	8	7	6	5	4	2	2	1,30	30
2002	28	27	28	27	26	24	24	22	21	21	20	19
2003	18	16	18	16	16	14	13	12	10	10	9	8
2004	7	6	6	5	4	3	2,31	30	28	28	26	26
2005	25	24	25	24	23	22	21	19	18	17	16	15

(Solar Calendar)

April

Day	Rise A.M.	☼	Set P.M.	☼
1	5:37	85	6:08	275
2	5:36	85	6:09	275
3	5:34	84	6:10	276
4	5:33	84	6:11	276
5	6:32	83	7:11	277
6	6:31	83	7:12	277
7	6:29	82	7:13	278
8	6:28	82	7:13	278
9	6:27	82	7:14	278
10	6:25	81	7:15	279
11	6:24	81	7:16	279
12	6:23	80	7:16	280
13	6:22	80	7:17	280
14	6:21	79	7:18	281
15	6:19	79	7:18	281
16	6:18	78	7:19	282
17	6:17	78	7:20	282
18	6:16	78	7:21	282
19	6:15	77	7:21	283
20	6:13	77	7:22	283
21	6:12	76	7:23	284
22	6:11	76	7:23	284
23	6:10	75	7:24	285
24	6:09	75	7:25	285
25	6:08	74	7:26	286
26	6:07	74	7:26	286
27	6:06	74	7:27	286
28	6:05	73	7:28	287
29	6:04	73	7:29	287
30	6:03	73	7:29	287

Notes:

1–7 Start of **Daylight Savings Time**. First weekend in April. Clocks go forward one hour (+1). GMT-7.

May

Day	Rise A.M.	☼	Set P.M.	☼
1	6:02	72	7:30	288
2	6:01	72	7:31	288
3	6:00	72	7:32	288
4	5:59	71	7:32	289
5	5:58	71	7:33	289
6	5:57	70	7:34	290
7	5:56	70	7:34	290
8	5:55	70	7:35	291
9	5:55	69	7:36	292
10	5:54	68	7:37	292
11	5:53	68	7:37	292
12	5:52	68	7:38	292
13	5:51	68	7:39	292
14	5:51	68	7:40	292
15	5:50	68	7:40	292
16	5:49	67	7:41	293
17	5:49	67	7:42	293
18	5:48	67	7:42	293
19	5:47	66	7:43	294
20	5:47	66	7:44	294
21	5:46	66	7:44	294
22	5:46	66	7:45	294
23	5:45	65	7:46	295
24	5:45	65	7:46	295
25	5:44	65	7:47	295
26	5:44	65	7:48	295
27	5:43	65	7:48	295
28	5:43	64	7:49	296
29	5:42	64	7:50	296
30	5:42	64	7:50	296
31	5:42	64	7:51	296

Notes:

25–31 **Memorial Day** Last Sunday in May. Start of summer holiday period.

June

Day	Rise A.M.	☼	Set P.M.	☼
1	5:42	64	7:51	296
2	5:41	63	7:52	297
3	5:41	63	7:53	297
4	5:41	63	7:53	297
5	5:41	63	7:54	297
6	5:40	63	7:54	297
7	5:40	63	7:55	297
8	5:40	63	7:55	297
9	5:40	62	7:56	298
10	5:40	62	7:56	298
11	5:40	62	7:56	298
12	5:40	62	7:57	298
13	5:40	62	7:57	298
14	5:40	62	7:58	298
15	5:40	61	7:58	299
16	5:40	61	7:58	299
17	5:40	61	7:59	299
18	5:40	62	7:59	298
19	5:41	62	7:59	298
20	5:41	62	7:59	298
21	5:41	62	8:00	298
22	5:41	62	8:00	298
23	5:41	62	8:00	298
24	5:42	62	8:00	298
25	5:42	62	8:00	298
26	5:42	62	8:00	298
27	5:43	62	8:00	298
28	5:43	62	8:01	298
29	5:43	62	8:01	298
30	5:44	62	8:01	298

Notes:

12 Earliest sunrise of the year.

16 Most northerly sunrise and sunset.

21 **Summer Solstice** Sun is farthest from the equator. Longest day of the year.

30 Latest sunset of the year.

Legend

Rise	When the sun will rise: Time in the morning (a.m.) the sun will cross the horizon.
☼	Where the sun will rise: Compass bearing in degrees from north. 90° = east.
Set	When the sun will set: Time in the afternoon (p.m.) the sun will cross the horizon.
☼	Where the sun will set: Compass bearing in degrees from north. 270° = west.

July

Day	Rise A.M.	☼	Set P.M.	☼
1	5:44	62	8:01	298
2	5:45	62	8:00	298
3	5:45	62	8:00	298
4	5:45	63	8:00	297
5	5:46	63	8:00	297
6	5:46	63	8:00	297
7	5:47	63	8:00	297
8	5:47	63	8:00	297
9	5:48	63	7:59	297
10	5:48	63	7:59	297
11	5:49	64	7:59	296
12	5:50	64	7:59	296
13	5:50	64	7:58	296
14	5:41	64	7:58	296
15	5:51	64	7:57	296
16	5:52	64	7:57	296
17	5:52	65	7:57	295
18	5:53	65	7:56	295
19	5:54	65	7:56	295
20	5:54	65	7:55	295
21	5:55	65	7:55	295
22	5:56	66	7:54	294
23	5:56	66	7:53	294
24	5:57	66	7:53	294
25	5:58	67	7:52	293
26	5:58	67	7:52	293
27	5:59	67	7:51	293
28	6:00	67	7:50	293
29	6:00	68	7:49	292
30	6:01	68	7:49	292
31	6:02	68	7:48	292

Notes:
4 **Independence Day**
4–6 **Aphelion**
Earth is farthest from the Sun (July 4–6).

August

Day	Rise A.M.	☼	Set P.M.	☼
1	6:02	69	7:47	291
2	6:03	69	7:46	291
3	6:04	69	7:45	291
4	6:04	70	7:45	290
5	6:05	70	7:44	290
6	6:06	70	7:43	290
7	6:06	71	7:42	289
8	6:07	71	7:41	289
9	6:08	71	7:40	289
10	6:08	72	7:39	288
11	6:09	72	7:38	288
12	6:10	72	7:37	288
13	6:10	73	7:36	287
14	6:11	73	7:35	287
15	6:12	74	7:34	286
16	6:13	74	7:33	286
17	6:13	74	7:32	286
18	6:14	75	7:30	285
19	6:15	75	7:29	285
20	6:15	76	7:28	284
21	6:16	76	7:27	284
22	6:17	76	7:26	284
23	6:17	77	7:25	283
24	6:18	77	7:24	283
25	6:19	78	7:22	282
26	6:19	78	7:21	282
27	6:20	79	7:20	281
28	6:20	79	7:19	281
29	6:21	79	7:17	281
30	6:22	80	7:16	280
31	6:22	80	7:15	280

September

Day	Rise A.M.	☼	Set P.M.	☼
1	6:23	81	7:14	279
2	6:24	81	7:12	279
3	6:24	82	7:11	278
4	6:25	82	7:10	278
5	6:26	83	7:08	277
6	6:26	83	7:07	277
7	6:27	84	7:06	276
8	6:28	84	7:04	276
9	6:28	85	7:03	275
10	6:29	85	7:02	275
11	6:29	86	7:00	274
12	6:30	86	6:59	274
13	6:31	86	6:58	274
14	6:31	87	6:56	273
15	6:32	87	6:55	273
16	6:33	88	6:54	272
17	6:33	88	6:52	272
18	6:34	89	6:51	271
19	6:35	89	6:50	271
20	6:35	90	6:48	270
21	6:36	90	6:47	270
22	6:37	91	6:46	269
23	6:37	91	6:44	269
24	6:38	92	6:43	268
25	6:38	92	6:42	268
26	6:39	93	6:40	267
27	6:40	93	6:39	267
28	6:40	94	6:38	266
29	6:41	94	6:36	266
30	6:42	95	6:35	265

Notes:
1–7 **Labor Day**
First Monday in September.
20–21 Sun sets due west.
22 **Fall Equinox**
Day and night are the same length.

Angular position of sun (azimuth) during the year

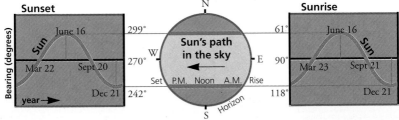

Sunset
Bearing (degrees)
Sun
June 16
Mar 22   Sept 20
Dec 21
year →
299°
270°
242°

N
Sun's path in the sky
W ← E
Set   P.M.   Noon   A.M.   Rise
Horizon
S

Sunrise
61°
90°
118°
Sun
June 16
Mar 23   Sept 21
Dec 21

October

Day	Rise A.M.	☼	Set P.M.	☼
1	6:42	95	5:46	265
2	6:43	96	5:46	264
3	6:44	96	5:47	264
4	6:45	96	5:48	264
5	6:45	97	5:49	263
6	6:46	97	5:50	263
7	6:47	98	5:50	262
8	6:47	98	5:51	262
9	6:48	99	5:52	261
10	6:49	99	5:53	261
11	6:49	100	5:53	260
12	6:50	100	5:54	260
13	6:51	101	5:55	259
14	6:52	101	5:56	259
15	6:52	102	5:56	258
16	6:53	102	5:57	258
17	6:54	103	5:58	257
18	6:55	103	5:59	257
19	6:55	103	5:59	257
20	6:56	104	6:00	256
21	6:57	104	6:01	256
22	6:58	105	6:01	255
23	6:59	105	6:02	255
24	6:59	105	6:03	255
25	7:00	106	6:04	254
26	7:01	106	6:04	254
27	7:02	107	6:05	253
28	7:03	107	6:06	253
29	6:04	107	6:06	253
30	6:04	108	6:07	252
31	6:05	108	6:08	252

Notes:
24–31 End of **Daylight Savings Time**. Last weekend in October. Clocks go back one hour (-1). GMT-8

November

Day	Rise A.M.	☼	Set P.M.	☼
1	6:06	108	4:58	252
2	6:07	109	4:57	251
3	6:08	109	4:56	251
4	6:09	110	4:55	250
5	6:09	110	4:54	250
6	6:10	110	4:54	250
7	6:11	111	4:53	249
8	6:12	111	4:52	249
9	6:13	112	4:51	248
10	6:14	112	4:51	248
11	6:15	112	4:50	248
12	6:16	112	4:49	248
13	6:17	113	4:49	247
14	6:18	113	4:48	247
15	6:18	113	4:48	247
16	6:19	113	4:47	247
17	6:20	114	4:46	246
18	6:21	114	4:46	246
19	6:22	114	4:46	246
20	6:23	115	4:45	245
21	6:24	115	4:45	245
22	6:25	115	4:44	245
23	6:26	115	4:44	245
24	6:27	115	4:44	245
25	6:27	116	4:43	244
26	6:28	116	4:43	244
27	6:29	116	4:43	244
28	6:30	116	4:43	244
29	6:31	116	4:43	244
30	6:32	117	4:42	242

Notes:
22–28 **Thanksgiving**. Fourth Thursday in November. Biggest travel weekend.

December

Day	Rise A.M.	☼	Set P.M.	☼
1	6:33	117	4:42	243
2	6:34	117	4:42	243
3	6:34	117	4:42	243
4	6:35	117	4:42	243
5	6:36	117	4:42	243
6	6:37	117	4:42	243
7	6:38	118	4:42	242
8	6:38	118	4:42	242
9	6:39	118	4:43	242
10	6:40	118	4:43	242
11	6:41	118	4:43	242
12	6:41	118	4:43	242
13	6:42	118	4:43	242
14	6:43	118	4:44	242
15	6:43	118	4:44	242
16	6:44	118	4:44	242
17	6:45	118	4:45	242
18	6:45	118	4:45	242
19	6:46	118	4:46	242
20	6:46	118	4:46	242
21	6:47	118	4:46	242
22	6:47	118	4:47	242
23	6:48	118	4:47	242
24	6:48	118	4:48	242
25	6:49	118	4:49	242
26	6:49	118	4:49	242
27	6:49	118	4:50	242
28	6:50	118	4:50	242
29	6:50	118	4:51	242
30	6:50	118	4:52	242
31	6:51	118	4:53	242

Notes:
4 Earliest sunset of the year.
21 Most southerly sunrise and sunset.
22 **Winter Solstice** Sun is farthest from the equator. Shortest day of the year.
25 **Christmas Day**

Notes:

Data only for San Diego. Location: W117deg 08' N32deg 45'

Consult a local newspaper for exact times or see our website for online calculators. California is in Pacific Standard Time (PST) which is GMT-8 hours. Daylight Savings Time adds one hour (GMT-7 hours) and lasts from the first weekend in April to the last weekend in October.

Sunrise and sunset times courtesy of Marc A. Murison, U.S. Naval Observatory, Washington, D.C. http://www.usno.navy.mil. Solar Azimuth calculations by Christopher Gronbeck, Center for Renewable Energy and Sustainable Technology (CREST).

59-Mile Scenic Drive

The Scenic Drive connects most of the city's major sights and takes about 3–4 hours to drive. There are several places where you'll want to stop and explore.

The route takes you to: The Embarcadero, Harbor and Shelter Islands, the Naval Training Center, Cabrillo National Monument, Sunset Cliffs, Mission Bay Park and SeaWorld, Pacific Beach, La Jolla, Old Town, Balboa Park, downtown San Diego, the Gaslamp Quarter, Seaport Village.

The route is marked by signs with a white seagull on a blue and yellow background. You can join at any point although the designated start is at Broadway Pier by Seaport Village. Bring a good street map in case you get lost or want to detour.

The Drive was first proposed by the San Diego Women's Club in 1963 and adopted by the City Council a year later.

One Day in San Diego

Probably the most popular and famous destination is the San Diego Zoo. Start early and there may be time to have dinner in the Gaslamp Quarter, Coronado or La Jolla. Alternatively, drive the Scenic Drive in the morning and spend the afternoon at your favorite part.

Scenic Tour

A good way to see a lot of the city is on the Old Town Trolley Tour. The tour is narrated and takes two hours. The distinctive red bus loops through the major sights including Old Town, The Embarcadero, Horton Plaza, the Gaslamp Quarter, Seaport Village, Coronado, the San Diego Zoo and Balboa Park. You can hop off the bus at any of the ten stops, explore an area, then hop on the next bus. 9–5. $24/$12. 619-298-8687.

For more than one day in San Diego, mix and match from the following:

The Big Attractions

SeaWorld, the Zoo, and the Wild Animal Park are the three big attractions. Each is well worth the visit and demands a full day. Brings plenty of film as there's lots to photograph.

Conventioner's Walk

Here for a convention and have some time to wander? From the Convention Center walk west to Seaport Village and continue on to the *Star of India*. Then head up Broadway to Horton Plaza and return via 5th Avenue and the Gaslamp Quarter.

Panoramic Overviews

Great views await you at the top of the Hyatt in Seaport Village, Cabrillo N.M. on Point Loma, and on Mt. Soledad in La Jolla. There's a good variety of cityscape views from the Ferry Landing on Coronado.

Resources

Tours
Old Town Trolley Tours:619-298-8687. Hop on and off at nine stops including: Old Town, Seaport Village, Horton Plaza, Coronado, Balboa Park. All day, $24/$12.

Gray Line Tours. 619-491-0011. City Tour includes: downtown, Gaslamp Quarter, Point Loma, Pacific Beach, La Jolla, Old Town, Embarcadero, Balboa Park, Mission Bay, Heritage Park. 1/2 day, $25/$11.

Bus Tours
San Diego Mini-Tours
619-477-8687
San Diego Scenic Tours
858-273-8687
Old Town Trolley Tours
619-298-8687
Grayline City Tours
619-491-0011
Five Star Tours
619-232-5049

Boat Tours
Bahia Belle
858-488-0551
Hornblower Dining
619-234-8687
Harbor Excursion
619-234-4111
Sea Maiden
619-24-0800

Helicopter
Skytours
619-291-4356

The Southern California Scene
Walk, bike or skate along the boardwalk, from Belmont Park to Crystal Pier, then return via Mission Bay.

History
Spend the day retracing San Diego's history. Start at Cabrillo National Monument (opens at 9am), where the first Europeans landed in 1542. Visit the excavated Spanish fortress (1769) on Presidio Hill and have lunch at Old Town (1822). Drive six miles east to the San Diego Mission (1774), then over to the Hotel del Coronado (1888) before dinner in the Gaslamp Quarter (1880s to 1920s).

Shopping
Horton Plaza and Seaport Village combine visual delights, entertainment and shops in open-air settings. La Jolla's Prospect Street is called the "Rodeo Drive of San Diego."

Missions
There are four missions to explore: San Diego De Alcalá (Mission Valley), San Luis Rey Francia (Oceanside), Pala (Pala) and Santa Ysabel (Julian).

For the Kids
Take your pick from: SeaWorld, San Diego Zoo, Wild Animal Park, Birch Aquarium, Belmont Park.

Other Ideas
Margaritas at Bazaar del Mundo in Old Town; lunch at George's at the Cove in La Jolla; afternoon tea at the U.S. Grant Hotel or the Horton Grand; Sunday Brunch at the Hotel del Coronado; explore the Gaslamp Quarter; ferry to Coronado and dining at the Ferry Landing; Jazz and dinner at Croce's; outdoor theater at the Festival Stage or Starlight Bowl in Balboa Park, or the amphitheater on Mt. Helix in La Mesa; the museums of Balboa Park; the houses of George Marston and Jesse Shepherd; ballooning over Del Mar.

PhotoSecrets®

Travel Photography Books

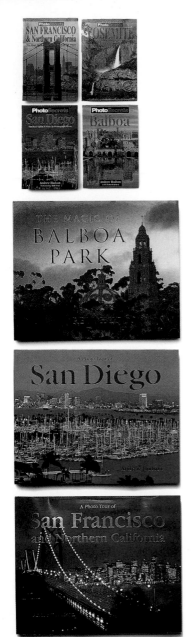

Resources

Also Available:

PhotoSecrets San Francisco
and Northern California
PhotoSecrets Yosemite
PhotoSecrets Balboa Park

A Photo Tour of San Diego
A Photo Tour of San Francisco
and Northern California
A Photo Tour of Orange County
A Photo Tour of Los Angeles
A Photo Tour of New York
The Magic of Balboa Park

Coming soon:
A Photo Tour of Las Vegas
A Photo Tour of Chicago

Grand Prize in the National
Self-Published Book Awards

Benjamin Franklin Award
for Best First Book

Visit The PhotoSecrets Web Site

for photo tips, travel photography
books and an extensive list of links.
www.photosecrets.com

Production Notes

Except where stated, all photographs were taken by Andrew Hudson using a Minolta X-700 SLR camera with a 20-35mm f3.5, 50mm f1.7, or 75–300 f5.6 lens. The rich colors are courtesy of Fuji Velvia (ISO 50) slide film and, for blue skies, a Tiffen polarizer.

Slides were scanned as Kodak Digital Science Photo CD files on a Kodak Filmscanner 2000. They were imported to an Apple Power Macintosh 9500/132 with 176Mb RAM running Mac OS 8.1. Basic touch up (levels adjustment and unsharp mask) was performed in Adobe® Photoshop® 4.0. Layout was performed in QuarkXPress® 3.32. Street maps were created in Adobe Illustrator 6.0. Proofs were made on a Hewlett Packard DeskJet 855C.

The entire book was delivered to the printer on five Iomega 1GB Jaz disks. The book is printed on 130 gsm gloss paper with a 260 gsm cover and threadsewn to lay flat. Printed in South Korea.

Photos

Many photographs of animals at the Zoo and Wild Animal Park are by Ron Gordon Garrison or Ken Kelley, copyright © 1998–2003 Zoological Society of San Diego, reproduced with permission. Most photographs of Sea-World are by Ron Couey or Ken Bohn, copyright © 1998–2003 SeaWorld San Diego, reproduced with permission. Photographs illustrating James Blank's article are copyright © 1998–2003 James Blank/Scenics of America. Photographs illustrating Jerry Schad's 'Afoot & Afield' article are copyright © 1998–2003 Jerry Schad.

Copyright

This book, including the text and photographs (except where stated), is copyright © 1998–2003 Photo Tour Books, Inc.

PHOTOSECRETS and PICTURES YOU CAN TAKE are trademarks of Photo Tour Books, Inc. When used in conjunction with the web site, PHOTOSECRETS is a service mark of Photo Tour Books, Inc. The names of many of the shows at San Diego Zoo and SeaWorld San Diego are trademarks or service marks of those organizations. All other trademarks and service marks are the property of their respective owners.

Send comments to:
Photo Tour Books, Inc.
9582 Vista Tercera
San Diego CA 92129

Visit the website at:
photosecrets.com

Distribution

PhotoSecrets books are distributed to the U.S. and Canadian trade by National Book Network (NBN), tel: 800-462-6420. For more information, contact Photo Tour Books at 858-780-9726.

Index

Resources

Andrew Hudson (author) loves to travel and take photographs. *"A camera is the perfect tool for travel"* he says, *"it pushes us to explore a location, to capture its essence, and to view the ordinary in an extraordinary way."*

Born in England, Andrew received his first camera from his parents on his 21st birthday and learned its art on trips through Europe and Africa. On business and vacation trips he always sought out the perfect shots, scouring travel books and postcard racks for ideas. He wondered why there wasn't a book that did this for him. *"For many travelers, coming home with a good set of photographs is a major objective of the trip."* Finally, on a trip through Asia, he decided to develop such a book himself. The PhotoSecrets series was born.

Andrew spent a year researching, photographing, and designing this, his third, book. Now the author of 10 books, he lives in San Diego with his wife, Jennie, and son, Redford.

Bob Krist (foreword) is a respected travel photographer. He writes the photography column for *National Geographic Traveler* and his photographs regularly appear in *National Geographic Traveler*, *Islands*, *Travel/Holiday*, and *Travel & Leisure*.

Visit the web site:
photosecrets.com